Work Less, Make More,
and Have Fun in Your Business

ENDORSEMENTS

"*Work Less, Make More, and Have Fun in Your Business* produces powerful results for business owners in their quest to create an extremely profitable business."

Dr. Nido R. Qubein, President, High Point University, noted Professional Speaker

"George Horrigan illuminates how to break through the financial or operational ceilings in your business you may have encountered, and take your enterprise to the next level."

Ron Wallace, Former President of UPS International, Serial Entrepreneur

"*Work Less, Make More, and Have Fun in Your Business* is a brilliant examination of an organization's Human Assets area (its personnel) and all the components required to maximize your enterprise's profitably and super-charge your company."

Dr. Tony Alessandra, Founder & Chairman of Assessments 24X7, creator of the world-famous DISC personality assessment, and author of *The NEW Art of Managing People* and *The Platinum Rule*

"Learn something, make money, and have fun – those are my conditions of satisfaction when I do business. George's book hits the nail on the head. His proven formula for success will take your business to the next level. It's about working smarter, not harder. Once you figure that out, you'll never work another day in your life."

Jeffrey Hayzlett, CEO of the C-Suite Network, Primetime TV & Podcast Host, Speaker, Author, and former Chief Marketing Officer & Vice President of Eastman Kodak

"*Work Less, Make More, and Have Fun in Your Business* is an excellent and practical business book. I have led many businesses over my 30+ year career and I have read many business books – however Work Less, Make More, and Have Fun in Your Business actually creates a practical formula for success.

Unfortunately, most authors or business executives who write books tend to generalize or story-tell as their method of teaching business success. Work Less, Make More, and Have Fun in Your Business creates a clear step by step approach that enables the reader to follow a proven, well documented methodology."

Bill Williams, Executive Vice President of Ameriprise

"As a small businessperson, I heartily recommend *Work Less, Make More, and Have Fun in Your Business* for anyone thinking seriously about starting a business and for anyone in the first years of their business to provide guidelines and a checklist on how you are doing.

For any business, the chapter on values and visions is essential—making money is the result of having values and a vision that provide the framework of the business. The author goes on to identify critical success factors—guidelines to keep the entrepreneur's focus. Subsequent chapters cover topics such as marketing, financing sources, technology, and the search for a team to assist in achieving success in the vision.

I found the text both readable and valuable in contributing to the success of any start-up business. Certainly, a must-read for anyone starting out. Yes, I am buying copies for my favorite young entrepreneurs."

John Silvia, CEO and Founder of Dynamic Economic
Strategy, former Chief Economist, Wells Fargo

"*Work Less, Make More, and Have Fun in Your Business* shows you how to take the failures in your business and turn them into successes."

Frank Abagnale, President of Abagnale & Associates and
person whose life was portrayed in the
award-winning movie "Catch Me If You Can"

"*Work Less, Make More, and Have Fun in Your Business* does an outstanding job of illuminating how the elements of a business' Operations area can be put together most effectively. Must read if you're looking for an innovative way of growing an organization."

Scott DiGiammarino, CEO and Founder of MovieComm

"*Work Less, Make More, and Have Fun in Your Business* unearths the secrets for creating a business that will provide you with a sustainable source of prosperity."

Marc Kidd, CEO of Captivate, former President of
Media Sales at the Outdoor Channel, Inc.

"Many people dream of owning their own business. What separates the dreamers from the ones who actually become business owners, is taking action. George Horrigan introduces you to the actions needed to get start on this dream. *Work Less, Make More, and Have Fun in Your Business* will show you how to turn your dream into your reality."

Bill Cates, Founder & CEO of Referral Coach International,
author of *Beyond Referrals* and *Radical Relevance*

"An alternate title for *Work Less, Make More, and Have Fun in Your Business* could be, "be confident, be excited and less stressed as you build a successful, profitable business of your dreams." Well written, in easy-to-understand language, here is the book every aspiring entrepreneur should have to read before launching their business.

Even seasoned business owners can benefit from a careful examination of all aspects of their business strategy, to bring it into even greater alignment for heightened success."

Dave Campbell, former Chief Operating Officer of FormFire

"There's an old saying: if you love what you do, you'll never work a day in your life. *Work Less, Make More, and Have Fun in Your Business* is an outstanding guide that delivers the keys to success. Gain the skills to grow your profits and have fun in your business too."

Maggie Linton, former Host of the SiriusXM Radio
program, The Maggie Linton Show

"*Work Less, Make More, and Have Fun in Your Business* is a must read for anyone starting a business or trying to grow one"

Aaron Young, Chairman of Laughlin Associates, Inc.,
Founder of "The Unshackled Owner"

"George Horrigan shares everything you will need to develop a Vision for your business that will guide you down the path of success, both personally and professionally. Who doesn't want to work less, make more and have fun?"

Shep Hyken, CEO of Shepard Presentations, Customer Service Expert,
former President of the National Speakers Association

"*Work Less, Make More, and Have Fun in Your Business* presents the ingredients required for you to overcome increased competition and create your recipe for success."

Dr. Simon T. Bailey, President of Simon T. Bailey International,
former Sales Director of the Disney Institute

"George Horrigan provides stellar insights in "*Work Less, Make More, and Have Fun in Your Business*" that show you how to operate a company so you can have the lifestyle you want."

Tom Antion, President of the Internet Marketing
Training Center, Internet Marketing Pioneer

"George Horrigan has hit a home run with this easy-to-understand book that walks a business owner down the path of creating a successful and thriving business."

Ford Saeks, CEO Prime Concepts Group Inc.,
author of *SUPERPOWER!*

"George Horrigan's book strengthens and helps you with simple and easy-to-follow principles to tackle, navigate and solve your business growth decisions. It's the ideal 'business bible' with the strength and help every business owner needs."

Mark Bortz, Founder & CEO of Premier Companies, Inc.

"The foundational building block approach that George Horrigan uses in *Work Less, Make More, and Have Fun in Your Business* will help you translate the frustrations you may be dealing with in your business into tomorrow's opportunities and successes."

John Greco, Cofounder & CEO of Greco Enterprises,
Recognized Business Thought Leader

"George Horrigan's genius shines again. In his latest book, "*Work Less, Make More, and Have Fun in Your Business,*" he reveals the path to maximizing your company profits. He does that while highlighting how to manage a corporation's marketing and sales operations more efficiently.

If you seek to maximize your operation's bottom line, I suggest reading *Work Less, Make More, and Have Fun in Your Business*. It will furnish you with the assurance that you can overcome the obstacles that may arise in pursuing the goals of your organization."

Greg Williams, CEO of The Master Negotiator,
Body Language Expert, and TV News Contributor

"*Work Less, Make More, and Have Fun in Your Business* utilizes a comprehensive business growth methodology that will result in you obtaining the assurance you are not missing opportunities for your business to grow and prosper."

Alan Urech, Managing Partner of Stoney River
Capital Partners, Serial Entrepreneur

"George Horrigan has hit another Home Run for business owners and Execs, seeking better ideas to grow their business with a clear plan that provides intuitive and insightful diagrams for those of us that are visual learners.

His latest book, "*Work Less, Make More, and Have Fun in Your Business*" provides numerous outside the box concepts, in an easily digestible fashion, that can quickly be put into action."

Joe Vidal, Channel Business Unit - Chief Technology
Officer at Hewlett Packard Enterprise

"*Work Less, Make More, and Have Fun in Your Business* conveys the keys for turning the pains you may be currently experiencing in your business into the promises of a better tomorrow."

Dan Janal, Entrepreneur, author of *Write Your Book in a Flash*

WORK LESS
MAKE MORE
AND HAVE FUN
IN YOUR BUSINESS

HOW *to* CREATE *the* BUSINESS
of YOUR DREAMS *in* 12 EASY STEPS

GEORGE HORRIGAN

NEW YORK

LONDON • NASHVILLE • MELBOURNE • VANCOUVER

Work Less, Make More, and Have Fun in Your Business

How to Create the Business of Your Dreams in 12 Easy Steps

Published in New York, New York, by Morgan James Publishing. Morgan James is a trademark of Morgan James, LLC. www.MorganJamesPublishing.com

Proudly distributed by Ingram Publisher Services.

ISBN 9781631957130 paperback
ISBN 9781631957147 ebook
Library of Congress Control Number:
2021945586

Cover and Interior Design by:
Chris Treccani
www.3dogcreative.net

Morgan James is a proud partner of Habitat for Humanity Peninsula and Greater Williamsburg. Partners in building since 2006.

Get involved today! Visit MorganJamesPublishing.com/giving-back

DEDICATION

For God so loved the world, that He gave His only begotten Son, that whoever believes in Him shall not perish, but have eternal life. John 3:16

TABLE OF CONTENTS

Foreword   xxi

Introduction   xxv

Chapter 1—Your Dreams Can Come True   1

Your Dreams   1
Their Dreams   1
What Does a Successful Business Look Like?   3
Overview of the Structure of Success™ Methodology   6
Why is this Framework Important?   11
What is Unique about the Structure of Success™ Process?   13
The Structure of Success™ versus The Traditional Business Plan   13
The Five Roles of a Leader   15
How is this Book Organized?   16

Chapter 2—Where is this Ship Going? (Step #1)   19

Your Values   20
A Vision for Your Company   25
Where Cometh a Vision   26
Your Vision Should be Powerful   27
Results of Having a Compelling Vision   28
The Importance of Having a Compelling Vision   31
Three Steps to Creating a Compelling Vision   31
The Five audiences of Your Compelling Vision   33
Creating a Win/Win Experience   37
Mission Statement versus Vision   39
Fostering and Encouraging the Development of Your Vision   40

Three Common Vision Problems 41
Chapter Summary 43

Chapter 3—How are You Going to Get there? (Step #2) 45
Your Strategy: The Road Map for achieving Your Vision 45
What is a Critical Success Factor for a Business? 46
Identifying Your Critical Success Factors 47
The Six Categories of Critical Success Factors 48
Combining Similar Critical Success Factors 50
Synchronizing Your Vision and Critical Success Factors 51
What Critical Success Factors Accomplish 51
The Two Different Parts of a Business's Vision 53
Critical Success Factors are the Foundation of Your Business 55
Creating Your Business's Strategy and Making it Measurable 56
Updating Your Time-Sequenced Vision 59
Input from Four of Your Business's Stakeholders 60
Preparing and Publicizing Your Vision and Critical Success Factors 63
Preface to the Remaining Chapters of this Book 65
Chapter Summary 65

Chapter 4—Getting the Word Out (Step #3) 67
The Importance of Marketing & Sales 68
Overview of Marketing & Sales 69
Number of Potential Buyers 70
Customer Awareness of a Need for Your Product or Service 81
Attractiveness of Your Solution 82
Awareness of Your Solution 88
Your Delivery Channels 96
Effectiveness of Your Sales Processes 100
Your Competition 107
Chapter Summary 110
Updating Your Critical Success Factors 111

Chapter 5—Five Ways to Beat Your Competition (Step #4)   113

Your Business is a Football Game   114

Chicken-Or-Egg Syndrome   115

Overview of Your Production Area   118

Developing a Sustainable Competitive Advantage   121

Exceptional versus Great versus Good versus Average   121

Your Product Cost Advantage   123

Your Product Quality   125

Your Delivery Time or Convenience   127

Your Customer Service   128

Your Product Uniqueness   131

Developing Your Unique Genius   133

Chapter Summary   135

Updating Your Critical Success Factors   135

Chapter 6—Growing Your Money Tree (Step #5)   137

The Importance of the Finance & Administration Area   138

Overview of Finance & Administration   139

Profitability   139

Asset Structure   163

Financing Sources   166

Financial and Administrative Controls   169

Chapter Summary   170

Updating Your Critical Success Factors   171

Chapter 7—You Can't Do it alone (Step #6)   173

The Significance of Your Human Assets Area   174

Overview of Your Human Assets Area   176

Correctness of Your Personnel   176

Effectiveness of Your Managers   179

Satisfaction and Morale Level of Your Employees   183

Training and Education Provided to Your Employees   190

Effectiveness of Your Leadership   192

Human Assets Infrastructure 199

Chapter Summary 202

Updating Your Critical Success Factors 202

Chapter 8—Technology to the Rescue (Step #7) **203**

Overview of Your Information Technology Area 204

Correctness of Data and Information 204

Accuracy of Information Captured 206

Utilization of Information in Processes 207

Your Use of Technology 209

Chapter Summary 212

Updating Your Critical Success Factors 212

Chapter 9—Double Checking Your Compass (Step #8) **213**

Your Role as a Chief Visionary officer 213

Scouting for Your Company 215

Scaling Your Business 217

Vision and Leadership 218

Perceived Benefit to Your Customers 219

Perceived Benefit to Your Employees 221

Perceived Benefit to Your Owners 222

Perceived Benefit to Your Suppliers 223

Perceived Benefit to Society 224

The First Step in Renewing the Vision for Your Business 227

The Three Stages of Visioning 228

The Process of Reconceptualizing Your Vision 231

Chapter Summary 235

Updating Your Critical Success Factors 235

Chapter 10—Effectively Calling the Shots (Step #9) **237**

Becoming an Effective Leader 238

Demystifying Leadership 239

Leadership Starts with Proper Planning 240

Group Business Management Team Retreats 244
Developing Your Leadership Skill Set 248
Working *In* versus *On* Your Business 250
Leading Your Team 254
Mentoring and Leadership Role Models 258
Chapter Summary 260

Chapter 11—Proper Execution Will Win the Day (Step #10) **263**
The *Busyness* Method of Execution 264
Leadership Burn Out 264
Structured Execution 265
The Five Components of Structured Execution 267
Systems 269
Personnel 273
Metrics 275
Quality Loops 279
Incentives 282
Impact of Company Size on Structured Execution Implementation 284
Development of Your Five Components of Structured Execution 286
Chapter Summary 287

Chapter 12—Building a Better Mousetrap (Step #11) **289**
Innovation Sees Every Problem as an Opportunity 292
How Ought the World to Work? 295
Innovation Teams 301
An Innovation Box 308
Systematizing Innovation 310
Rewarding Innovation 312
Chapter Summary 314

Chapter 13—Putting it all Together (Step #12) **317**
Update the Strategy for Achieving Your Renewed Vision 319
Updating Your Organization to Accomplish Your Vision 322

Working on the Future of Your Business 327
Your Business is Your Product 331
Succession/Exit Planning 333
Oversee Your Business's Operations and Manage it via Metrics 335
Chapter Summary 336

Conclusion **337**

About the Author **341**

Free Special Bonuses **343**

Additional Resources **345**

FOREWORD

I was introduced to George Horrigan by two of my favorite people on the planet, Rick Frishman and David Hancock and I soon discovered George and I shared a passion for helping people create successful businesses, which in turn gave their customers/clients exactly what they were looking for.

I soon realized we shared the same principles. In the more than 80 books I have written on various Guerrilla Marketing™ techniques, they mirror the concepts contained in the Structure of Success™ methodology that George presents in *Work Less, Make More, and Have Fun in Your Business*.

One of my first books, *Earning Money Without a Job* (Holt 1991), particularly parallels the Structure of Success™ with regards to starting a new business. They are two sides of the same coin—meeting people's needs and creating vibrant, thriving enterprises to meet those needs.

As a marketing expert working with business owners and leaders, I learned long ago that many of them were so intimidated and worried about making mistakes, that they never fully pursued their dreams.

Relatedly, I discovered that George and I had a mutual concern for business owners and the frustration and sometimes heartbreak they go through in trying to create the business they long for.

George is the perfect person to write this book because he has personally started nine businesses, seven which were successful, and two which were failures—but as he says, he learned a lot from these failures. So, he personally knows the anguish of not being able to take a company where you want it to go, as well as the joy that comes from fulfilling the dreams for your business.

His experience with his nine companies and the understanding he gained from working with the over 1,200 enterprises that have employed the Structure of Success™ methodology have qualified him to write a book like this, which specifically shows you how to take your company where you want it to go.

His hands-on involvement with these many companies has provided him with the knowledge, insights, and wisdom to be able to guide businesses to the success they desire.

This guidance starts with George showing you how to create a vision for your company that will enable you to create a quality product or service that is focused on what your customers will benefit from it.

This starts with creating products and services based on knowledge of your customer, business sector, and competition, and then he shows you how to effectively market your product/service. This continues with learning various ways to grow a company, scale it to multiple levels, as well as profitably sell it.

My expertise in employing Guerrilla Marketing™ as an unconventional marketing tool to emotionally connect with your customer is completely in synch with the numerous concepts contained in *Work Less, Make More, and Have Fun in Your Business.*

I have found that purchase decisions are often made by the unconscious mind. Therefore, the concepts in this book—understanding your customer's short-term and long-term goals related to your product/service and comprehending the emotional state your customers desire to experience related to your product/service—are absolute marketing nuggets of gold.

George also provides unique insights involving how to get your customer to talk about themselves and establishing a meaningful relationship with them by understanding their needs—all things that are necessary for converting prospects to customers. This effort also includes developing the chemistry to form long-term relationships.

The concepts he presents around the value and power of Branding—setting an expectation of the experience your customers will have with your product/service—are extremely insightful.

His observations are particularly astute regarding how to turn customers into your advocates by "Creating Experiences Worth Repeating™" so they will tell others about your product/service.

Another thing I appreciated about *Work Less, Make More, and Have Fun in Your Business* is that all of the Structure of Success™ methodology concepts are presented in very appealing graphical images, because I learned long ago that our brains use images to help us internalize and fully understand ideas.

I thoroughly recommend this book to you. It shows you clearly and concisely how the moving parts of an enterprise fit together and the order in which they need to be addressed. This is crucial because I have seen many business owners and leaders wrestle with trying to understand how all the pieces of a business interrelate to each other.

The understanding George provides regarding effectively meeting your "stakeholders'" needs will give you the ability to create a truly powerful engine for meeting your customers', employees', suppliers', and society's needs, as well as you own objectives for your enterprise. As the book's subtitle says, George accomplishes this by detailing "The 12 steps to creating the business of your dreams."

George's prior book, *Creating a Thriving Business*, was very helpful to many, many readers, and this book will be even more beneficial because it covers many more topics, including putting the things in place to develop an exit strategy for your company.

Related to these other topics, I am sure you will greatly benefit from this book as it shows you how to get your employees on board with where you want to take your company, and make sure they stay happy and fully engaged in their work.

It is important to note that *Work Less, Make More, and Have Fun in Your Business* is very easy to read, and implementing the concepts it describes is straightforward because it includes many examples, as well as a companion *Workbook* that guides you through applying its principles.

So, do yourself a great favor, read this book and apply the concepts it contains so you can create the business of your dreams.

Jay Conrad Levinson
The Father of Guerrilla Marketing™

INTRODUCTION

Congratulations, the book you are about to read, will change your business and your life!

I have personally used the Structure of Success™ methodology, which is covered in this book, with over 1,200 companies and it has enabled these businesses to:

- Grow their revenue
- Increase their profits
- Scale their operations
- Reduce the risk to their enterprise
- Decrease the owner's personal stress level
- Make their business easier to operate
- Break through ceilings in their company

Starting a new business or trying to grow an existing one should not just be a leap in the dark, merely a process of hoping and praying, or purely trial and error, but it should be based on sound and proven business principles.

That is just what this book provides.

By utilizing the approach which is laid out in this book you will create a business that will make you very happy, continually refresh your soul, and produce a sense of fulfilment - as compared to having a company which is emotionally, physically, and mentally draining.

Furthermore, use of the Structure of Success™ methodology will produce a work environment that creates engaged, productive employees, who will thrive in your company.

Not only will we examine how to develop a successful, thriving business, but we will cover how to grow and scale your enterprise and how to create a business you long for, that is, the "business of your dreams."

To accomplish this, I will show you how to:

1. Establish a compelling vision for where you want to take your business
2. Develop a strategy for taking it there
3. Execute this strategy in a systematic manner
4. Apply innovation to your enterprise
5. Create a self-regenerating economic system within your company

Additionally, we will accomplish the above in a way which has a positive impact on society, because it is crucial that one's company is part of making the world a better place. As you will see, a by-product of using the Structure of Success™ is you will develop a "socially responsible business" that will improve your society and community.

Therefore, let's get started on creating the business of your dreams, so that you can *Work Less, Make More, and Have Fun in Your Business!*

Chapter 1

Your Dreams Can Come True

• • • • •

YOUR DREAMS

In this book you are about to embark on a potentially life-changing voyage of taking your company from where it is to where you want it to go. Take a moment to journey back in time to when you started your business. What were your initial goals, hopes, and dreams? Have you achieved those dreams? All? Some? A few? Even more importantly, ask yourself, "Am I on target for reaching my current goals, hopes, and dreams?"

THEIR DREAMS

Let's start by looking at three business owners, how they went about creating the businesses of their dreams, and if they were successful in reaching their goals.

Michael

Michael, a tall man in his late 50's had begun his health care company 10 years before he came to our firm for help. A serial entrepreneur, Michael had started and sold several businesses in the past and was very familiar with his particular market segment in the health care industry. He knew where he wanted to take his enterprise, figured out the things that needed to be accomplished, and had a plan to get there. His plan was to scale his organization quickly, and he executed it well.

As his business grew—from one to two to three locations—so did his profits. After 10 years in operation, his annual net income was about $2.5 million. He had an exit strategy—sell the business to a large national company in his same industry. When an ideal buyer who wanted to expand into his city came knocking and made him an offer, he could not refuse. Michael took the offer and walked away with over $14 million.

Janice

Janice was a driven woman in her mid-thirties who was an architect and had run her business for about 12 years. She was an expert in her industry and put together a system to understand and consistently fulfill her customers' needs. She had identified the goals for her company, knew the specific things that needed to be done to be successful, and had a strategy to achieve her plan—which she executed methodically. However, her plan did not include growing her entity to the next level nor expansion to other cities. Janice's business was very profitable, so she decided to sell her business and start another one. A competitor who wanted to expand bought it for $900,000.

William

A friendly man in his early sixties, William had been in the commercial construction industry his entire adult life. He had run his own company for a number of years, growing it to about $2.5 million in revenue per year. His dream was to pass it on to his son. His business was successful and profitable, but he had not figured out how to create an organization that was more than himself and several other individuals who worked for him.

Meanwhile, William's son had a secure, well-paying job with a separate large construction company. Although having worked part time for his father over the years, when William approached his son about taking over the business, his son said, "Thanks, but no thanks." Since none of the individuals who had worked with William over the years wanted to purchase the company—and he did not want to run it the rest of his life—he just shut it down.

> Throughout this book I will predominately use the term
> *business owner*. Please note that this term also includes
> business leaders and managers.

What Went Right, What Went Wrong?

Several things went right, and several things went wrong in these businesses.

Michael executed his plan for his health care business, and his yearly profits grew and grew. He had fun running the business and he walked away with a huge bundle. After he sold it, he went on to do it again in another city. Brilliant!

Janice created a very successful organization. However, though she rigorously executed her strategy, she did not develop a strategy that would enable her to scale her business to the next level. However, she was able to sell her business for a tidy sum and start another business.

While William knew that he wanted to pass his business on to his son, his business model was an unsustainable one requiring constant maintenance from William and his friends. His son perceived this and did not want to operate an unstructured business with his father's friends. Unfortunately, the business was not attractive to a buyer, and ultimately William shut it down. Unlike Michael and Janice, William did not get even a penny for his company.

WHAT DOES A SUCCESSFUL BUSINESS LOOK LIKE?

Fruit Stand versus Factory

What lessons can we learn from these three businesses?

Having worked with over 1,200 companies during the past 17 years, I have found two basic scenarios about how businesses operate: the fruit-stand model or the economic factory model.

Metaphorically speaking, in the fruit-stand model the owner shows up Monday, sets out the fruit, and has revenue. Tuesday and Wednesday, same thing. On Thursday the owner doesn't show up—therefore no revenue. Friday, the owner shows up, sets out the fruit, and has revenue.

Under the fruit-stand model, more or less the business is totally dependent on the owner. If the owner doesn't do things, compel others to do certain tasks, or scold others for doing something the wrong way and do the task him/herself, the business does not operate properly.

In the economic factory model, the owner shows up Monday and builds the factory but has no revenue. On Tuesday the owner hires personnel, trains them, and puts the equipment in place, but still has no revenue. On Wednesday, the owner comes in, starts the factory, oversees operations, and has revenue. Thursday, the owner comes in, oversees operations, and has revenue. However, on Friday, Monday, and going forward, the owner doesn't show up but still has revenue.

Under the factory model, a business owner initially invests the time to develop, implement, perfect the products (or services, which are a "product"), and optimize the systems that are necessary for the business to operate without the owner's constant supervision. Consequently, an economic factory-type enterprise takes longer to develop, but the payoff is enormous.

So how do you move from a fruit-stand model to a factory model? Developing a systematic approach to operating your business and fully satisfying your customers are the keys to transforming a business from a fruit stand to an economic factory!

Please don't think that a fruit-stand model means that the organization is small. We recently ran into a $20,000,000 company in which the owner was personally doing a key component of the operations. When the owner got too busy and stopped doing this vital task, the company almost failed.

Keep in mind that the difference between a fruit stand and an economic factory business is not black and white but a continuum. Also, fruit-stand operations are present within businesses of all sizes. One of our Fortune 500 clients periodically says, "We have various fruit-stand operations within our multi-billion-dollar company!"

The important thing to take away from this book is that there are specific steps that must be undertaken to turn your business into an "economic factory" so that it still operates smoothly while you can be off doing whatever you want!

Example

Bruce, a congenial man in his early 50's, owned a commercial construction company that had gone through various feast-to-famine business cycles. He told me of his frustration that when his business seemed like it was going great, it would hit a downward spiral and sputter to a stall.

After discussing the concept of a Fruit Stand versus an Economic Factory, Bruce realized that even in the best of times for his company, it was only him pulling the strings to make things happen with his subcontractors. He had no construction superintendents, no support staff, and no infrastructure in place. Just like a typical Fruit Stand owner, he had not developed any policies and procedures for his company because he carried all this information in his head. Likewise, he orchestrated every aspect the construction process, instead of having staff to take care of these actions.

As I worked with him to start moving his business from a Fruit Stand to an Economic Factory mode, Bruce established company policies and procedures, hired the personnel to supervise the various aspects of the commercial construction cycle, and began managing the overall operations of his enterprise.

Complete exercise 1-1 in workbook

The Many Moving Parts of a Successful Business

Let's dig into the overall themes of what went right and what went wrong in Michael's, Janice's, and Will's businesses.

Experts on learning and thinking say we need to have a framework within which to interpret and comprehend things to make sense of them.

This framework enables us to gain understanding and perspective on what is taking place.

To truly understand what happened with these business owners' companies, I need to introduce the methodology we use at Fountainhead Consulting Group, Inc. for analyzing a business. This framework is necessary because businesses are very complex operations with many, many moving parts. We use this framework both with start-ups and existing organizations.

This is the five-step approach we use to analyze a business:

1. What values does the owner embrace and what is his/her vision for the business?
2. Has the owner identified the specific things (its objectives) the company must do to be successful?
3. Is there a comprehensive strategy in place to achieve the vision for the organization and to accomplish its unique objectives?
4. Is there a practical execution plan in place for achieving the vision for the business, accomplishing the unique must-do actions, and carrying out the strategy?
5. Is the business owner applying transformational innovation to the entire organization that will separate it from its competition?

We call this framework the Structure of Success™.

OVERVIEW OF THE STRUCTURE OF SUCCESS™ METHODOLOGY

Over the years our clients have discovered that understanding the above five concepts have been very insightful in comprehending where their organizations were and deciding what steps would take their businesses to the next level. We have found that one of the things that perplexes many company owners is how this thing called a "business" is supposed to fit together and operate.

I have found that a business is like an intricate jig-saw puzzle where one piece of the organization fits with another piece, and when all the pieces are put together properly, they form a company that functions correctly and is an attractive mosaic of its components.

> Our definition of a *dream* business is much more than having a certain amount of revenue or profit. It includes having fun in your business and enjoying it. It should also provide you with a work/life harmony and allow you to spend time with your family, have adequate recreation, and not come home overly stressed out.

However, many business owners view their businesses as one cohesive unit—kind of a big earth ball the owner is trying to push in one direction or another. Therefore, many are frustrated because their operation is not responding to their efforts. This is because they do not fully realize how the different components of a business fit together.

The above five steps of analyzing a company along with the details that make up strategy and execution areas provide the tools that enable an owner to determine what must be accomplished to create a thriving business. These five steps translate into the five building blocks below.

Without these tools to understand the big picture, business owners usually gravitate to the area of a company in which they are most comfortable: If they are most at ease in finance, that is where they spend the majority of their time. Or if they don't particularly like working with people, but really enjoy the operations area, they get consumed with that aspect of the business. This leads to the neglect of the other areas within their organization, sometimes with disastrous results.

There is an old analogy of three blind men describing an elephant. One grabs the trunk, one the tail, and one a hoof. Each describes a completely different animal. So, it is with a business; depending on the orientation of the leaders, they could analyze a company completely differently and then enact drastically differing plans for moving the entity forward. Understanding the concepts below will prevent that from occurring.

With this analogy in mind let us look at how these five building blocks of an organization fit together.

Building Block One: Understanding Your Values and Developing a Compelling Vision

The foundation of any organization is the values you hold near and dear. Once you have identified those values very specifically, you use them to determine where you want to take your business; this becomes your Vision. It is the direction or destination where you want your company to go. It elucidates what a successful and thriving business looks like to you. This cannot be a pie-in-the-sky Vision, but a concrete, specific, and detailed description of what you want your enterprise to look like.

Fig. 1-1 Structure of Success—Vison & Values

Building Block Two: Identify Your Critical Success Factors

You need to identify the unique make-or-break, must-do activities for your business. We call these your Critical Success Factors—the things that your company must absolutely, positively do, and do correctly every day, to be successful.

Fig. 1-2 Structure of Success—Critical Success Factors

Building Block Three: Create a Comprehensive Strategy

This step involves the formulation of a detailed plan for how your business will achieve its Vision and accomplish its unique Critical Success Factors. This strategy needs to address all six of the functional areas of your company, which are:

1. Vision and Leadership
2. Marketing & Sales
3. Production
4. Finance and Administration
5. Human Assets
6. Information Technology

Fig. 1-3 Structure of Success—Strategy

Building Block Four: Establish a Practical Execution Plan

Next you need to develop and implement a plan to execute your strategy. The execution plan is a day-by-day, week-by-week and month-by-month plan of the tactical things that must be done to achieve your overall strategic plan.

Fig. 1-4 Structure of Success—Execution

Building Block Five: Innovate Your Business

Lastly you want to establish a spirit of innovation within your company that will allow you to apply transformational innovation to your entire organization. This will enable you to differentiate your business from your competition.

Fig. 1-5 Structure of Success—Innovation

When you combine these five building blocks, this is what the Structure of Success™ process looks like:

Fig. 1-6 Structure of Success

WHY IS THIS FRAMEWORK IMPORTANT?

There are two reasons why the above concepts are critical.

First, studies by McKinsey & Co. and the Harvard Business School have shown that 55% to 70% of a business's success is tied to proper execution. However, you cannot properly execute a Strategy without first having one to execute. Next, you cannot develop an effective Strategy without knowing your unique Critical Success Factors. Finally, you cannot determine your Critical Success Factors without knowing where you want to take your business (i.e., your Vision).

Second, without a cohesive and comprehensive operational plan, invariably a business will revert to functioning in a crisis management mode and dealing with the "crisis du jour" while putting out fires all day long. This may mean you end up functioning in what I refer to as a "tyranny-of-the-urgent" syndrome.

The result is that your company ends up going nowhere fast. This is often the cause of business-owner burnout. This burnout sets in because the company owner ends up doing the same thing day after day, week after week, month after month and year after year, getting no closer to his/her overall goals. If you use the Structure of Success™ process, you will not only achieve your company goals and avoid burnout, but you will also create a business system that ends up maximizing the market value of your business.

The essence of this book is that a structured methodology will create the business you long for—that is, the business of your dreams. Please note the Structure of Success™ process utilizes a systematic approach—but not a cookie-cutter one—to achieve a company's objectives. No two businesses will implement the concepts detailed in this book the same way.

Enormous amounts of your time, money, effort, thoughts, and energy are currently going into your business. Why not reduce the margin of error you deal with in pursuit of your goals? The systematic approach we will examine will also eliminate the guess work in taking your enterprise to the next level. The methodology we will consider leaves nothing to chance.

Talk to several people who have truly been successful in their businesses and you will find that they have in some way done what is included in this book. But you will also find that they most likely accomplished these things through years and years of trial and error. By following the concepts contained in this book, you will catapult your business forward because you will benefit from what others have discovered the hard way.

The concepts and ideas we will examine are game-changing. I promise if you implement the methodology, concepts, and ideas we will cover, your business will be changed forever!

Example

Joel was a very bright, articulate, and creative person in his late 40's who had been the Creative Director of several large advertising agencies. He had grown tired of the stress and demands of the positions, and as a result had started his own creative marketing agency.

After meeting with me to discuss the Structure of Success™, Joel understood how the moving parts of a successful business are supposed to fit together. He further grasped the concept of a Fruit Stand versus an Economic Factory business, and he did not want to continue the Fruit Stand model he was currently operating, so he invited his three adult children to join the company, added staff to carry out the details of the business's operations, and developed a game plan to grow his enterprise.

To do this, together they identified their Critical Success Factors, developed a comprehensive go-forward Strategy, and established a structured Execution Plan. As a result of these actions, the company grew to several million dollars in annual revenue and garnered a number of Fortune 1000 clients.

WHAT IS UNIQUE ABOUT THE STRUCTURE OF SUCCESS™ PROCESS?

There are five unique attributes of the Structure of Success™ methodology:

1. It is graphical in nature and because of this, it is easy to understand and intuitive. This enables company owners to see a clear picture of how the various parts of their businesses fit together.
2. It is built on the concept that the use of a structured and systematic approach in an enterprise will create one that is not overly dependent on its owners and allows them to scale and grow their companies.
3. The entire methodology uses concepts that enable an organization to perform an ongoing series of self-assessments. This empowers a company to effectively *plan*, then *execute*, then *evaluate*, which leads back to planning. As the entity continues to cycle through this process, it is continually improving itself.
4. It is scalable to the size and complexity of the business and can be implemented in small steps.
5. It is not meant to be only an exercise but consists of actionable concepts and ideas that move you, step by step, closer to your goals.

THE STRUCTURE OF SUCCESS™ VERSUS THE TRADITIONAL BUSINESS PLAN

Do not confuse the Structure of Success™ process with a traditional business plan; there is one key difference. Because of how a traditional business plan is constructed, and the fact that it does not lend itself to actually being executed, many times a business plan ends up sitting on a shelf collecting dust because it is *not* actionable.

Think of the Structure of Success™ process as a traditional business plan on steroids because every step is executable. They both contain the same basic elements but the Structure of Success™ process gives your enterprise a very quick payback because you are taking actions, implementing concepts, and harvesting the benefits from these actions almost immediately.

Looking at the typical components of a traditional business plan, here is how it compares to the Structure of Success™ model:

Typical Business Plan	Structure of Success™ Area
Describe your business	Values and Vision
What is your product/service?	Marketing & Sales, Producing Your Product or Service
What is your target market?	Marketing & Sales
Define your customers' needs and your ability to meet those needs	Marketing & Sales
Show that your customers can and will pay for your product/service	Marketing & Sales
Show the size of your market	Marketing & Sales
What are your competitors' strengths and weaknesses?	Marketing & Sales
Address impediments to success	Marketing & Sales, Producing Your Product or Service
Communicate your business's management and their expertise	Human Assets, Becoming a World-Class Leader
State your marketing strategy	Marketing & Sales

Communicate your business's goals and objectives	Values and Vision, Renewing Your Vision
Communicate your funding needs and targeted financial outcomes	Finance and Administration
Inform investors and lenders of their expected return on investment	Values and Vision, Renewing Your Vision, Becoming a World-Class Leader, Finance and Administration

Table 1-1

THE FIVE ROLES OF A LEADER

As we delve into this framework in the remainder of this book, keep in mind that from my experience in working with over 1,200 companies during the past 17 years, I have observed there are five roles of a business leader:

1. Develop and cast a compelling Vision for the organization
2. Develop a strategy for achieving your Vision
3. Create the organization to accomplish your Vision
4. Oversee the business's execution and manage it via metrics
5. Apply transformational innovation to the entire organization

Let me flesh these out a little.

Develop and Cast a Compelling Vision for the Organization

You must figure out where you want to take your business (the Vision for your company) and then present that Vision to the people you want to affect.

Develop a Strategy for Achieving your Vision

While it is great to have a Vision for your business, you must also have a plan for accomplishing it. This plan is your strategy.

Create the Organization to Accomplish the Vision

If you have a Vision for your business, and you have a strategy for achieving your Vision, you will also need an organizational vehicle for accomplishing your strategy. This organization is the company, the personnel (if you have any), the methodologies, the processes, etc. that you will need to realize your goals.

Oversee the Business's Execution and Manage it via Metrics

Once these prior elements are in place, your game plan must be properly executed and since businesses do not run by themselves, you will need to monitor, direct, and oversee your business's operations. This involves the use of administrative and financial controls and measurements (known as "metrics"). We will examine effective execution and metrics in detail in Chapter 11.

Apply Transformational Innovation to the Entire Organization

Lastly, to differentiate your business and separate it from the competition, transformational innovation needs to be applied to your entire company. We will focus on this step in Chapter 12.

If the above steps sound familiar, it is because they are a recap of the Structure of Success™ methodology. The five roles of a business leader flow directly from the Structure of Success™ methodology, which makes it straight forward to understand what it takes to become a world-class leader.

Complete exercise 1-2 in workbook

HOW IS THIS BOOK ORGANIZED?

Within the above five building blocks you will find the following 12 steps for creating the business for which you long. Each of these 12 steps is separately addressed in the chapters listed below:

Chapter	Description	Step
2	Where Is This Ship Going?	#1
3	How Are You Going to Get There?	#2
4	Getting the Word Out	#3
5	Five Ways to Beat Your Competition	#4
6	Growing Your Money Tree	#5
7	You Can't Do It Alone	#6
8	Technology to the Rescue	#7
9	Double Checking Your Compass	#8
10	Effectively Calling the Shots	#9
11	Proper Execution Will Win the Day	#10
12	Building a Better Mousetrap	#11
13	Putting It All Together	#12

One of the most frustrating things in life is when you have a dream, desire, or goal, but no way to achieve it. The methodology we will examine in detail in this book provides you with a path to the Vision for your business.

With this in mind, I want to say one last thing to business owners or leaders who are thoroughly discouraged with their companies, about to throw in the towel, or give up on their dreams. If you are open and willing to change your company, you can exchange your discouragement for the success, satisfaction, and peace of mind of knowing your company is the on the path to becoming the business of your dreams!

Chapter 2

Where Is This Ship Going?
(Step #1)

• • • • •

The first step in taking the business that you have and turning it into the business of your dreams is to develop a compelling Vision for it. However, your Vision for your company is founded on and reflects what you value. Therefore, we need to begin by identifying the values, principles, and philosophical underpinnings you hold near and dear.

This process is important because it is incumbent that you anchor your beliefs and values into the bedrock of your company. This is crucial because you want to avoid the pressures of the marketplace that may cause you to stray from the original purpose and values for which you started your business.

INNOVATION

EXECUTION

STRATEGY

CRITICAL SUCCESS FACTORS

VISION & VALUES

Fig. 2-1 Structure of Success—Values

YOUR VALUES

Values are the beliefs you live by, espouse or hold in high regard. They are the concepts you hold close to your heart, such as honesty, thriftiness or diligence. These values may be personal or business related. In many companies, identifying your values is an often-overlooked step in trying to create a successful business. Once you have identified these, use them to determine where you want to take your enterprise.

Why Are Values Important?

Values are the assumptions about how things work and beliefs that drive and shape how a business owner wants to operate the company. Two equally successful competitors could have completely different philosophies or principles on how they operate. For instance, business owners who have train locomotive companies could decide that they want to produce their product (locomotives) in very different ways based on their respective Values.

Company A may believe that using a single, fully integrated manufacturing and assembly team that operates in one large, centralized manufacturing facility yields the highest quality product with the lowest manufacturing cost. This business feels that utilizing one team to build the locomotive end to end will produce the highest quality product.

Company A believes in using a craftsman's-like team environment that creates pride of workmanship. It believes the related ownership that comes from this being "their locomotive" and operating in an old-world craftsman environment, in which there is mutual accountability for the quality of the product will consistently produce the best product in the most cost-effective manner.

Conversely, Company B's world view (what it values) is that contracting out as many components as possible and then using a traditional assembly line approach provides the highest quality locomotives at the lowest cost.

It has incentives for high quality and punishments for substandard quality built into their supplier contracts. Since it is using an assembly line approach, it has employed a rigorous quality control process to ensure the highest quality locomotives.

Company B believes that it is impractical to be an expert on everything, so it utilizes suppliers who have developed expertise in various areas for components and assemblies. To ensure the highest quality, it uses very exacting engineering specifications for its component and assembly suppliers.

If we boil down these two scenarios into their core philosophies, we would see that business A has a foundational principle of the "pride of workmanship" whereas business B has a foundational principle of "specialization."

Neither philosophy is right or wrong, better or worse, but what is paramount is that A's and B's entire Execution Plan will be totally different. If you tried to use Company A's Execution Plan for Company B or vice versa, you would have a disaster because foundationally each business wants to achieve the same result (high quality locomotives), but by an entirely different route.

In assessing your beliefs, philosophies, values, principles and ideologies, you may find you do not have any strong persuasions about how to operate your business and want to do things in the traditional or standard way for your industry. That is a perfectly acceptable realization, but you will do yourself a favor by at least considering your values and how they may impact your business.

There are six types of Values, namely:

1. Values that apply to all humans
2. Values that apply to all businesses (no matter where they are located)
3. Industry-specific Values
4. Market subsegment Values
5. Values that apply only to your business
6. Your personal Values

Keep in mind Values can apply to any area of your company.

Values That Apply to All Humans

These are Values that are common to all humans, no matter in which country they live, no matter what their society is, no matter what their socioeconomic group is.

Example—No matter where people live, they like relaxed environments where they feel welcomed, safe, and befriended.

Application of example—In the Production area of a business, you have created a restaurant that is a cross between a Starbucks® and the Cheers television program, where people want to drop in throughout the day and eat, talk and just "hang out."

Values That Apply to All Businesses

These are Values that are relevant to all businesses, regardless of where they are located, no matter what kind of business it is, and not subject to the size of the enterprise.

Example—Wherever a business is located, it will operate better when it understands, relates to and addresses the emotional state of its customer.

Application of example—You invest in software for your telephone Customer Support personnel which analyzes a caller's words and voice inflexions to determine their emotional state and stress level. The system shows this information on the Customer Support person's computer display and suggests words that can be used to address and sooth the customer's emotional state.

Industry Specific Values

These are Values which are unique to certain industries or business segments.

Example—Certain industries, such as the pharmaceutical industry (that is selling to heath care professionals) have found that using a "hard sales" approach does not work as well as educating the customer on how their product meets their needs.

Application of example—You use a consultative sales approach where you primarily educate the heath care professional customer about your product. Your Marketing & Sales personnel operate as a "consultant" to their customers instead of a "salesperson."

Market Subsegment Values

These are Values that pertain to specific markets or industry subsegments.

Example—Customers feel most connected to a business when the company asks them for input and recommendations on how to improve their products. This is especially true in the Baby Care Market subsegment of the Consumer Products market.

Application of example—Knowing that some of the best ideas for improving current or developing new Baby Care Products come from the parents of the babies, you set up a website to solicit input from the parents who buy your products.

To do this you include an eye-catching insert in every Baby Care Products package you produce which solicits input through a website. Each week you give awards to the top three submissions.

Values That Apply Only to Your Business

These are Values which are unique to how you want to operate your business.

Example—You feel that you want to have a business which is not only very profitable, but also allows people to eat healthy.

Application of example—You create a line of healthy ice cream, which is high in antioxidants, high in fiber, and uses green and white tea as ingredients. It utilizes organic ingredients and comes in natural fruit flavors that are healthy for your customers like strawberry, blueberry, and mango. Finally, you develop a signature flavor which is a red-grape ice cream that is naturally high in resveratrol.

Your Personal Values

These are your personal Values by which you live, and they may or may not impact how you operate your business.

Example—You feel that it is desirable to give people who have run afoul of the law a second chance in life.

Application of example—To give wayward youth a second chance in life, you hire 10% of your employees from the roll of juveniles who have had legal problems but are now trying to change their lives.

Example

Debbie, who was a kind-hearted woman in her mid-40's, had started several successful businesses before, but didn't find much personal fulfillment in any of them. However, when she was trying to find care for her elderly mother, she realized that a senior living and care search business could be something that she would find personally satisfying.

This kind of business met the basic human need that almost all people have of wanting to care for others. It, it provided a valuable service of finding the proper living arrangements or care for a senior person, and she built it in such a way that it was a blessing to both the families that were looking for care of their loved ones as well as to the facilities providing the care.

Her great knowledge of people in general, a wish to serve others, and her personal desire to help people just like her mother enabled her to create a very successful business that was built upon many values that were important to her.

Complete exercise 2-1 in workbook

A VISION FOR YOUR COMPANY

Fig. 2-2 Structure of Success—Vison

We need a starting point for developing a compelling Vision for your company, so I would like you to stop and write down the current Vision you have for your business. It will only take a few minutes. Try to be as specific as possible and don't assume the Vision for your enterprise is so obvious that anyone can see it.

Everything in life is created at least twice. First it is created in the mind of the creator and then in the real world. This truism applies to anything, whether you are building a deck, planting a garden, or starting a business. What you are trying to do must be first formulated in your mind and then your body can do the actual actions needed to create the item.

However, I believe everything, including your business, should be created *three times*. First it is created in the mind of the creator, then secondly on paper, and thirdly in the real world.

Why is the writing-down step vitally important? It is because our minds have a curious tendency to take two or more things that do not synchronize and fit them together. In your mind, your business may seem to be a perfect mosaic that fits together so all its "if-thens" are in perfect harmony, but this may not be the reality of your situation. This can lead to prerequisites being accidently glossed over.

Writing down the Vision for your business helps to identify those gaps. When you create something on paper you can analyze it for logic and completeness, look for the loose ends and gaps in your reasoning, and recognize the dependencies of actions that must take place in a certain order. Writing your Vision down also enables you to review what you have recorded before and edit, clarify, and improve it based on items discussed in this book.

Also, I suggest you have someone review and "punch holes" in what you have written as a result of reading this book. Does this phrase need to be removed? It appears you're asking the person to do this before reading the book. However, you do not want to choose someone who tends to pour cold water on virtually everyone's ideas. Conversely, don't pick someone who is an unrealistic optimist, does not want to hurt your feelings or does not have the appropriate background to provide you proper feedback. Your objective should be to find someone who would give you both positive and negative constructive feedback.

Complete exercise 2-2 in workbook

WHERE COMETH A VISION

A Vision can come from five main sources:

1. Dreaming (or daydreaming) about a business or an invention that could lead to a business.
2. Reading books, listening to tapes or CD's, or attending seminars or conferences which cause you to think about possibilities for a company.
3. Talking with other people who stimulate your thoughts.
4. A synthesis of the above that involves an intuitive leap of thinking. For instance, you attend a seminar and then discuss some of the things the speaker brought up with a friend. All of sudden you have an "aha" moment when multiple things come together and

springboard you to an entirely new thought and a business idea that is different from either the seminar topic, or discussion with your friend.

5. Dreams or visions you received from God regarding your business. While this is not a particularly common way of developing a Vision for a business, the Bible and other holy books record various situations where a person received divine guidance on a matter.

No matter the source of your Vision, the goal is to clarify your business idea and develop a Vision in such a way as to make it so inspiring in your mind it becomes the compulsion necessary to take your organization where you want it to go. It must be motivating enough to overcome the possibility of a "gale force wind" of issues and problems you may face in your business. The end result of developing this Vision is it will lead you to create a company that will be a fountainhead of profitability and personal satisfaction.

YOUR VISION SHOULD BE POWERFUL

> "Vision"—The desired or intended future state of a specific organization or enterprise in terms of its fundamental objective and/or strategic direction.

Each of us grew up in a particular neighborhood and while most of us no longer live in those same neighborhoods, in a split second we can remember in detail the sights, sounds, smells, and memories of our childhood neighborhood. Recalling these can transform your emotional state in a moment or cause you to recollect something you have not thought about in a long time.

The Vision for your business should be every bit as powerful as your childhood memories. It should affect your emotional state in a moment. It should transport you into the future where you can envision what your company will look like.

There are two related concepts which are unbelievably powerful and motivating:

1. Where is your business going?
2. What will it look like when it gets there?

Studies have shown the human mind is much better at *moving toward* something rather than *moving away from* something.

For instance, if I say to you, "Think about a beautiful beach with soft white sand, gently lapping waves, and palm trees swaying in the breeze," that is what you are going to think about. It is the same way with your company—the first step in having the business of your dreams is to state very clearly and in detail what that dream looks like. What does a successful and thriving business look like to you?

Relatedly, to develop and maintain a Vision you must be optimistic; in particular, you must be expectant about what your company will look like in the future. Great leaders are always optimists! By being positive about your desires for your business I am not suggesting that you be totally unrealistic, but you must have encouraging thoughts about your business so even when trying circumstances arise, you can very clearly see in your mind's eye the end in sight.

RESULTS OF HAVING A COMPELLING VISION

At the beginning of this chapter I mentioned the objective is to have a compelling Vision, not just a "check it off" your to-do list type of Vision. These are the results of having a compelling Vision:

- It becomes the North Star for your business
- It provides the "fire in your belly" that motivates you each day
- It becomes your sales process
- It is how you deliver your product/service

Let's look at each of these more closely.

Your Compelling Vision Becomes Your North Star

For thousands of years people have navigated by the North Star—a beacon guiding them to their destination.

Your Vision is the North Star for your company. No matter what gets thrown at you on a daily, weekly, monthly, or yearly basis, you have a guide to help you navigate in this world. Your Vision will lead you to your intended destination by acting as a compass to assist you with decisions, issues, and problems.

Your Compelling Vision Becomes the "Fire in Your Belly" that Motivates You Each Day

Earlier in this chapter we discussed the gale force wind that company owners may run up against as they move their businesses forward. Each issue, time pressure, deadline, decision, challenge, problem, disappointment or derailment may seem like a gale force wind blowing directly in your face. This wind might keep you from doing virtually anything at all or conversely it might challenge you to summon your drive and determination to deal with the issue du jour. Having a compelling Vision is key to finding that fire in your belly which yields that drive and determination to overcome those challenges.

Your Compelling Vision Becomes Your Sales Process

A properly conceived Vision becomes your Unique Selling Proposition which is foundational to your Marketing & Sales processes. A compelling Vision is not only motivating to you—it is also motivating and inviting to your customers. By simply communicating your Vision, customers will want to do business with you because of what you can do for them. We will discuss this in the pages ahead and in Chapter 4, Marketing & Sales.

Your Compelling Vision is How You Deliver Your Product/ Service

While it is wonderful to have a North Star for your business, a fire in your belly to motivate you each day, and a Marketing & Sales processes that are a natural outgrowth of your Vision, unless you can provide your product/service to your customer, all of the above are wasted efforts.

There is a straightforward answer to this challenge. A properly conceived and executed Vision guides you in delivering your product/service. In other words, your delivery process is the execution of your Vision (we will discuss this more in Chapter 5, Producing Your Product or Service).

Example

When we started working with this tree-service company, the owner Roberto, a greying, friendly man in his early 50's, told me they were struggling mightily with how to get all of their 25 employees on the same page and working together. They had experienced high personnel turnover, and Roberto rushed from trying to address one problem to another. He was frustrated and beginning to get exhausted from constantly having to put out "fires" all day long in his company.

As we began implementing the Structure of Success™ in his company, he and his management team were able to flesh out a Vision that became their North Star, and it also put a "fire in their belly" to do the things that would move the company toward its Vision each and every day.

They had wrestled with two key concerns: first, how to get their sales personnel to properly quote tree jobs so they would end up being profitable, and second, ensuring the tree crews did the job the way it was quoted. These two issues were crucial because there were multiple ways a specific tree job could be quoted and thereafter actually done, and both the sales and production areas refused to fully communicate and coordinate with each other. Each area continually blamed the other area for the various difficulties they were encountering.

By both departments being fully involved in the Visioning process, they bought into the company Vision, which led to the Vision becoming part of their sales process and how they delivered their tree services. This decision to fully work together as a result of a shared Vision transformed the company into one of the largest tree service organizations in their metropolitan area.

THE IMPORTANCE OF HAVING A COMPELLING VISION

We all live very busy lives and are bombarded every day with three basic types of information: facts, people's opinions, and advertising. In response, we either internalize or reject this input, which impacts the decisions we make.

A Compelling Vision Gives You a Clear Signal

All this information intruding into our lives can feel like hearing a countless number of AM and FM radio signals simultaneously. This would sound just like a cacophony of noise.

However, when you tune your radio to a specific station, you get a clear signal. The Vision for your organization is this clear signal—the only one that should be guiding you.

A focused compelling Vision enables you to process and interpret these countless facts, opinions, and advertisements that come into your life and use this information to assist in achieving the goals for your enterprise. However, continually and drastically changing your Vision based on this incoming information would be like switching radio stations every second—not a good experience.

THREE STEPS TO CREATING A COMPELLING VISION

How do you create a compelling Vision? By using the "Three C's of Visioning:"

1. Conceptualizing your business
2. Crafting a compelling Vision
3. Casting your Vision

Conceptualizing Your Business

You start by conceptualizing your business, which is dreaming, envisioning, and pondering (possibility thinking)—what your business could look like three years into the future. For this dreaming process, one year is too short of a time to really get past where your business is at today.

Conversely, once you pass five years, things become so nebulous they are not helpful. I have found that looking three years out is both far enough and near enough to give you the best results.

While more than simply wishing or hoping, conceptualizing your Vision is letting your imagination create a clear image of what you want your business to be. The result should be so clear, so specific, that it becomes as real as those memories of your childhood neighborhood!

Crafting a Compelling Vision

After you figure out in your mind what you want your enterprise to look like, you need to craft this image in words. Translate the thoughts in your mind into a "word picture" so appealing, so compelling, it will motivate a listener to become involved with your business.

The goal of your Vision Statement is to emotionally connect with your target audience by aligning your business objectives with their personal or business goals by using words, terms, and expressions that demonstrate that your company exists for them, not vice versa. Regarding a prospect or customer, your Vision should make it clear to them that purchasing your product/service will move them closer to their goals in life.

Your Vision Statement should be three to five paragraphs long, generally one paragraph for each of the five stakeholders of your business (introduced in the next section). It must clearly state the Win for each stakeholder.

Casting Your Vision

The final step of the three C's of Visioning is to share the crafted Vision with your target audience. You can do this in many ways. For instance, you may say it to a customer, discuss it with an employee, or display it on your website.

Who is your target audience? Everyone! If you are so excited by your business's Vision, then everyone you meet will be drawn to it, just like an object in space is drawn to a star by its gravitational pull. Your Vision should be so attractive, captivating, and compelling that someone who was not interested becomes interested.

More specifically, your external audiences are your customers, suppliers, and society. What should a compelling Vision do for them?

- Attract potential customers
- Provide the framework to retain customers for life
- Engage your suppliers to want to provide you with the best products/service and customer service
- Communicate how your company will benefit society

Additionally, the internal audiences of your Vision are your employees and owners. Internally, what should a compelling Vision accomplish?

- Inspire and motivate personnel
- Guide operations
- Attract and satisfy owners

THE FIVE AUDIENCES OF YOUR COMPELLING VISION

Your Five Stakeholders

As was mentioned above, there are five stakeholders of your business, and your Vision Statement should address the needs and wants of each of these stakeholders by resonating with and motivating them. Many times, I read Vision Statements that address only one stakeholder, the business owner. To be truly successful, your company needs to provide a Win/Win experience for everyone involved with it. Your Vision should be:

- Crucial to customers
- Essential to employees
- Imperative to owners and investors
- Significant to suppliers
- Support to society

Crucial to Customers

A business exists to serve its customers and meet their perceived needs. If a business fulfills this, it has accomplished the main task for which it exists. Therefore, your customers have a stake in your company's existence and operation.

Your Vision Statement must clearly and unequivocally state the Win your customers will receive by dealing with you. They must see that:

- Your product/service is better at meeting their perceived need than your competitors
- They can trust you to deal with them in a desirable manner
- The value they perceive they are receiving is worth the cost

The words and images in your Vision Statement must communicate how you will meet your customer's perceived needs, and this is the most important part of your Vision.

Most of us have heard that word-of-mouth advertising is the most effective form of advertising. For a customer/client to become an advocate for a company, they must feel they have had an experience they would like to repeat or tell others about.

A current customer recommending you is much better than you speaking to a prospect—because unlike you, your customers has little to gain from that action. You can only create customer-advocates by identifying their needs, exceeding their expectations, and delivering something they consider to be a very good value—and your Vision statement should state how you will accomplish this.

Essential to Employees

Most businesses cannot survive without employees. People will only work for you if they feel it is in their best interest. Therefore, your employees have a stake in your company.

Your employees' stake hold in your business manifests itself two ways.

1. First, your employees must feel that by working for your company they are a partner with you in serving your customers. Therefore, employees want to know you are taking care of them and giving them a fair deal. In essence, how will you provide a Win employment experience for them. Your Vision Statement must plainly and explicitly communicate this.
2. Second, you need to cast your company's overall compelling Vision to your employees, so they feel they are part of something bigger than themselves.

If both areas are properly addressed in your Vision Statement, your employees will go the second and third mile for you and your customers.

I have found that a compelling Vision acts to rally employees to a better future. To fulfill this role of rallying employees you must inspire, motivate, and encourage your personnel by use of your Vision. When you combine a compelling Vision with the knowledge and resources to accomplish the tasks at hand, you empower your employees. Empowered employees can change the world!

When you communicate a compelling Vision to employees they will respond positively to big requests and sacrifices because they want to be part of a team making a difference. They feel challenged in a good way with the compelling Vision you have cast to them.

Depending on how your enterprise is structured your independent contractors can be included in this stakeholder section.

Imperative to Owners and Investors

You obviously have a stake in your company because it is your future income, livelihood, and where you are going to spend a great amount of your time and mental efforts. Additionally, other investors (whether through an equity investment or a loan) have a stake in your enterprise's success.

Your business may start with you as the only investor, but at some point, you may need additional capital or want to sell some or all of it. Your company and consequently your Vision Statement must be compelling to potential owners and investors. This portion of your Vision Statement needs to state in general terms what the enterprise's owners and investors want to obtain from it.

Significant to Suppliers

The vendors who provide services or products to your business (different from independent contractors) are also its stakeholders. If your business doesn't succeed, they no longer have the opportunity to serve you as their customer.

Therefore, except in the case where a supplier is so large that you are insignificant to their revenue stream, there is a stakeholder relationship between your entity and its suppliers.

Your Vision Statement should communicate how your enterprise will be an asset to key suppliers and vendors so they will be drawn to partner with you to meet your customer's needs.

Support to Society

Because all businesses operate in the context of and benefit from the society in which they exist, a Vision Statement should state how the company intends to provide a Win to society. You may be thinking, "What debt does a business owe to society and what is the nature of this stake hold?"

A business would not be able to exist without the rule of law provided by its society. Without police, fire, and national security services, it could not operate. Roads being provided for its customers, employees and suppliers to reach it are fundamental for its survival. The infrastructure that is necessary for a company to conduct business is part of the society that businesses need to appreciate and therefore support.

This gratitude needs to take the form of companies being "good corporate citizens" and supporting and giving back to the society to which they owe their very existence. Therefore, this part of a company's Vision Statement should state how it will be a responsible part of the community in which it operates, make the world a better place, and improve the economic wellbeing of the people that comprise the society in which it resides.

Example

A security-guard company that was owned by Carol, a tall, thin woman in her mid-30's, was in the process of developing a compelling Vision for her business. Carol and her small management team had completed the first version of its Vision statement. As I reviewed it, I found they had developed one that was very inviting to both their Customers and to Carol herself as an Owner.

However, the Vision statement did not include anything that addressed their Employees, Suppliers, or Society. As I worked with Carol and her management team, they realized that they had not thought through the process of how to create a company that was attractive not only to their Customers and Carol, but one that provided a resounding benefit to their Employees, Suppliers, and Society.

Thereafter, they were able to establish a Vision statement that motivated their Employees and was a guide to them in developing an enterprise that would deliver a substantial reward to their Suppliers and Society.

Complete exercise 2-3 in workbook

Having this expanded understanding of a compelling Vision, you should begin to see your business in a significantly different light.

CREATING A WIN/WIN EXPERIENCE

In Steven Covey's book *The 7 Habits of Highly Effective People,* the fourth habit he discusses is "Think Win/Win." A compelling Vision has Think Win/Win at its core. Specifically, you want everyone who interacts with your business to have a Win/Win experience.

Why is this so important? Have you ever gotten the short end of the stick in a transaction or plainly been ripped off? That person or business practiced Win/Lose. It was a "win" for them but a "lose" for you.

When you practice Win/Lose, you do not have repeat customers, happy, contented, long-term employees, satisfied owners, or suppliers who will go the extra mile for you. Win/Lose is a self-destructive cycle, but Win/Win is a self-perpetuating cycle! When a business does not consciously practice Win/Win they may end up operating with some variation of Win/Lose.

To accomplish Win/Win you need to continuously create goodwill. To do this your Vision must be clearly thought out, regularly communicated, and consistently achieved.

Developing, communicating, and delivering your Vision is like laying a course of bricks; they must be all in a line, otherwise after a few courses of brick the wall will weaken.

If you conceptualize your business one way, but you cast your Vision in a different way, then your target audience will be confused. Likewise, if you don't deliver on your Vision, your target audience will say, "They talked a good game, but they did not play a good game."

To practice Win/Win you first need to clearly identify your customers then build your business to meet your customer's perceived needs. All great visionaries have done this with their companies.

Example

Lisa, a wife and mother in her late 30's, owned a large landscaping business, and she and her leadership team were trying to solidify their Vision statement. Once they were introduced to and comprehended the concept of Think Win/Win, they were well on their way of establishing a compelling Vision that had Think Win/Win at its core.

They ended up doing such a great job of articulating and delivering a Win/Win experience to their customers, they created tons of repeat homeowners who loved the experience of dealing with Lisa's company. By effectively executing their Vision, they also produced happy, engaged long-term employees. Because they not only "talked a good game, but played a good game," they ended up winning numerous landscaping design and installation awards.

Additionally, as result of clearly defining, consistently communicating, and effectively executing their win/win Vision statement with the people who interacted with their business, they created a large amount of community goodwill.

MISSION STATEMENT VERSUS VISION

Now that you have a rough version of your Vision Statement, you may be wondering how it differs from a traditional Mission Statement.

From my perspective, a Mission Statement focuses on the fundamental purpose for the existence of the business, whereas a Vision Statement is focused on what the company will look like at a particular point in time.

Specifically, your Mission Statement differs in three ways from your Vision Statement.

1. First, your Mission Statement can be likened to the road your business is on; while your Vision is the view or scenery you see on the road. Your Vision Statement is a snapshot of your company and its relationship with its five stakeholders you will see when you arrive at your destination.
2. The second difference is that a Mission statement is typically entirely focused on the targeted customer, whereas a Vision Statement should address all five of the stakeholders of the business.
3. Third, Mission Statements mainly appear in Marketing & Sales literature, websites, and various marketing and advertising documents, while Vision Statements are generally used more strategically.

Relatedly, your slogan is a shortened version of your Mission Statement that tells others where your company is going. For instance, on a personal level if you were traveling to the Florida Keys you might say: "I'm going to the beach" or "I want to catch some sun" or "I'm going to chill out." Your slogan should utilize terms and words your target audience understands and can relate to in an appealing manner, so it provides a shorthand version of the benefit they will obtain from your organization.

Now that we have gone through the initial step in understanding how to create a business that is a Win/Win for your customers and how to translate that to a compelling Vision Statement, we can easily create a compelling Mission Statement.

To do this take the customer portion of your Vision Statement, generalize it, and ensure that is it focused on what the overall purpose of your business and the "road" your business in on. A Mission Statement should be no longer than two sentences.

Complete exercise 2-4 in workbook

FOSTERING AND ENCOURAGING THE DEVELOPMENT OF YOUR VISION

There are a number of things you can do to foster, encourage, and incubate the development of your Vision.

First, focus your time, energy, and thinking on what you want your business to look like three years from now. Focusing your thought process is the key! As we discussed previously, everything in life is first created in your mind, and if your mind is not focusing on what you want your company to look like, then it is doubtful you will develop a compelling Vision.

Related to this concept is that as you regularly think and plan about what you want your business to look like, those dreams and Vision become the "fire in your belly" that motivates you each day. While it is necessary to deal with and confront the negative thoughts that everyone has regarding their company, it is not productive to focus on them too much. Remember focusing on the obstacles means you are not concentrating on the Vision for your business.

You need to be like a "laser" rather than like the light bulb when it comes to your business and your Vision. Both the light bulb and a laser are light; the difference is that the laser is completely focused, while the light bulb is defused. Use your free time to focus your mind on your company and how to make it an incredible success. For instance, turn off the radio in your car and think about your Vision and what you are going to do today to move closer to it. Or listen to an inspirational CD while driving. Always have reading material with you so when you take a break for lunch or need to wait at an appointment, you can stimulate ideas for your Vision.

THREE COMMON VISION PROBLEMS

I have typically seen the following three problems with the Vision area for an organization:

- There is no Vision
- There is a Vision, but it is not current
- The business owner creates the Vision with no input from any of the company's other personnel

There Is No Vision

When there is no Vision for a business, the company basically muddles along with the same activities day after day, putting out fires, but not doing much to move it in a meaningful direction. Because of this they may lose customers and employees who decide "this business is going nowhere fast."

There is a Vision, But It is Not Current

A Vision was created, but when the business changed, the Vision did not. Thus, the Vision is irrelevant to the ongoing operations of the business.

The Business Owner Creates the Vision with No Input from any of the Business's Personnel

If the business only has one person, then the business owner has no choice but to create the Vision himself or herself. However, if the business has other key personnel who will be instrumental in determining its destiny, they should be included in the Visioning process.

If you get your key employees involved in developing a shared Vision, you will have a much better and more complete Vision than if you do it by yourself—and everyone will be on board with it. To do this you follow the above Visioning process in a group setting with your key employees.

Please keep in mind the employees you have now may not be the same ones who will be with you a couple of years from now. So, you may need to revisit this Visioning process as your enterprise grows.

Besides the business owner, who are the key employees that should participate in these meetings? Generally, they will be the head of sales, operations, finance and accounting, personnel and information technology. In a larger company they may have the titles of VP of Sales, Chief Operations Officer, VP of Finance, Director of Human Resources and Information Technology Officer. In smaller organizations they may have Director or Manager titles.

In addition to the above personnel, depending on the nature of the company, there may one or two other people who may participate in developing your Vision. Normally, there will no more than six to eight people in these meetings otherwise the group's operation becomes too unwieldy. Throughout this development process, the important thing is to solicit input from the people who are in charge of all aspects of your organization.

There are a couple of reasons to solicit your key personnel's opinions when it comes to creating your Vision. First, as the adage goes, two heads (or more) are better than one. Each person will bring a unique perspective on how to create a Win/Win experience for each of your stakeholders.

Second, because it will be their Vision for "their company," buy-in occurs. Once you have buy-in from your key employees, they can in turn obtain buy-in from your remaining employees. Developing a shared

Vision also produces a more harmonious and peaceful work environment because of the unifying nature of having common goals and purpose.

Example

Carl was a serious, focused man in his mid-20's, who owned a software company and he was in the process of developing his business' Vision statement. While he and his wife (who also worked in the business) had done a very good job of understanding their customers and their needs, he was not a person who liked to interact with his management team and employees. Therefore, he developed the Vision statement himself and did not solicit input from others.

There were two consequences of this omission. First, he missed out on obtaining valuable input from his employees that could have made the Vision statement better and more comprehensive. Second, the Vision statement was not fully embraced by his personnel because it was "his" Vision statement, not theirs. The ultimate outcome was that the Vision Statement was not as powerful and impactful as it could have been if his entire leadership team and some of his employees had participated in the Vision-statement creation process.

> Your employees' involvement in this process is like many tributaries coming into and combining with the main river, thereby making the river larger, more powerful, and able to provide more benefits because of its size.

CHAPTER SUMMARY

Creating a compelling Vision is the first step in realizing the business of your dreams. You then need to cast that Vision to the five stakeholders in your company.

Once you have developed a compelling Vision, it becomes the motivating factor by which all other aspects of your business pull together. When you feel you are starting to lose your way, you can always go back and reground yourself in your Vision. In the next chapter, we will examine how to develop a strategy for achieving your Vision.

Chapter 3

How Are You Going to Get There? (Step #2)

• • • • •

In Chapter 2 we learned how to create a compelling Vision for your business. Now that you know *where* you want to take your business, the next question is *how* do you get there?

YOUR STRATEGY: THE ROAD MAP FOR ACHIEVING YOUR VISION

While having a compelling Vision is the start, you still need a road map of how to realize your Vision. This is your Strategy.

Your Strategy includes your objectives, policies, and resource-utilization plans stated in such a way that it will provide a plan to achieve your Vision.

Components include:

- What business a company is in (the product line as well as the markets for which products are designed)
- The channels though which these markets with be reached
- The image it will project to key stakeholders
- The means by which the company will be financed
- The profit objectives
- The eventual size of the business

45

Let's start by setting this book aside and writing down your Strategy for accomplishing the Vision for your business.

Complete exercise 3-1 in workbook

Next, look at what you have written and ask yourself: Does it address the specific things I must do to achieve the Vision for my business? Does it capture all the things that are indispensable for my company to accomplish its Vision? Is it not only comprehensive, but is it also an *executable* Strategy?

I have seen a significant number of Strategic Plans lack a definition of all the things a business must do to achieve its Vision. These "must do" items are called your Critical Success Factors. By identifying and addressing all your Critical Success Factors, you ensure you have a *comprehensive and executable* Strategy.

WHAT IS A CRITICAL SUCCESS FACTOR FOR A BUSINESS?

Critical Success Factors are the items or actions a company must achieve to reach its Vision—the things that will either make or break the business. Identifying your Critical Success Factors will determine the destiny of your business; they are the foundation of your Strategy. Focusing on Critical Success Factors allows you to formulate your Strategy in small, easily accomplished steps.

Every business has limited time, money, and talent; identifying your Critical Success Factors enables you to channel your effort into the most important areas for your business and utilize your resources most efficiently to achieve your Vision.

As we discussed in Chapter 2, the lack of having a clear Vision can lead to being stuck in a "tyranny-of-the-urgent" syndrome in which the organization functions in a reactive mode instead of a strategic mode. Consequently, the creation of a Strategy based on Critical Success Factors will move an organization away from simply dealing with the crisis of the day to the strategic execution of your game plan. This will ultimately allow you to move from working *in your business to working on* your business. Further, by operating in a strategic fashion, you will have a better chance of creating a business that has a saleable value.

Think of Critical Success Factors like the body's central nervous system—just as your central nervous system directs the muscles of your body, so should your Critical Success Factors direct the actions of your business.

Fig. 3-1 Structure of Success—Critical Success Factors

IDENTIFYING YOUR CRITICAL SUCCESS FACTORS

The first step in determining your Critical Success Factors is to analyze your business and look for things that must absolutely, positively be done correctly or your company will fail. These are not only nice things to have or do, but items that will either make or break your business—things that you must do well every day to be successful.

For any business, there are generally between 15 and 25 Critical Success Factors. To use Critical Success Factors to monitor how your business is performing, you need to translate them to a measurement system (or a set of metrics) sometimes called Key Performance Indicators. A number of studies have shown the maximum number of Key Performance Indicators a business owner can practically monitor is in this same 15 to 25 range. I have personally found that very rarely will a business have more than this number of "make-or-break" factors.

Complete exercise 3-2 in workbook

THE SIX CATEGORIES OF CRITICAL SUCCESS FACTORS

No matter the size of an organization there are six areas of a business. A startup company has these six areas; IBM and Microsoft have the same six areas. While IBM, Microsoft . . . may be a lot more complex than a startup, every business has the same six areas.

1. **Vision and Leadership**—What is the Vision for your business and what Leadership are you providing to drive your company toward this Vision? Your Vision and Leadership area leads to your Marketing & Sales area.

2. **Marketing & Sales**—How are you going to market your products/services and what will be your sales process? Your Marketing & Sales area leads to your Production area.

3. **Production**—How are you going to produce what you are marketing and selling? Your Production area leads to your Finance & Administration area.

4. **Finance and Administration**—What will you do to manage your finances and handle administrative activities? Your Finance & Administration area leads to your Human Assets area.

5. **Human Assets**—How will you best manage your personnel or "team"? Your Human Assets area leads to your Information Technology area.

6. **Information Technology**—What can you do to leverage your internal Information technology area, so it provides you with a strategic competitive advantage?

Your Vision and Leadership, Marketing & Sales and Production areas are the core, the foundation of your company. Whereas your Finance and Administration, Human Assets and Information Technology areas function as a support to your core areas.

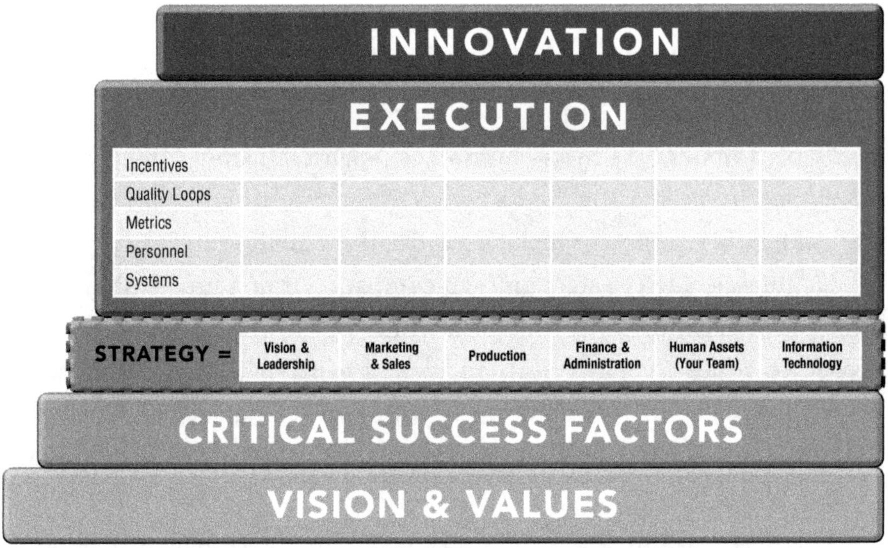

INNOVATION

EXECUTION

Incentives					
Quality Loops					
Metrics					
Personnel					
Systems					

| STRATEGY = | Vision & Leadership | Marketing & Sales | Production | Finance & Administration | Human Assets (Your Team) | Information Technology |

CRITICAL SUCCESS FACTORS

VISION & VALUES

Fig. 3-2 Structure of Success—Six Strategy Areas

Therefore, Critical Success Factors must be identified for each of the following areas:

- Vision and Leadership
- Marketing & Sales
- Production
- Finance and Administration
- Human Assets
- Information Technology

Chapters 4, 5, 6, 7, 8, 9, and 10 will discuss each of these areas in detail.

Now, examine the above list of Critical Success Factors and write down your company's Critical Success Factors. Keep in mind that these are "big picture" type things that you need to do successfully each and every day to create a truly successfully business. As you list them, don't limit yourself, write down every one you can think of.

Example

The concept of Critical Success Factors and the six areas of a business they relate to was crucial for Tim, in righting his business. Tim was the owner of commercial fitness-equipment repair company. A mechanically gifted man in his late 20's, he had worked for another company as a commercial fitness-equipment repair technician for eight years.

He then decided to start his own company. At first it consisted of just him, and everything went fine for a while. But as the company grew, he needed to add a second technician, then a third, and then a fourth. He eventually got up to 10 technicians. However, it became clear that by the time the second technician was added, the business was increasingly out of control.

Tim was a technician—not a businessperson, and the entire concept of managing and running a company was completely foreign to him. Therefore, "tyranny of the urgent" set in across the company. When he was introduced to the concept of Critical Success Factors and the six categories they fall into, he finally began to see what things he needed to do throughout his company for it to be a success. By using this tool, he understood how he could take control of it and operate it without the stress he was currently experiencing.

Complete exercise 3-3 in workbook

COMBINING SIMILAR CRITICAL SUCCESS FACTORS

Now that you have a complete list, examine this list and combine similar items to get down to the manageable goal of between 15 and 25.

Start by sorting your Critical Success Factors into the above six categories in the order they were listed. You may find a Critical Success Factor falls into two or more areas; if so, choose the area to which it is most closely tied.

The second step is to check if any can be combined—perhaps they say basically the same thing, one is dependent on another one, or one is an amplification of another item.

Once you have done this if you have more than 25 items, don't worry, just use your current list because you will have other opportunities later in this book to combine items.

Complete exercise 3-4 in workbook

SYNCHRONIZING YOUR VISION AND CRITICAL SUCCESS FACTORS

Next you need to make sure your Critical Success Factors and the destination for your company (your Vision) are in synch. To do this, review your Vision Statement and verify that you have identified a Critical Success Factor for each of the major items in your Vision Statement.

If you have an area in your Vision with no corresponding Critical Success Factor, most likely you need to add one. Keep in mind a Critical Success Factor can relate to multiple areas in your Vision Statement, so there is not a one-to-one relationship between the two. Not all Critical Success Factors need to be represented in your Vision Statement, only the ones that tie directly. However, you may have a Critical Success Factor that is not reflected in your Vision Statement and upon your review you may realize you need to modify your Vision Statement to include that area.

Complete exercise 3-5 in workbook

WHAT CRITICAL SUCCESS FACTORS ACCOMPLISH

There are four things you will accomplish by using your Critical Success Factors as the foundation of your Strategy. They are:

- Identifying company-wide goals

- Providing for the proper allocation of resources
- Inspiring and motivate personnel
- Providing ongoing operational guidance

Identify Company-Wide Goals

Because your Critical Success Factors are defined as the things that you must accomplish to achieve the Vision for your business, they are automatically focused on Company-Wide Goals. Conversely, if you randomly identify a number of business goals, you may end up achieving various objectives while not necessarily bringing the company closer to its ultimate objective, the fulfillment of its Vision.

Provide for the Proper Allocation of Resources

The Critical Success Factor methodology by its nature incorporates a holistic approach to operating your company because you are examining all the areas of your business to ascertain the make-or-break factors in each area. All areas are put on a level playing field and your resources are not allocated until you have identified how you will address each of your make-or-break areas.

Inspire and Motivate Personnel

Studies have shown that people generally want to be part of something bigger than themselves—not just a job in a company, but something that has more purpose and meaning than earning money simply to pay the bills.

When your personnel are made aware of your business's Vision and Critical Success Factors, they will be inspired, motivated, and challenged by their work -making it more than just a job.

Provide Ongoing Operational Guidance

By using your Critical Success Factors as the framework of your Strategy, you will ensure you have purposefully laid out a plan for your ongoing operations that avoids the endless loop of crisis management where everyone may work hard, but the company is beset continuously by the same problems. We will discuss this area in more detail in Chapter 11.

Example

Doug, a quiet, low keyed man his mid-30's, owned a large commercial construction company that on the surface looked quite successful. It employed a number of people and did a large amount of construction work. However, it was not nearly as profitable as it should have been and had not achieved its true potential.

The problem was that each area of the company operated somewhat independently of the other areas. There was no unifying force for the enterprise.

When Doug and his management team discovered the concept of Critical Success Factors, he said, "This is it, this is what we have been looking for." By determining their Critical Success Factors, they were able to identify their company-wide goals, which enabled them to provide for the proper allocation of resources across their organization.

Thereafter, by letting personnel throughout the company know its Critical Success Factors, they were able to inspire and motivate their employees. In addition, when they established the objectives that would guide their ongoing operations, everyone got on board with them because of having a shared foundation of understanding their Critical Success Factors.

THE TWO DIFFERENT PARTS OF A BUSINESS'S VISION

You may be wondering how you tie Vision and Critical Success Factors together? This is achieved by creating a Time-Sequenced Vision that connects these two. In reality, there are two different parts of a business's Vision:

1. The General Vision
2. The Time-Sequenced Vision

The General Vision

In Chapter 2 we defined Vision as the "The desired or intended future state of a specific organization or enterprise in terms of its fundamental objective and/or strategic direction." We must now separate this definition into two sections. The portion "in terms of its fundamental objective and/or strategic direction" refers to a General Vision, which addresses: Where your business is going? What are you trying to accomplish? The nature of a General Vision is that it is not time-specific or bound by any planning horizon.

The Time-Sequenced Vision

The "desired or intended future state of a specific organization or enterprise" portion of the definition relates to a Time-Sequenced Vision. This section focuses on—in very *specific* terms—what your business will look like in the future.

The future can refer to various time horizons—a week from now, a month, one year, five years, etc. This means we need a method to measure the major items in your Vision Statement in the future.

Let me give you an analogy of what this would look like. Using our previous example of traveling by car to the Florida Keys, your General Vision is to arrive at the Florida Keys by driving there. Your Time-Sequenced Vision is each view that you will see at various mile markers as you progress to your destination: what the scenery looks like as you get to Atlanta (sunshine and warm weather), as you get to the Florida border (live oaks and pine trees), as you get to Orlando (Disneyworld®), as you get to Miami (sandy beaches and waves) and finally what the scenery looks like as you arrive in the Keys (a sub-tropical paradise).

Example

The concepts of a general and Time-Sequenced Vision were instrumental to James in accomplishing his goals. An intense man in his late 40's, James owned one of the largest plant nurseries in Atlanta, Georgia, and he had a unique overall objective.

Several years before, James had established a large plant nursery just outside of the developed area of Atlanta. This location was the third one he had owned and since he had been in the nursery business all his adult life, it was run very successfully. His unique perspective was that he knew the Atlanta metropolitan area would continue to grow for many years to come and developers would then want to purchase his large acreage for a sub-division or shopping center because he had established each of his nurseries on major roads.

Therefore, the concept of establishing general and time-sequenced Visions was perfect for him and his management team. It provided the blueprint for: establishing a new nursery; running it properly; and as the area around it started to develop, starting another nursery eight to ten miles further out from the current one; progressively moving their nursery stock to it; and selling the current one to a developer.

The concepts of general and time-sequenced Visions allowed James to plan for and make large amounts of income both in the short-run and the long-run.

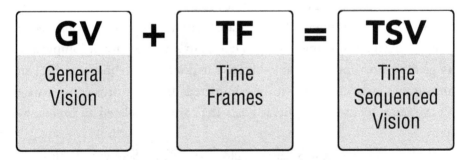

Fig. 3-3 General and Time Sequenced Visions

CRITICAL SUCCESS FACTORS ARE THE FOUNDATION OF YOUR BUSINESS

The key to making use of the power of Critical Success Factors is to use them to develop your Strategy. To do this we must first lay some conceptual underpinning.

In Steven Covey's book, *The 7 Habits of Highly Effective People*, the second habit is: "Begin with the End in Mind" and the third habit is: "Put First Things First." What we want to do is examine each of your Critical Success Factors and apply these two habits to them.

To do this, first consider what outcome you desire because of accomplishing each Critical Success Factor? This is how you "Begin with the End in Mind."

Once you have a clear picture of what the desired outcome looks like, then ask yourself: What is the first step in achieving this goal? The second step? The third step, and so forth until the goal is accomplished. This is how you "Put First Things First." This will translate your Critical Success Factors into your Strategic Plan, which will then lead you to your Execution Plan, which in turn will guide you on a day-by-day basis to achieving your Vision for your business.

CREATING YOUR BUSINESS'S STRATEGY AND MAKING IT MEASURABLE

If you closely consider your Critical Success Factors, you will discern that you have the framework of a Strategy for accomplishing your Vision. This is crucial because many times a company's Strategy for accomplishing its goals is not implementable because it does not identify specific and measurable tasks that need to be completed. In these situations, instead the Strategy focuses on general goals that are not related to executable steps.

Using your Critical Success Factors and Time-Sequenced Vision as your business's Strategy solves this dilemma. Your Strategy can be created by identifying the above steps for each of your Critical Success Factors and determining how you can measure your progress at attaining them.

Measuring the correct things in your business and then taking actions based on those measurements becomes the Strategy that will guide you to your Vision. Please note while you may have 15 to 25 Critical Success Factors, only the ones that directly tie to your General Vision will comprise your Time-Sequenced Vision.

While it is imperative to have a Vision for your business and identify your Critical Success Factors, it is the *achievement* of these tasks that is the important thing.

> We define a measurement as a specific indicator that allows for the evaluation of whether or not the target value for a Critical Success Factor is being attained.

There is a saying that what gets measured (using specific information, not just guesses) gets managed and improved. This is because you cannot improve what you do not measure. How can you tell if your actions have made it better or worse?

To accomplish this, you want to measure all your Critical Success Factors at the same point in time. Just imagine you go away on a one-year sabbatical and someone runs your business while you are away. When you return you stop by your company to see how it is doing. You would talk to your personnel and ask them how each area was going. You would then evaluate your financial statements, other financial measurements, and other indicators of your company as of the date you return.

This process would be tantamount to what would occur periodically with your Time-Sequenced Vision.

There are two types of measurements with regard to your Critical Success Factors (i.e. your Time-Sequenced Vision). The first type is "financial measurements" and we will examine this in Chapter 6. The second type is "metrics," and this will be covered in Chapter 11.

Complete exercise 3-6 in workbook

Mile Markers

At what intervals should you set up these Time-Sequenced snapshots of your business?

For smaller business, I have found that a one-year, three-year, and five-year Time-Sequenced Vision is most effective. However, for larger companies it is feasible to have an additional ten-year Time-Sequenced Vision. But bear in mind that a ten-year Time-Sequenced Vision is more for strategic planning purposes than for true measurement purposes.

Of these, the three-year Time-Sequenced Vision is the most important planning horizon; one year comes in no time and five years is so far in the future that many factors can change, making it too much of a guesstimate to be truly predictive.

To enable you to evaluate and quantify where you are on the road to reaching your Vision, these mile markers need to very specific measurements that are related to your Time-Sequenced Vision, not something that is different from or is tangentially unrelated to it.

> Your Mile Markers should be SMART, an acronym standing for Specific, Measurable, Attainable, Relevant, and Time-bound. This rule of thumb is critical in defining and developing each goal of your *Time-Sequenced Vision.*

Remember back in Chapter 2 we discussed the pleasant emotions that can come to mind in an instant when we reflect about our childhood neighborhood? Now do the same thing regarding your business. Imagine that the measurements in your Time-Sequenced Vision have been achieved and allow yourself to feel the full range of emotions—happiness, pride, and relief—this would generate.

So, let's recap: Your Time-Sequenced Vision is comprised of your Critical Success Factors that directly relate to your General Vision, and they provide a set of synchronized objectives that are mile markers on the path to your ultimate goal—achieving your Vision.

Example

Dan, the owner of a large residential remodeling business, had a big challenge in his company. He was a very friendly and congenial man in his late 50's, and he wanted to pass his company equally on to his son and daughter. The problem was that the business needed to up its game and become much more professional and high-end—in an increasingly competitive housing market.

Dan was stymied with how to identify all that needed to be improved in his business, and then prioritize these tasks. Learning about Critical Success Factors was a godsend to him and his children.

As they identified their Critical Success Factors and fleshed out the mile markers for the various facets of the company that needed to change to take the business to the next level, a sense of calm and control came over him. He realized that he could put targeted objectives in place so that he, his leadership team, and all his staff would be able to monitor their progress toward taking the company to the next level and successfully passing the business on to his son and daughter.

> **Complete exercise 3-7 in workbook**

UPDATING YOUR TIME-SEQUENCED VISION

At the one-year mark of the planning process, you should review not only your one-year goals but your three- and five-year Time-Sequenced Visions as well. Then ask yourself, are you on track to achieve these? Do you need to make adjustments?

Next, each year you will want to create a new set of one-, three- and five-year Mile Markers and update and roll your prior three- and five-year Time-Sequenced Vision Mile Markers forward one year.

You may be wondering if you can have other goals or objectives besides the goals or objectives that comprise your Time-Sequenced Vision. Yes, of course. Additionally, for complex initiatives that relate to your Vision Statement or Critical Success Factors, you may have many other goals and objectives. But they are separate from your Critical Success Factors that comprise your Time-Sequenced Vision. Lastly, you may have various other targets or points of calibration along the way to your ultimate goals or objectives for your enterprise.

But I say this with two points of caution: First, don't let goals or objectives that are not part of the items in your Vision Statement and your Critical Success Factors lead you away from the most important point of why you have your business—the attainment of your Vision.

Second, each organization has a limited amount of time, money, and talent and, therefore, you need to carefully consider how much of these limited resources you want to devote to items that are not part of the items in your Vision Statement and your Critical Success Factors. Consequently, yes, there are many, many other things that you will want to and need to address in your company, but always make sure that your Critical Success Factors are being addressed—*these are the things that will make or break your business.*

As we will see in Chapters 4 through 10, planning for and then creating the organization to reach the goals that are part of your Time-Sequenced Vision are the major parts of achieving your Vision. Therefore, the measurement of where your company is currently with regard to its Mile Markers will provide you the information you can use to possibly modify your overall strategy so you will be able to realize your intended Time-Sequenced Vision.

INPUT FROM FOUR OF YOUR BUSINESS'S STAKEHOLDERS

One way to continually access and improve the above discussed Time Sequenced Vison and Strategy is to request input from your company's stakeholders. Since you can't really solicit responses from Society, you are left with the four remaining stakeholders. The closeness and openness of your current relationship with each of your business's four remaining stakeholders—customers, employees, owners/investors, suppliers—determines how much you can solicit input from each of them.

Customers

This is the trickiest of the four stakeholders from whom to obtain input because you don't want to put doubts in their minds about your business. However, if you have a solid, good relationship with your customers and they are the type who embrace partnership-building, then you can obtain invaluable information regarding your Critical Success Factors. You can even try "casting" your Vision to them as you are still working on it. But be very, very careful and watch very closely for signs that you customer is beginning to think twice about doing business with you.

Employees

At the end of Chapter 2 we discussed how to receive input, and therefore buy-in, for your Vision from your key employees. The exact same process is used here to solicit participation from them to identify your Critical Success Factors. Additionally, because of your relationship with your key employees, it is advisable to involve them in determining the goals that comprise your Time-Sequenced Vision.

Thereafter, you could use your key employees to dialog with all the employees who report to them regarding the Vision for your business and your Critical Success Factors. We will discuss the related topic of publicizing the Vision for your business and Critical Success Factors later in this chapter.

Alternatively, you could complete each of the above steps with a smaller group of key employees and then meet with some or all your other employees in which you ask for input from them. Then take that input back to your group of key employees and determine what, if any, changes you may want to make to the Vision for your business, your Critical Success Factors, and the goals that comprise your Time-Sequenced Vision based on that input. But be very cautious in following this approach because it can be become a three-ring circus with everyone wanting to give you input on your strategy.

Owners/Investors

Of course, this is the easiest of the four stakeholders from which to obtain input if you are the sole owner with no investors. However, if there are many owners/investors, or some are not very involved with the business or they are physically located a large distance away, it can be impractical to involve them. That said, if other owners/investors can be included in this process, you will end up with a more comprehensive Vision, a more complete list of Critical Success Factors, and a more accurate Time-Sequenced Vision.

Suppliers

Depending on how engaged you are with your suppliers, you may be able to obtain valuable input from them. Generally, the input will be quite narrow in the overall scheme of things because they are only involved in one small area of your business. However, most suppliers will be quite forthcoming in sharing with you how from their perspective you can improve your company. I have found that best way to initiate this process is by casting your initial Vision to them as you work on it and then solicit input regarding identifying your Critical Success Factors as they apply to them.

Example

Obtaining input from their customers, employees and suppliers was decisive to Pauline, the owner of a large commercial sign company, and her management team in turning the business around.

Pauline had owned the company for over 20 years, but it had continually underperformed and lacked the profits that should have been generated. With almost 100 employees, the task of identifying all that needed to change in the company was a daunting task.

However, since her customers, employees, and suppliers had a long-term relationship with Pauline and the company, there was sense of trust present. After her and her management team identified their Critical Success Factors, General Vision, Time-Sequenced Vison, and overall strategy, the presence of the long-term trust then allowed them in confidential, one-on-one meeting share those with certain customers, employees, and suppliers.

The resulting feedback enabled Pauline and her management team to improve all the previous work performed and fix any area they had not adequately addressed. This resulted in a comprehensive turn-around plan that put them firmly on the road to the profitability they desired.

Complete exercise 3-8 in workbook

PREPARING AND PUBLICIZING YOUR VISION AND CRITICAL SUCCESS FACTORS

Most likely at this stage your list of Critical Success Factors is a bit rough with regard to grammar and overall wording. Therefore, we now need to go through the same "crafting" process we went through with your Vision Statement in Chapter 2.

There are three steps in getting your list of Critical Success Factors ready to be publicized. First, since you have added some more Critical Success Factors during the above steps, resort them into the six business areas:

1. Vision and Leadership
2. Marketing & Sales
3. Production
4. Finance and Administration
5. Human Assets
6. Information Technology

Second, expand the description of each Critical Success Factor. I also suggest making each one a declarative statement by adding the words "We will" or something similar to that to the beginning of each item.

Third, examine the grammar and wording of each Critical Success Factor and edit as necessary to make each one more understandable. I recommend that each Critical Success Factor be one sentence long; however, if you have combined two or more of your initial Critical Success Factors into a single Critical Success Factor you may end up with a compound sentence.

Complete exercise 3-9 in workbook

Posting your Vision Statement and Critical Success Factors

Once you have completed the above process, print your Vision Statement and your final list of Critical Success Factors, mount them in a nicely matted frame, and hang them in a prominent place, perhaps your break or lunchroom. However, I *do not* recommend posting them in any public area in which customers or suppliers may see them because they are private documents for you and your employees. (Your Mission Statement is something you can post in more public areas.)

Why do you want to post your Vision Statement and Critical Success Factors? Because you are looking to build awareness and a commitment from your employees and owners to achieving your business's Vision. Additionally, your Critical Success Factors are the vehicle through which your business will realize its Vision. Therefore, it is essential that each of your employees know why your company—and they as the employees of it—are doing certain things.

As a result of seeing your Vision and Critical Success Factors, employees and owners will be reminded daily why the business exists in the first place, why they came to work that day, the importance of their effort in making a difference in customers' lives and in the world, why they should go the extra mile, and why they are going to all the effort to FILL-IN-THE-BLANK. It's easy to lose sight of "why are we doing this?" Posting your Vision Statement and Critical Success Factors can be the encouragement needed on a regular basis for you and your employees to pursue your Vision with renewed vigor and devotion.

PREFACE TO THE REMAINING CHAPTERS OF THIS BOOK

In Chapters 2 and 3 we have covered how you create a compelling Vision for your business and the identification of your business's Critical Success Factors.

The next seven chapters will cover how to take your general Strategy and create a detailed Strategic Plan. This includes the structure and organization you will require to accomplish the *Vision* for your business and achieve your business's Critical Success Factors. I will also cover how to use your Strategic Plan in a systematic way to identify your strengths, weaknesses, opportunities, and threats throughout your company.

> Throughout the remainder of this book I will refer to the concept of General Vision as just Vision. When I refer to Time-Sequenced Vision it will always be spelled out specifically.

CHAPTER SUMMARY

A Strategic Plan needs to be developed for achieving the Vision for your company. Creating a Strategic Plan begins with identifying your organization's Critical Success Factors, which are the make-or-break factors of your business. Then using your Critical Success Factors, you can establish a Time-Sequenced Vision that is the foundation of your Strategic Plan, which lays down the Mile Markers that allow you to measure your progress in attaining your Vision. By following these steps, you can determine the activities that will take you down the road to achieving your Vision.

Chapter 4

Getting the Word Out (Step #3)

• • • • •

W e saw in Chapters 2 and 3 that everything flows from having a Vision for your business. And that Vision is not just something checked off a to-do list; it is a compelling Vision that will drive your organization forward. Additionally, we understood that you must cast your compelling Vision to your target audiences to achieve the goals for your company. Then we identified your Critical Success Factors so that you know the things you must accomplish to achieve your Vision.

Next, we took the elements from your compelling Vision and your Critical Success Factors analysis and developed goals for each of them so you could measure your progress. Lastly, we took these goals and stratified them by establishing future planning horizons in creating a Time-Sequenced Vision using one-, three-, five- and perhaps 10-year milestones which led us to developing a Strategy for accomplishing all of the above.

In this chapter, we will drill into the items listed above by developing your Strategy for Marketing & Sales. You will learn how to effectively cast your compelling Vision to your target audience to obtain revenue for your business.

Please note that due to the significant volume of content in this book, this Chapter only covers the Marketing & Sales area at a high level. For a much more detailed examination of this all-important area, please refer to my previous book, *Creating a Thriving Business*.

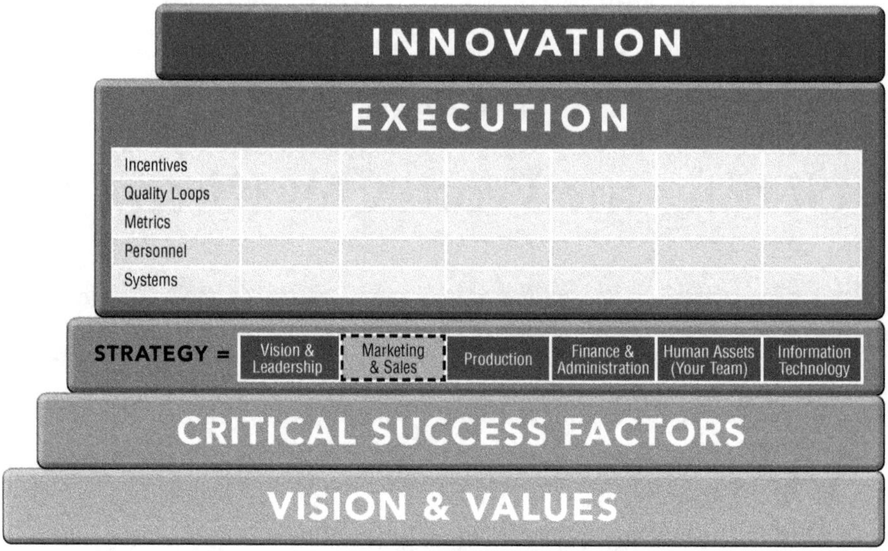

INNOVATION					
EXECUTION					
Incentives					
Quality Loops					
Metrics					
Personnel					
Systems					

STRATEGY =	Vision & Leadership	Marketing & Sales	Production	Finance & Administration	Human Assets (Your Team)	Information Technology

CRITICAL SUCCESS FACTORS
VISION & VALUES

Fig. 4-1 Structure of Success—Marketing and Sales Area

THE IMPORTANCE OF MARKETING & SALES

Marketing & Sales is imperative to your business because without revenue from selling your product, all you have are the expenses of creating or providing it. So, unless you want to put all your own money into your business and perhaps eventually go to the poor house by operating in the red, you must generate revenue. After Vision, Marketing & Sales is clearly the most crucial area of your organization.

Some business owners feel their product sells itself. Unfortunately, nothing sells itself. As we will see, some type of marketing must be done for your product no matter how easy it is to sell.

Other business owners undervalue Marketing & Sales and consider Production or Finance & Administration the highest priority area of the business. Some company owners view Marketing & Sales as a necessary evil that has to be tolerated just to be in business. If you go to all the trouble to create a product that wonderfully meets your customers' needs, but they don't know about it or you cannot convince them to buy it, then unfortunately you have wasted your time and resources.

The initial validation of a business is when a customer pays you for your product; the ultimate validation of a business is when a *repeat* customer pays you for your product a *second* (third, fourth . . .) time.

In fact, it is very possible for a competitor's product to be inferior to yours but because it has a better Marketing & Sales function, it may outsell you at every turn. The perception created in a customer's mind is what causes a customer to purchase a product, not the actual product. Therefore, it is of utmost importance to have the best possible Marketing & Sales operation.

Back in Chapter 3 you identified the Critical Success Factors for your business, and you separated your Critical Success Factors into the six areas of your business. Now please take a minute and review your Critical Success Factors for the Marketing & Sales area. As we work through this chapter you will have the opportunity to update and add to the Critical Success Factors that you have already identified.

OVERVIEW OF MARKETING & SALES

When you think of Marketing & Sales you should think of the word *Opportunity*. This is the key to your Marketing & Sales.

You must first determine the size of the opportunity that presents itself to you—who is your customer and how large is the market for your product? Then you need to determine how you can take advantage of this opportunity; this is your strategy for taking advantage of the potential market for your product.

The formula for understanding the components of and then the creation of a strategy for your Marketing & Sales area is presented below.

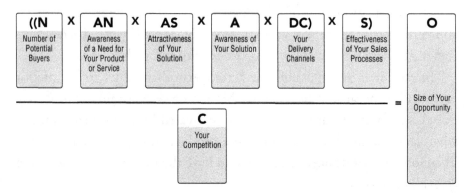

Fig. 4-2 Marketing and Sales Area—Overview

Please note the abbreviations at the top of each element of the formula because they will be used at the end of this chapter.

We will examine each of these components in detail to assess the strengths, weaknesses, opportunities, and threats of them to your organization.

NUMBER OF POTENTIAL BUYERS

The two main components that comprise the size of your opportunity are:

- Your target buyer
- Your geographic area

To determine the size of your opportunity, you want to analyze the market that presents itself to you and your *solution* for this market.

> For the remainder of this book I will frequently refer to the product or service you sell as your *solution*, because that is what it is—your solution to their perceived need.

To determine the number of potential buyers in your market, these six questions need to be answered:

1. Who is your customer?
2. What is your customer's perceived need?
3. Are there segments to your market?
4. What segment do you choose to pursue?
5. What does your customer look like?
6. What is actual the size of your market?

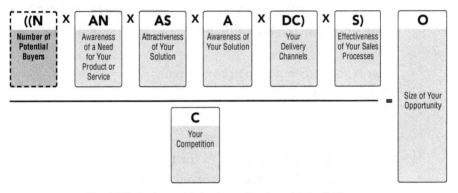

Fig. 4-3 Marketing and Sales Area—Number of Potential Buyers

Who Is Your Customer?

From a practical standpoint, a customer is a person or entity that has a real or perceived particular need. A customer in some way, shape, or form provides revenue to your business because of your company providing something to them that fulfills that need.

It's important to be sure you are getting to your true customer. For example, say your business represents construction tools and you call on Home Depot. You have to sell to Home Depot for you to be able to place these construction tools in Home Depot stores. However, the true customer is the end user—the consumer who will go to Home Depot and purchase your products. Therefore, Home Depot is your *primary* customer. However, even though the buying public is your *secondary* customer, if your products do not make the buying public happy, there is no way you can make Home Depot happy.

What Is Your Customer's Perceived Need?

> A group of customers who have a common need
> is called a "market."

The first part of determining the size of your market is to ascertain what your customer wants. You can easily be led astray in this process; answering questions like the following will help keep you on track:

- What is your customer's perceived need?
- Who will need my product?
- Who will benefit from my product?
- How will my product help them?
- Why is my product important to the target buyer?
- If my product did not exist, how would it impact my target buyer?
- Are there substitutes for my product?
- Who is the *ideal* customer for my product?

Most businesses make assumptions about who their customer is, but sometimes after close examination, they may get a different answer—perhaps a different member of the household or a different individual in the business. For instance, you might assume that the customer for interior house paint is a male, thinking that he will most likely be the one to paint the room. However, after you investigate the market, you may find out that the actual customer for certain types of paint is a female because she is buying the *outcome* of a room being painted in a certain color.

Next, interview some of your potential customers about what they want from a product. As you consider their answers, however, be aware that sometimes what people say regarding a product and what they think are two different things. This may occur for several reasons. They may be experiencing cognitive dissonance between what they think and what they say. There may be social norms that may cause people to say something that is different than what they are thinking because "you just don't say that." Also, for whatever reason, they may not be telling you the truth about how they truly feel. Gaining valid insights into your potential customers may be accomplished by having marketing professionals perform interviews with prospects and customers or by using a focus group.

> The many other details of these steps are outside of the scope of this book; however, there are many marketing books available where you can learn more about market research processes. Or you could hire a market research professional.

While truly and deeply listening to what your potential customer says are their needs and wants is vitally important, you also want to use this information to forecast what your target customer and market will look like in the future.

Here are some of the questions you want to ask regarding the future:

- How will lifestyle changes affect your business?
- How will changes in population demographics affect your business?
- Over time, will your overall market increase or decrease?
- How will customer expectations change over time?
- Are there any current trends that may influence your target market?
- Are there any trends that are foreseen in the future that will influence your target market?

In answering the last two questions, you want to look for trends that affect your market, not fads. Trends are long-lasting (i.e., aging population, interest in locally sourced foods) and are things on which you can build your overall Marketing & Sales strategy. Whereas fads are short-lived (i.e., pet rocks, brown plants, beanie babies) that will eventually present you with a precipitous and disastrous fall in revenue when the fad disappears.

Once you have ascertained the need of your target customer, you can go back to the original question that we were attempting to answer: Who is our *actual* customer?

Now you have:

- Determined the specific need or want of your potential buyer
- Isolated your actual customer
- Defined a "market" as a group of customers who have a common need

You have now completed the first step in determining the number of potential buyers.

Are There Segments to Your Market?

Now that you understand your overall customer/market, you want to determine if any market subsegments exist.

If the identified needs were uniform across your potential buyers, then your target market is not fragmented (there is no market segmentation) and you can skip this step; the average customer in your market is your target customer. However, if your research finds that your overall market is separated into various segments then you should decide which of the segments you will pursue.

You may quickly realize that we have a chicken-or-egg syndrome between market segmentation and determination of the needs of your target customer. To identify your possible market segments, you must first understand your customers, and to understand a specific group of customers, you must first separate your entire market of potential customers into segments. Another term for market segmentation is "niche marketing." Niche marketing is a key to your analysis of your market and the development of your Marketing & Sales area.

There can be an untold number of market segments. Listed below is a sample of potential market segmentation factors that may affect you.

- Gender
- Age
- Family size

- Education level
- Income level
- Spending habits
- Industry or SIC code
- Quality/durability
- Functional use of your product
- Need for customization
- Geographical area
- Demographics/culture/religion
- Social status
- Special needs or interests
- Early adopter of new products/service (e.g., Apple devotees)

To determine if your market is divided into various segments, analyze a sample of your universe of potential buyers. Do they separate themselves out into various groups based on the above or similar criteria? How does this play out in the real marketplace? For example, the market for portable computers may seem to be only one market, but in fact it can be broken down based on the functional use of a portable computer:

- Full-sized Laptops
- Lightweight laptops
- Ultra-lightweight laptops
- Notebook laptops
- Tablets
- Convertible tablets
- Ruggedized laptops
- Gaming-specific laptops

What Segment Do You Choose to Pursue?

Once you are armed with this customer information, decide which market segment you will pursue in your marketing, engineering, and/or production. One of the biggest mistakes that a business owner can make is trying to "specialize" in too many market segments. Obviously, you want to target the markets in which you are most likely to succeed and obtain the highest profits.

> Be conservative in estimating the size of your target market.
> Many business owners think and feel that everyone is a
> potential customer when that is simply not realistic.

If you have chosen to pursue only one market segment, any additional analysis that you perform is straightforward. However, if you are going to pursue more than one segment, you will need further detailed analysis. There are two ways to proceed with this:

1. Perform further detailed analysis for each one of your market segments. With this approach, you will have more detailed information regarding each of the segments that comprise your entire target market. However, this approach will take longer, cost more, and some of the information you obtain may be redundant because the same information may apply to other market segments as well.
2. Combine all your target markets segments and analyze these markets at the same time. Thereafter, you only perform an additional segment-level analysis on the factors that differ between each segment. While this option is quicker and less expensive, the risk with this approach is that you may overlook some very important information that would only be uncovered with the more detailed analysis of each market segment.

What Does Your Customer Look Like?

We've discussed who your customer is in general and what are your target market segment(s). An important related question is: What does your customer look like? One of the first steps in creating the marketing systems and processes for your Marketing & Sales area is to develop a profile of your target customer. As you more fully understand what your customer looks like, you have the information with which to analyze and decode what your customer's motivating factors are in making a purchasing decision. To do this, you need to develop a profile of your target customer by listing specific characteristics that are common to that customer.

Here is sample of items that could be included as attributes in your customer profile. You'll note that some were already researched for potential market segmentation factors.

- Age
- Gender
- Marital status
- Family size (adults, children)
- Education level
- Geographic data—if they live in an urban, suburban, exurban or rural area
- Total income level
- Discretionary income level
- Occupation
- Employer
- Spending habits
- Hobbies/interests
- Source of information (TV, radio, internet, social media, trade magazines, neighbors, the coffee shop)
- Social status
- Ethnic and cultural background and practices
- Resident status (tourist, seasonal, or permanent)
- Other factor special interests

Once you have created the above profile, one additional step is to use it to define your ideal customer—the customer whose needs and decision criteria fit perfectly with your business model and product. This is a key additional step because, as you will see later in this chapter, it will allow you to very specifically target your Marketing & Sales effort at a precise slice of your overall market. For instance, for a hospitality type of business you could build a profile of your ideal customer by using the above general information and the following additional information:

- What kind of car they drive?
- What kind of clothing shopper they are?
- How often they eat out?
- What kind of restaurant they frequent?
- How hectic is their lifestyle?
- How much they travel?
- To which locations they travel?
- What mode of travel they prefer to use?

What Is Your Target Geographic Area?

The next thing to determine is your target geographic area.

In the above steps, we have clarified who your target customer is and what they look like, but to provide your product to them, you must be able to support a marketing and sales function in their geographic area, deliver your product to them, and provide post-sales support to them—all where they are located.

Determining your target geographic area could play out in four possible ways. You could:

1. Choose a market segmentation structure strictly based on the location of where your customer lives or works.
2. Find that your target customer is concentrated in a certain geographic area.
3. Identify the fact that a specific customer need only exists in particular locales.
4. Choose to start or expand your business based on certain geographic boundaries. For instance, first you start your business in the city where you are located, then expand to the neighboring

city, next expand to your entire county, then grown to serve your whole state, and finally become a national company.

Pricing Your Product or Service

The last thing to consider before using all this information to determine your number of potential buyers is some idea about what price you will charge for your product. To determine this, we must refer to economics principles: the demand for a product depends upon the price of the product. This economic reality is referred to as "elastic": The lower the price, the more sold; the higher the price, the fewer sold. To calculate the quantity of the product that you will sell, you must estimate the selling price.

What Is the Actual Size of Your Market?

After you do all the above steps to determine the total number of *potential* customers in your target market or market segment, the following steps will calculate the *actual size* of your potential market:

1. Eliminate customers who are already entrenched in an existing supplier relationship.
2. Determine the average usage rate for your product per customer (you can use industry publications, or you own research for this data).
3. Calculate your market potential using this formula: (Number of available customers) x (Average purchase volume per year) x (Average selling price per unit) = Your market revenue potential.
4. Based on your selling price, the competition in your market, and the strength of your Unique Selling Proposition, calculate a realistic percentage of the market that you could obtain. This will provide you with a preliminary estimate of the size of your market.

An additional step you should undertake is to compare the size of your market to the product quantity you will calculate in determining your break-even point in Chapter 6. If your initial projected quantity is below your break-even quantity, then you should determine how you will finance your business during the time that you are operating below your break-even point.

Example

Bob, a laid-back man in his late 40's, had owned a construction firm that had focused on various markets over the past 20 years. His challenge was that he would move from one market to another based upon what seemed to "hot" at the time.

The problem this created was that he was always a late entry to the market or sub-market, and by the time he learned the ins and outs of the market, it would begin to dry up, and he would then have to look for a more robust market.

Once Bob understood the process of identifying who was his customer, what was their perceived need, and determined which market was the most attractive to his company, he was able to put down long-term roots in a specific market.

During this process, he was able to establish what his customer looked like and what was the potential size of the market he decided to focus on. He decided to focus on the build-out of franchised locations for large, national restaurant chains. This laser focus led to his company's growth and increased profitability as it became the go-to company for the build-out of franchised restaurant chain locations.

Complete exercise 4-1 in workbook

CUSTOMER AWARENESS OF A NEED FOR YOUR PRODUCT OR SERVICE

The next part of the formula for creating your Marketing & Sales strategy is to assess how aware your target customers are of the existence of your product—*not your business* but just a general awareness of your specific product. This does not mean they are aware of your (this product is fictional) smart phone app called "Family Shopping List" that allows family members to share grocery shopping needs and that is automatically updated as anyone in the family purchases something on the list. It means are they aware that shopping list smart phone apps exist at all?

If your target customers are fully aware of the product, then your Marketing & Sales will be easier—you simply need to convince them to purchase your product instead of your competitor's product. However, if your product is new to your customer, then your sales plans and processes will be a lot different than if they were already aware of your product in a general sense. This is because for a product that is new to them you must do some initial educating on what it does before you can sell them on your specific product. This preliminary education of your target customer enlarges your marketing effort and increases your cost.

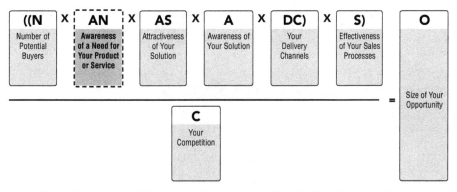

Fig. 4-4 Marketing and Sales Area—Awareness of a Need for Your Product or Service

Example

The challenge for this large printing company was how to pivot to their new business model. Samantha, an energetic, driven woman in her mid-50's, had started the business over 25 years earlier, but during this time the profit margins had greatly decreased as a result of increased competition.

In talking to other printing companies, she discovered they were dealing with the same situation. She devised a plan, which was for her company to move into the sign-printing market—but do it as printer/supplier of signs to smaller printing companies who were located far from her market. This could be a symbiotic relationship because the equipment to print large, commercial signs was very expensive, and printers in smaller markets could not afford to make that kind of investment.

This was a new business model where her company would become the fulfillment house for other printers to increase not only Samantha's profits but the profits of the other printers as well.

Since her potential customers were not aware of this new option for getting into the sign production business, we worked with Samantha's company to develop a communications and marketing plan that would educate other printers about this new product and how her company could provide the necessary signs at a very reasonable price for their local printed-sign market.

Complete exercise 4-2 in workbook

ATTRACTIVENESS OF YOUR SOLUTION

You now have

- Gained an understanding of your customer base
- Ascertained the size of your market
- Determined if your potential customers are fully aware, partially aware, or totally unaware of your product.

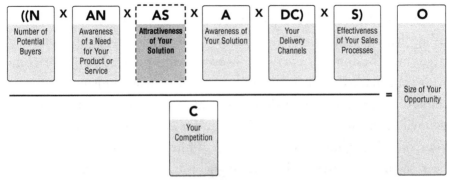

Fig. 4-5 Marketing and Sales Area—Attractiveness of Your Solution

Now you can begin to establish how you will present your product to your target market.

To develop an effective Marketing & Sales program, you must first gain a thorough comprehension of the attributes of your product that will make it appealing to your customer. But before we get to that, you must understand the following two foundational concepts:

Enable Your Customers to Achieve their Goals

If you take the entire discussion regarding how attractive your solution is to your customers and distill it down to one concept, that concept would be this: People make purchasing decisions based on their perception of a product's ability to enable them to achieve their goals in life.

Furthermore, it is not really the achievement of their goals that motivates them, but it is the (likely subconscious) emotions they perceive they will feel when they achieve their goals. These goals may be short-term (getting a better interest rate, lowering their cholesterol), intermediate-term (building retirement savings, becoming physically fit), or long-term goals (living a certain lifestyle, financial security).

If your product is a short- or intermediate-term type, then your marketing can express not only the immediate benefit to the buyers but also the long-term benefit to them with regard to them trying to reach their overall goals in life.

Marketing directed toward meeting customers' short-term needs by using their intermediate- or long-term goals related to their short-term needs must be done very, very subtly or you will appear to be overreaching with your marketing claims. Use images rather than words in this case—think of those beer commercials that seem to claim if you drink their beer you will gain a bunch of great friends and have a great-looking partner at your side throughout your happy life. While the short-term need is the beer, the intermediate- or long-term goal is happiness in life.

Complete exercise 4-3 in workbook

Create Experiences Worth Repeating

Almost as important as meeting or fulfilling your customers perceived needs is the overall experience, they have in dealing with your company. We have all had experiences where our wants or needs were met but the overall experience ranged from mediocre to awful—the fast food restaurant that was anything but fast, the car repair that cost more than the car was worth, the home repair job that had to repaired again, the vacation that was anything but relaxing, the tool purchase that didn't solve the problem, the meal at a fine dining restaurant that was not a "fine" experience, are all examples.

An experience worth repeating is one that meets the immediate needs of your customers. They perceive it moves them closer to their long-term goals, and the overall experience is something that, if they have the need again, they would want to repeat. From a customer standpoint, the goal of your business should be to Create Experiences Worth Repeating™! This concept is the most powerful concept known to the business world; if you practice it consistently, your business will become a world-class business as a result of creating repeat business and a ton of referrals.

Back in Chapter 2 we discussed creating additional goodwill from each transaction by providing a Win/Win experience for your business and your customer, resulting in an upward (positive) spiral in your relationship. To Create Experiences Worth Repeating™ is the personification of this concept.

Example

Brian, a quiet man in his early 50's, owned a large tree-service company. But the difficulty he and his organization faced was how to differentiate themselves from their competition, because in this highly competitive market, cutting a tree down or trimming it was a "commodity" service.

As we worked with him and his company, they realized they already provided very good services, so if they just slightly improved their game, they could create an experience for their customers that would be so good, they would want to repeat it, by having future tree work performed. This would also lead to garnering referrals from their many customers.

They implemented two actions to achieve this. First, they provided a guaranteed completion time for the job. If they did not finish by the time quoted, they would deduct 25% from the overall price of the service. Second, they implemented a "leave no trace" program, where they guaranteed that there would be no logs, sticks, nor piles of sawdust left when they completed the job.

Their customers ended up being thrilled with the higher level of service, which ended up creating an experience worth repeating. Relatedly, in the year after these actions were implemented, their revenue from referrals grew by 35%.

Complete exercise 4-4 in workbook

Benefits versus Features

Next, we want to figure out which of your product's benefits will be most appealing to your target market. The attributes that determine the attractiveness of your solution are the benefits you should use to promote and sell your product.

Benefits are different than features in two ways:

1. Features are generic descriptions of something, while benefits are the results that a person obtains because of purchasing your product. For instance, "four-wheel drive" versus "you will never get stuck in snow or mud"; or "side air bags" versus "your family will be safe in a side impact accident."

2. Features have no emotions attached to them, but benefits do. Compare "this disability insurance policy pays 65% of your compensation" to "with this policy you can rest assured that you and your family will be able to continue living in your house for the rest of your lives."

Determining the Attractiveness of Your Solution

To determine the Attractiveness of Your Solution, use this formula:

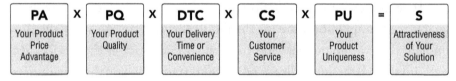

Fig. 4-6 Attractiveness of Your Solution Formula

The factors that comprise this formula are the five basic things that determine the attractiveness of your solution that you can use to position and market your product to set you apart from your competitors.

Your product price advantage—Your first option is to position your product as having a price advantage over your competitors. This option is viable if in fact you will be selling your product at a lower price than your competitors, but be careful not to risk the overall viability of your business just to obtain a price advantage.

Your product quality—Your second choice is to use the superior quality of your product (or the perceived superior quality of your product) as your promotional strategy. If you decide to do this, you need to be sure that you truly have a quality advantage and determine if your customers care about this aspect.

Your delivery time or convenience—Third, if you can consistently deliver your product/service more quickly or are you more convenient than your competition and you have determined your customers care about quick delivery or convenience, then this could be part or all the attractiveness of your solution.

Your customer service—Your fourth option is to build your Marketing & Sales strategy on the claim that your business's customer service is better than your competitor's customer service. Once again, you would need to be sure it is and that this is a key concern for your customers.

Your product uniqueness—Your remaining option is to base your Marketing & Sales strategy on some unique feature of your product. This can be a result of a patent or copyright protection; a design feature that makes it unique from your competitors; or simply a feature your competitors have not chosen to use in their promotional strategy which makes your product seem unique.

As you can see, the attractiveness of your solution is a result of your product's differentiators. Therefore, it is imperative to know everything about how your product differs from your competition in each of the above areas. Furthermore, as we discussed previously, it is equally imperative that you describe the attractiveness of your product in terms of the benefit your customers will obtain in emotional expressions that have meaning to them.

> Ultimately, it is paramount to understand what your customers truly want; once you know this you can also alter or revise the Attractiveness of Your Solution by applying your product's differentiators to focus on a new or different market segment.

Example

Developing the attractiveness of their solution was crucial to a small, on-line photography equipment company. The company had been started by Derrick, a serious, studious man in his mid-50's and his wife several years before. However, there were a number of large players in the market already. The challenge for him and his wife was how to identify, develop, and dominate a niche market.

By understanding their customers' short, intermediate, and long-term goals related to their photographic equipment needs—and the difference between benefits versus features, Derrick and his management team were able to utilize the Five Elements of the Attractiveness of Your Solution to create and communicate an attractive remedy for their customers' needs.

The definition, communication, and delivery of an attractive solution (value proposition) enabled them to become the go-to on-line retailer for specialized, high-end photography equipment. This in turn allowed them to grow and greatly increase their profits.

> **Complete exercise 4-5 in workbook**

AWARENESS OF YOUR SOLUTION

You next need to develop a marketing program so that potential customers are aware that you have a solution to their needs. There are lots of resources available that tackle this subject specifically; I encourage you to seek them out. Here we will cover just the foundational pieces of your marketing program to introduce you to the concepts that you need to fully understand and apply. These are the basic steps to an effective marketing program:

- Determine if the profile of your decision maker is different from your customer
- Determine your customer's and decision maker's buying criteria
- Create your value proposition
- Construct a brand identity
- Determine how to meet and exceed your customer's expectations

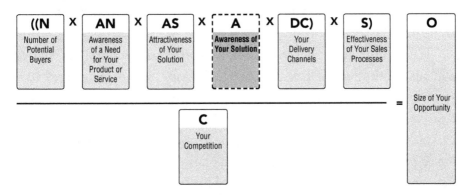

Fig. 4-7 Marketing and Sales Area—Awareness of Your Solution

How is marketing different from advertising? Advertising is a single component of marketing—it is the most visible and generally the most expensive component of your overall marketing plan.

Advertising is accomplished through various media or channels and it mainly includes:

- Choosing the media (direct mail, newspaper, television, radio, internet)
- Creating the advertisement
- Placing the advertisement
- Evaluating the advertisement

Marketing is a process—not just a specific event—and is intended to create awareness of your business, product, or brand. If you want to take your marketing to the next level, once you have completed the steps outlined in this chapter, consider engaging a qualified marketing consultant who will bring a wealth of experience, education, and training to your marketing efforts.

Is the Profile of Your Decision Maker Different from Your Customer?

The person who makes the decision to purchase your product may or may not be the customer. If not the same person, you may be faced with a two-tracked Marketing & Sales program: one track to reach your true customer and one track to reach the decision maker. If you have this situation, you will want to develop a profile of your decision maker, and if the decision criteria for him or her and your customer are the same, then a similar marketing strategy can be used for both.

For instance, if a father (the decision maker) was buying a car for his teenage daughter (the customer) their decision criteria would be different. His most likely would be focused on safety and reliability and hers would be centered on how cool and attractive the car is. Therefore, you would need to develop different decision maker and customer profiles from which to create dual marketing efforts.

Complete exercise 4-6 in workbook

Determine Your Customers' and Decision Makers' Buying Criteria

Is your product faster or better? Do you provide better customer service than your competitor? Is your product less expensive? Greener? Locally made? These motivating factors are known as "buying criteria." You need to understand both your customers' and decision makers' buying criteria.

Buying criteria have two levels. The first level is easy to identify by asking straightforward questions or looking at the obvious facts. For instance, someone wants to buy an automobile because it gets great gas mileage; or it has enough room for a family; or it has a high safety-crash rating. For simple products like gasoline and toilet paper, the buying criteria may not go any deeper. However, many business owners get tripped up here because they do not ask the deeper questions. For more complex purchases, the initial or obvious answers don't get to the subconscious motivating factors. For those, you need to dig deeper to discover:

- Why your product is important to your customer?
- What your customer's true need is?
- What the true benefit of your product is to your customer?
- What the Win is for your customer?
- What your product allows your customer to accomplish?

The key in this process is to peel away the layers: Ask questions and then ask the questions of the answers and then ask questions again of those answers until you have drilled down to the most basic motivating factors. This will allow you to understand the core need or want that you are addressing in your target audience.

Here are some examples of this progression:

1. A person is buying a new front door for her house. The first reason is a physical need for a door; the next is to have an attractive yet strong, secure front door; next is for physical protection for her family; next is that she wants to have a door that is welcoming and attractive to neighbors and guests coming to her house; finally, in her mind's eye she can envision her grandchildren remembering grandma's house by the inviting front door it had.

2. A person is choosing a flavor of cake to buy. The first reason for his choice is that it is his favorite flavor; next is that his family wants a certain favor cake; next is that eating this cake will produce a happy family event; next is that this cake provides emotional comfort; next is that this cake brings back happy family childhood memories or family experiences.

3. A couple is choosing a restaurant. The first factor on the list is the kind of food they like; next is that the restaurant has an attractive appearance; next is where they feel most relaxed in its friendly atmosphere; next is that they feel welcomed at the restaurant;

next is that they have a relationship with the business manager or owner and feel like part of their family when at the restaurant; lastly, it reminds them of their previous happy memories.

4. A person is deciding where to have her prescription filled. The first reason considered is the cost of the prescription; next is the ease of the purchasing process; next is the location of the pharmacy so it's easy to fit the stop into her schedule; next, will this choice reduce, not increase, her stress level; finally, will the experience reassure her that she is taking care of her long-term health?

You see that while you are peeling away layers to get to the core of a person's decision, you are progressing from micro-level choices (i.e., cost) to macro-level choices (i.e., not stressful).

Complete exercise 4-7 in workbook

Create Your Value Proposition

Your Value Proposition defines the unique value that your business offers to your customers—why your customers will want to do business with you. It lays out the factors that you will use throughout your marketing effort to separate you from your competition. Your Value Proposition is a statement that is constructed from four foundational concepts we discussed earlier in this chapter.

1. You must enable your customer to achieve their goals in life. This concept is the bedrock foundation of your Value Proposition.

2. You need to fully understand the desired emotional state of your customer; stress benefits not just its features to connect at an emotional level with your customer.

3. You want to design and build your whole business and its processes so that your customer's entire experience in dealing with

your company is so good that they cannot wait to do it again—you need to Create Experiences Worth Repeating™.

4. Figure out which of the five elements of the Attractiveness of Your Solution (Price, Quality, Delivery Time or Convenience, Customer Service, Uniqueness) are your customer's buying criteria and how you are going to use these to make your solution attractive to your target customer.

Later in this chapter we will cover how your Value Proposition leads to your detailed Unique Selling Proposition, which summarizes the selling strategy you will use to convince your customers to purchase your product.

***

Complete exercise 4-8 in workbook

***

Construct a Brand Identity

Your brand identity starts with making a psychological connection to your market and continues to the actual experience a customer has with your product or business. The purpose of your marketing program is to create a certain brand image in the mind of your target audience. The intention is to create expectations in your customers' minds that your product is better suited for their needs than that of your competitors'. The actual customer experiential aspect includes the combination of all interactions they have with your business or its product. This is what is known as their "brand experience."

While the standard definition of brand is "the name used to identify and distinguish a specific product or business," the true power of branding is that it sets an expectation of the experience they will have with your product or business in your customer's mind. This expected experience reduces the risk in your customer's eyes of making a purchase. If this expected experience becomes a known commodity in the marketplace and it is a desirable experience, you are able to catapult your product or company ahead of your competition.

Having a recognized brand is one of the most beneficial and powerful elements in your marketing plan, which provides unique marketing opportunities to your product or business.

There are five steps to fully developing a brand:

1. Determine your intended brand identity.
2. Validate your brand identity by asking questions of your prospects and customers such as:
   a. What do they think when they hear about or see your business or product brand?
   b. How do they describe your business or product brand to others?
3. Fully develop your branding by making changes to your brand based on step 2.
4. Determine how you want to communicate your brand to your target audience.
5. Implement the marketing and promotion of your brand throughout all your marketing materials and efforts.

Complete exercise 4-9 in workbook

Meeting and Exceeding Your Customers' Expectations

To meet or preferably exceed your customers' expectations, you must properly set and manage your customers' expectations. If your customers' hopes are too high, you will end up disappointing them. We have all heard the saying about how it can take a lifetime to create a great reputation, but it can be lost in moment; you can lose an enormous number of customers or potential customers as the result of negative advertising from a disappointed customer.

Setting and managing your customer's expectations begins with the development of the Attractiveness of Your Solution. As we will discuss in the next chapter, there is a chicken-or-egg syndrome between your Marketing

& Sales area and your Production area; nowhere is that more evident than in the definition of the Attractiveness of Your Solution. You need to not just talk a good game (Marketing & Sales), you need to play a good game (Producing your Product). Otherwise, you will over-promise, set yourself up to disappoint your customer, and lay the groundwork for problems.

Related to this overall discussion is the goal to have someone who is not an employee—and therefore has nothing to gain or lose by speaking favorably about your business—become its powerful, but unpaid marketing force. How do you create satisfied customers who become your advocates?

1. Create the most Attractive Solution possible for your customer.
2. Build into your Production process that you will provide this exact Solution, day in and day out, without fail.
3. Set the expectations for your product or business in your customers' minds high enough to get their business but not so high that you will not be able to consistently fulfill their expectations.

> To produce raving fans who will become your advocates, set the proper expectations by fully understanding what your customers really want and then consistently exceed their expectations!

Example

This mid-sized industrial-coatings company that was owned by Bill, a friendly man in his late 60's, did a brilliant job letting prospects know about their unique product. His product was a coating that was applied to large buildings like warehouses, data centers, and manufacturing plants. It was applied to both the roofs and exterior walls, and it reduced their energy consumption in both hot and cold weather by 15%. It truly was a product that paid for itself in only a few years, and he built his value proposition upon this fact.

Using the Structure of Success™, he developed profiles of their target customer and the decision maker, along with their buying criteria.

He then built a brand identity around the fact that his product was a "no-brainer" because it paid for itself in energy savings in one to two years.

Bill then developed three very convincing post cards that shared the above information, which were sent to the prospect 60, 30, and three days before he or his sales staff would call the decision maker. Because he had done such a good job of creating the awareness of his solution to their energy challenges, he and his sales staff had over a 20% sales closing ratio. Additionally, because they delivered on the 15% energy reduction promise, they got many referrals as a result of meeting and exceeding their customers' expectations.

Complete exercise 4-10 in workbook

YOUR DELIVERY CHANNELS

Your delivery channels are the methods by which you distribute your product to your customer. The concept of delivery channels is addressed near the end of Marketing & Sales because you must first develop your marketing function to have sales for you to have the need to deliver products to customers.

So, to review, the steps covered so far in developing your Marketing & Sales area are:

1. Determine the need that you are going to fulfill.
2. Figure out who your customers are and the number of potential buyers in your market.
3. Assess their awareness of a need for your product or service.
4. Develop the attractiveness of your solution for their perceived need.
5. Create an awareness of your solution in your buyer's mind.
6. Determine how many delivery channels you will use to provide your solution to your customer.

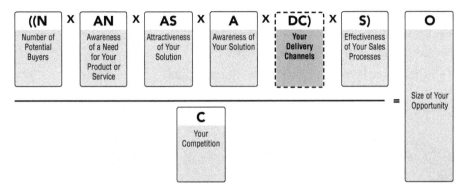

Fig. 4-8 Marketing and Sales Area—Your Delivery Channels

While dealing with your delivery channels may come near the end of considering your whole Marketing & Sales function, it may in fact be a part of the foundation of your Vision for your business and the key to your solution. Your product and everything else about your business could be the same as your competitors except *how you deliver*—for instance, buying stamps over the internet versus going to a post office.

The more delivery channels that you have, the more sales you can have because while you may be providing the same product, you are getting the product to more customers.

> Several terms are used for delivery channels: sales channels, distribution channels, marketing channels. However, we will use the term *delivery channel* because all these terms refer to how your product will be provided to your customer.

As an example of a product with multiple delivery channels, if we look at the Coca-Cola soft drink, we see it is delivered in three basic ways:

- Various containers purchased at stores
- Fountain drinks purchased at restaurants, sporting events, etc.
- Containers purchased via vending machines

Consequently, the Coca-Cola Bottling Company can easily obtain additional revenue from the sale of one product, the Coca-Cola soft drink, because it has multiple delivery channels.

There are three considerations regarding delivery channels:

1. Which is the best and most appropriate delivery channel for your product?
2. Which additional delivery channels are cost-justified? Because there are additional costs to develop and maintain each delivery channel, you must compare your incremental revenue to your incremental costs to verify that the effort of creating additional delivery channels makes sense.
3. Will the marketplace be confused?

There are two related secondary benefits that your business may obtain from using multiple delivery channels:

1. The same marketing efforts can be used to promote and drive multiple delivery channels. For instance, a television advertisement for a physical store can have a website listed at the bottom and the words "shop online at" added at the end of the commercial.
2. Synergies can be obtained by a business as a result of promoting a product by showing it being purchased from different delivery channels. For instance, a television advertisement shows a soft drink being served at a cool, relaxing, and pleasant pool party which would encourage physical store sales. However, when the consumer passes a vending machine in the middle of a hot bustling city and remembers the advertisement, her or she would be enticed to purchase the product via this different delivery channel because of the cool, relaxing and pleasant pool party image that was recalled from the ad.

Determination of the delivery channel for your product and the possible use of multiple delivery channels are influenced by the following factors:

- How your customer has traditionally purchased your product
- The amount of risk involved in the purchase (potato chips are low risk; an automobile purchase is high risk)
- Demographics/culture/religion of the purchaser
- Who is the decision maker?
- Motives of the purchaser
- Perceptions about your product
- Ability of and knowledge of the purchaser
- Attitudes toward your product
- Personality of the purchaser
- Lifestyle of the purchaser
- How opinion leaders shape your market
- How people's roles and family influences affect delivery channels
- Social class of the purchaser
- The culture and subculture of the purchaser

Example

Dwight, a pleasant and likeable person in his late 20's, started a brick-and-motor health foods and vitamin store before online retailing had taken off. They had a wide variety of items, but within five miles of his store, he had eight direct competitors.

As we worked on his company, we discussed the various possible delivery channels he could employ. Because of his wife's challenging health situation, he ended up being very knowledgeable about vitamins and nutritional products for women.

This led him to start an on-line retail operation as a second delivery channel that specialized in vitamins and nutritional products for women. Soon after, the website delivery channel grew to be almost as large in terms of revenue as his brick-and-motor store.

> **Complete exercise 4-11 in workbook**

EFFECTIVENESS OF YOUR SALES PROCESSES

The Effectiveness of Your Sales processes comes as the last piece which will define how large an opportunity you have in front of you because you should set the stage for closing the sale with the prior five steps before you can construct your sales process. The five prior steps of the Marketing & Sales formula fall into the category of marketing, while this step is specifically sales related. Now you are now ready to complete a sales transaction. The crucial question is how effective is your entire sales function in converting potential buyers into customers?

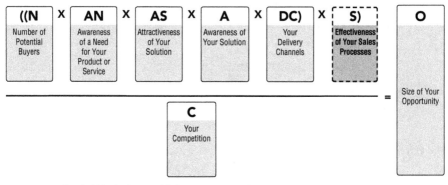

Fig. 4-9 Marketing and Sales Area—Effectiveness of Your Sales Processes

How Marketing & Sales Interrelate

Marketing & Sales go hand in hand. Without setting the stage with marketing, you will have no sales and without sales, marketing efforts are worthless. Your sales process involves closing the sale, and it usually involves a personal interaction—sales calls, presentations and meetings, networking events, interaction on your website (a customer's interaction with your company on a website is a personal, sales type of activity), etc., that engage the target customer on a personal level.

Bad News: Your Customer is a Walled City

People tend to have a defensive wall up against all sales efforts all the time. However, the good news is that is not typically the case with regard to marketing efforts. The marketing function does not encounter the same resistance that the sales process does because of two things: First, good marketing generally is not presented in a way that tries to invade a person's walled city but is usually very subtle and even entertaining. Second, marketing is not interpersonal, but the sales process is always interpersonal.

How does a business overcome this wall? By connecting with target customers so that they take the wall down themselves. It is almost impossible for you or your business, as an outsider, or an invading army if you will, to take the wall down. The customer must personally dismantle the wall for you to enter.

The height and strength of their wall is determined by their temperament, personality, upbringing, the nature of your product, and the setting in which they find themselves. A person who would be considered very cynical would have the highest and strongest wall. People's walls are overcome by connecting with them from the start with something that is of emotional importance to them before going into the details of your sales presentation.

The emotions your customer feels—either positive or negative regarding the need for which your business offers a solution—are the ladder that will enable you to get over the wall. The benefits, in the form of the facts and the claims of your product, are what are carried by your salesperson on the ladder. Therefore, you want to present the attractiveness of how your solution fulfills your customer's needs or wants in words and concepts that emotionally reverberate throughout his or her mind, heart and soul.

Your Unique Selling Proposition

An effective sales process brings the attractiveness of your solution to life. The phrase "so that" highlights the outcome-based benefits of your solution. An outcome-based sales approach is very successful because it identifies the need, lack, want, or desire that a potential customer is feeling and presents your product in terms of the emotional outcome. The most effective process I have found to accomplish this is to develop and utilize what is called your product's Unique Selling Proposition (USP).

Your Unique Selling Proposition is a sales pitch that has been clearly thought out to fully resonate with your customer. It utilizes your customer profile, their buying criteria, and your value proposition to understand what motivates your target customer to purchase your product and then frames that in terms of the emotional benefit to your customer.

The elements of your Unique Selling Proposition are:

- A thorough comprehension of the needs of your customer
- A complete understanding of the market trends that are affecting your customer
- A detailed list of major features of your product (as defined in the Attractiveness of Your Solution)
- An awareness of the uniqueness of your product
- A recognition of the usefulness of your product to your customer in terms of the emotional state they want to be in
- A selling proposition that conveys with *simplicity how your product fulfills the customer's needs*

Your Unique Selling Proposition is put together in four steps by identifying and stating four things to your customer:

1. Your Big Idea
2. Your Big Benefit
3. Your Big Promise
4. Your Proof of Your Claims

Your Big Idea

This is a theoretical statement that captures the imagination of your target customers and gets them excited. Your Big Idea is not your product, but it is a "what if" statement: "What would the world look like if

_____?" Your Big Idea is outcome-based, and it opens the door to the next step, the Big Benefit. Your Big Idea is a statement that says, "think about this concept as if you could wave a magic wand" and you could experience it, or it was a reality. Some examples are:

- What if exercise was fun?
- What if you could make everyone your friend?
- What if we could operate the world using renewable energy?
- What if you could find your ideal soul mate?

To create a Big Idea statement, you first must thoroughly understand:

- The *needs* of your customer
- *Market trends* affecting your customer

Your Big Benefit

If your Big Idea was played out very specifically in real life, what would your customer's world look like? In this step, you are now beginning to connect with her or him at an emotional level in terms of the outcomes that your target customer desires from your product. For instance, using the above examples:

- "If exercise was fun, I would exercise regularly and look and feel great."
- "If I could make everyone my friend, I would never be lonely; I would be incredibly happy, could not wait to meet the next person in my life and would look forward to every day."
- "If we could operate the world using renewable energy, we could virtually eliminate pollution, enable everyone to improve their lives, and alleviate many of the financial, political, and military stresses in the world."

- "If I could find my ideal soul mate my life would totally be worth living; every day would be paradise, and I would want to spend every minute of every day in joyful happiness with that person."

To develop your Big Benefit, you must—as in developing your Big Idea—know the needs of your customer as well as have:

- A detailed list of major *features* of your product (as defined in the Attractiveness of Your Solution)
- Recognition of the *usefulness* of your product to your customer

Your Big Promise

Your Big Promise is comprised of the specific things that your product will provide to your customer with regard to the above Big Benefit. The bottom line is that the closer your Big Promise is to their imagined Big Benefit, the more powerful it is and the more effective is your entire Unique Selling Proposition. This Unique Selling Proposition concept works because people make purchasing decisions based on their perception of the expected outcome from the purchase.

Keep in mind, the goal in this sales process is that their desired outcome is in fact your Big Benefit. What you are trying to do is to subtly and in a non-patronizing way tap into your target customer's hopes and dreams, because, as we discussed back in Chapters 2 and 3, hopes and dreams are incredibly motivating factors in our lives. To be effective, your Big Promise must be significant, important, or attractive enough to motivate a person to act but still believable enough to not raise doubts.

To create your Big Promise, you must first have all the things needed for your Big Idea and Big Benefit as well as:

- An awareness of the *uniqueness* of your product.
- A selling proposition stated in such a way as to convey with simplicity how your product fulfills their needs

The Proof of Your Claims

What are the documented results that customers have obtained from using your product? These results could be in the form of testimonials, reported results from customers, customer statistics, surveys that support your claims that relate to your Big Promise, or statements made from observations of customers using your product.

To support the Proof of Your Claims you must have everything needed for your Big Idea, your Big Benefit, and your Big Promise as well as documented results from customers' use of your product.

Understanding your Unique Selling Proposition and successfully using it as the conceptual foundation of your entire Marketing & Sales Program is a critical concept.

When you fully comprehend all the facets of your Unique Selling Proposition, utilize these concepts in developing your Marketing & Sales Plans, and then use your Unique Selling Proposition in the execution of your daily Marketing & Sales processes, you will have the most effective results in reaching your target customers.

Complete exercise 4-12 in workbook

Sales Is an Ongoing Process

Keep in mind that just like Marketing, Sales is an ongoing process, not an event. Additionally, a sales process should be tested and refined so that it is the optimal sales method for your business, so it is used consistently by *all* your personnel. It is *imperative* that everyone use the same sales process. If you leave it up to each salesperson to do what works for him or her, you have no real sales process. You will receive less than ideal results, and you will lack the ability to properly oversee your sales operation.

> One thing that you can do to verify that your intended sales process is being used, used properly, and to assess its overall effectiveness is to test your sales process by hiring people to pose as supposed potential customers (secret shoppers).

Part of your sales process or sales presentation needs to be a request for the potential customer to take an action. Ideally you ask for an order, a sale, or a commitment on their behalf to do something—something for them to consider or think about, a referral to someone else, providing of a contact—all with the intention that there is some action they will take. By them agreeing to do something, the door is opened so you can reconnect with them regarding what they agreed to do. If you did not obtain a sale in the encounter with them, this overt or unapparent commitment on their behalf sets the stage for the next step in your sales process.

Example

This software development company was owned by Ray and his two adult sons who were in their mid-30's. One of biggest challenges they faced was that they had virtually no sales system in place. All three of them came from a programming background, and they did not like sales, or anything related to it. Consequently, they did everything they could do to avoid it.

Even though they had developed a very good software package, they had virtually no revenue. We worked with them to determine who was their ideal customer, the profile of their target customer and decision maker, and their buying criteria. We then helped them develop a brand identity.

Next, they created great marketing materials based on their Value Proposition, identified their Unique Selling Proposition, and fully developed their big idea, big benefit, big promise and proof of their claims.

Lastly, they placed the father in charge of sales and established ongoing sales processes. Within one year they had substantial revenues and added several salespersons to assist the father.

YOUR COMPETITION

As we move on to the last step in our Marketing & Sales formula, let's set the stage for the last element of the formula by using an example.

Let's say you have determined the need that you want to fulfill is women's need for deodorant and that your potential buyers are all the women in the world. You have determined that virtually all women are aware of a need for deodorant. Your solution for their need will be very attractive because your deodorant comes in various fragrances, and it serves the multiple purpose of being a deodorant, skin conditioner, and a perfume.

You will create awareness of your perfumed deodorant in your buyer's mind by use of a well-planned and generously funded marketing campaign to give out free samples in newspapers, women's magazines, and via direct mail. You will use two main delivery channels to provide your perfumed deodorant solution to your customer—retail and mail. You have created an effective sales process built on all the above that uses a Unique Selling Proposition model.

In this example you have developed a very desirable and comprehensive Marketing & Sales program, and you have defined an enormous market opportunity. However, you still have not addressed one issue: unless your product is the only women's deodorant on the market, then you are going to have to deal with competitors and your competition's products. This means that unless you can drive them out of business, you will not control the entire market. Therefore, you must evaluate your competition to determine the size of the market opportunity you will be able to achieve.

But before you can do that, you must assess your competitors. This includes determining:

- Who your competitors are?
- What their strengths and weaknesses are?
- How much market share you will garner now and in the future?

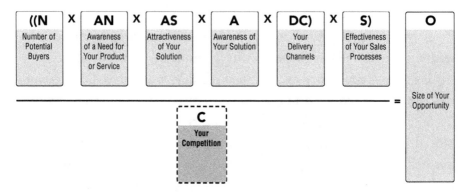

Fig. 4-10 Marketing and Sales Area—Your Competition

Know Your Competition

To beat your competition, you must first thoroughly understand who your competition is. You will want to collect at least the following general information about your competitors and use this information to perform an analysis. There can be many more factors, some of which are related to the characteristics included in the profile of your customer earlier in this chapter:

- Revenue
- Profits
- Financial strength
- Number of employees
- Region served
- Target (urban or rural markets)
- The demographics of their target market
- Marketing orientation
- Brand strength

The first action is to create a list of your competition (remember to include your direct competitors, indirect competitors, and those with products that can be substituted for your product). You can develop a complete list of your competitors just by doing an internet search based on the keywords related to your product. You can obtain quite detailed information about each of your competitors' businesses and their products just by visiting their websites.

> Some business owners think that they have no competitors. This is hardly true, but if it were, you would still have some indirect competitors because someone can almost always substitute another product for your product.

You should also answer the following questions regarding your competitors:

- What are the strengths and weaknesses of their product?
- What are the strengths and weaknesses of their company?
- What is their reputation in the marketplace?
- Is their market share increasing or decreasing?
- What is their overall marketing plan or strategy?
- What is their pricing strategy?
- What delivery channels do they use?
- What do you anticipate each of your competitors will do in response to you?
- Over time, will you have new or different competitors?

What do you do with this analysis? You use it in four ways:

1. To validate or, if necessary, modify your definition of the need that you are going to fulfill (i.e., your opportunity), who your customers are, and what is your target market segment
2. To develop or refine the Attractiveness of Your Solution for your target customer market now and for the future
3. To expand or modify your delivery channel strategy
4. If necessary, to modify your Marketing & Sales strategy to set your product apart from your competition

Example

Not knowing your competition went from being a weakness to a strength with this landscaping business that was owned by John and his friend, who were both in their mid-20's. They had met each other while working for another landscaper several years before and thereafter decided to start their own company.

Their problem was that there were hundreds of landscaping companies in their city, so how could they differentiate themselves from their competition? When they came to us, their business was just limping along, making enough to survive, but not earning a sufficient amount for them to really prosper and be able to take care of each of their young families.

To differentiate themselves from their competition, they needed to know who their competition was, their strengths and weaknesses, and how they marketed themselves. While it was a daunting task to research all these companies, once they completed it, they knew there a niche market they could target—landscaping with drought-tolerant plants (Xeriscaping). Once they made the decision to refocus their business, they ended up being a key player in this market, all because they took the time to research and understand their competition.

Complete exercise 4-13 in workbook

CHAPTER SUMMARY

Please note that due to the significant volume of content in this book, this chapter only covered the Marketing & Sales area at a high level. For a much more detailed examination of this all-important area, please refer to my previous book, *Creating a Thriving Business*.

Marketing & Sales are intertwined. To have sales, potential customers must be aware your product or service exists. Create a marketing plan by determining who your potential buyers are, how aware they are that your product in general exists, and then develop a marketing strategy that makes them consider your solution to their need as the most attractive one compared to your direct and indirect competitors. This step includes determining which delivery channels you will utilize to get your product to your customer. Then create a sales process that takes all the factors from your research into consideration. Next, ensure your sales process is used consistently by all your sales personnel. Finally, assess your competition and have a plan to overcome them.

UPDATING YOUR CRITICAL SUCCESS FACTORS

Back in Chapter 3 you identified the Critical Success Factors in the six areas of your business. Now that you have worked through this chapter, please review all that we covered and determine the strengths of, weaknesses of, opportunities of, and threats to your business in the Marketing & Sales area. Then, if necessary, modify and/or add to the Critical Success Factors that you have already identified. Once you have done this, then add a column to your list in which you note which element of the Marketing & Sales area formula pertains to each Critical Success Factor.

Below is an example of what this table should look like:

Critical Success Factors	Element of Formula
Sample critical success factor #1	N, AS, S
Sample critical success factor #2	AN, DC
Sample critical success factor #3	AS

Chapter 5
Five Ways to Beat Your Competition (Step #4)

• • • • •

N ow that we have Marketing & Sales processes in place to produce revenue, we need to focus on how we are going to produce the products or services we are selling. The definition of Production is the area of your business in which you create the product that you are providing to your customers to generate revenue. When most people hear the word "Production" they think "manufacturing"; however, you will need to expand your concept of Production because *every* business has a production area.

For instance, if you were a bank, your Production area would be providing banking services and if you were restaurant, you would be producing food and beverages in your Production area.

Furthermore, Production includes more than just producing the actual product. For example, continuing on with the restaurant analogy, Production would include: choosing the location, creating and decorating the restaurant, creation of the emotional experience (i.e., the ambience) of which you wish customers to partake, welcoming them, seating them, taking their order, procuring and storing your food, creating new menu items, preparing the food, serving them, resolving problems, charging and collecting the payment for their food, obtaining feedback from their experience at your restaurant . . . and many steps in between.

As you can see, your Production area is the core of your business.

Please note that due to the significant content in this book, this Chapter only covers the Production area at a high level. For a much more detailed examination of this all-important area, please refer to my previous book, *Creating a Thriving Business*.

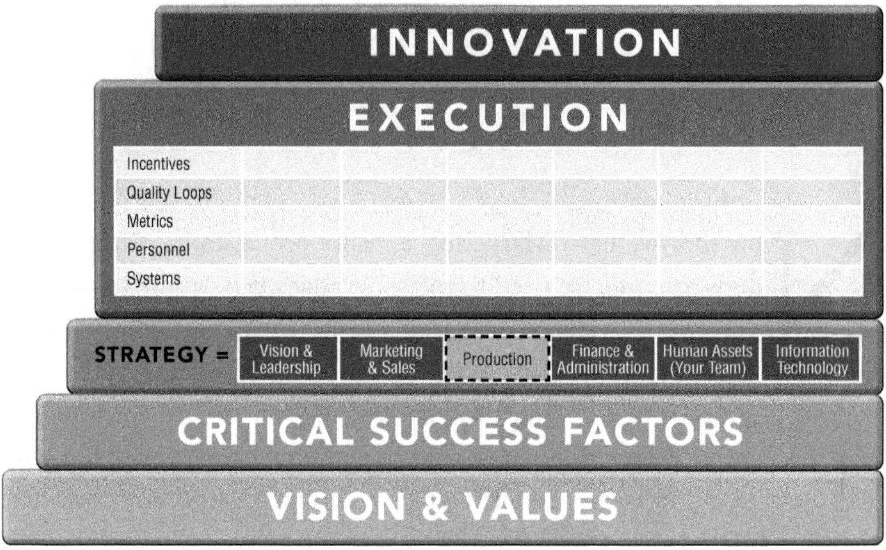

INNOVATION					
EXECUTION					

Incentives
Quality Loops
Metrics
Personnel
Systems

| STRATEGY = | Vision & Leadership | Marketing & Sales | Production | Finance & Administration | Human Assets (Your Team) | Information Technology |

CRITICAL SUCCESS FACTORS

VISION & VALUES

Fig. 5-1 Structure of Success—Production Area

YOUR BUSINESS IS A FOOTBALL GAME

Think of your Production area and your Marketing & Sales area in terms of a football game. In this metaphor the activities in your Marketing & Sales area include the process of coming up with the game plan for winning the game; however, it's your Production area that is going out on the field and executing the game plan.

As we have already discussed, it is one thing to talk a good game, and it is an entirely different thing to play a good game. If a person talks a good game—(I am using "good" because it is the common analogy; you want your business to be great or excellent not just good)—but then falls on his/her face in the actual football game, then he/she becomes a laughingstock to all of the people viewing the game or discussing it afterwards.

We see this in the literal sense each year before the Super Bowl. As game day draws closer and closer, the hype of what one team will do to the other team becomes louder and louder and some very grand predictions are made. These predictions are very similar to the claims that are made as part of a business's marketing efforts. In the actual game, these words may, or may not be backed up by actions.

It is the same way with your business. If you make claims that are not consistently backed up by your actions, then your customers will doubt your business and its products, they will no longer be your customers, and they will likely tell other potential customers not to do business with you. So, your Production area includes the entire realm of playing a good game, which is how you go about producing revenue for your company.

> In this book, I will use the terms *equipment* and *tools* in a generic not a literal sense. For instance, "equipment" may be used to connote a personal computer, and "tool" may be used to indicate an electronic spreadsheet for a personal computer. So "equipment" and "tools" or other terms that generally apply to a manufacturing environment should all be viewed as something that is of assistance to you in producing your product, whatever it is.

CHICKEN-OR-EGG SYNDROME

There is such a close interrelationship between your Production area and your Marketing & Sales area that the proverbial "chicken-or-egg syndrome" (i.e., the unanswerable question of which comes first) exists between Production and Marketing & Sales.

As we saw in Chapter 3, your Marketing & Sales area leads to your Production area. Additionally, in Chapter 4 we looked at your solution to the market opportunity that presents itself to you, and we discussed the process for determining and fully developing the Attractiveness of your Solution considering the opportunity that is presented in your target market. Listed below is the formula that we discussed in

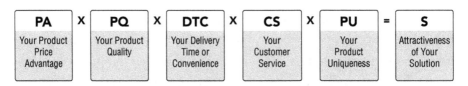

Fig. 5-2 Attractiveness of Your Solution Formula

So, where does the chicken-or-egg syndrome come into play? How do you know what you can bring to the marketplace with regard to the Attractiveness of Your Solution (*talking* a good game) without first working on Production to determine how you plan to *play* a good game? Furthermore, are you positive that can you execute your game plan? Or might you fall on your face?

Hence the chicken-or-egg syndrome; that is, while your Marketing & Sales area (what are you going to market and how are you going to sell it) leads to your Production area (how are you going to produce what you are marketing and selling), your expertise in your Production area drives your Marketing & Sales area. You must, to some degree, figure out how you will meet the expectations (which you do in your Production area) that you are creating in your potential customer's mind (your Marketing & Sales area) before you engage in the effort to create these expectations via your Marketing & Sales area.

Three Passes Through Your Production Area

Like the answer to "What comes first, the chicken or the egg?", there is no perfect solution to this dilemma between your Marketing & Sales and Production areas; the best solution is that you make three passes through your Production area.

The first analysis of the Production area should be part of the process of conceptualizing what your business is all about while you are developing your Vision. This initial analysis is where you are constructing the overall conceptualized game plan for delivering the Win to your customer. This first step would be like figuring out if you should even play the proposed football game; that is, can you realistically compete with the other teams (your competitors) in this league?

The second analysis of your Production area is to (continuing with our football analogy) review what players you have on your team—including an introductory assessment of their capabilities—to figure out a preliminary game plan. The result of this initial analysis is your overall game plan for the upcoming contest of how you will meet the game-day expectations (Production) that you are creating in viewers minds by talking a good game to the public (Marketing & Sales) before you engage in the effort to create these expectations.

This is exactly what we did back in Chapter 4 when we looked at using the above formula to determine and develop the Attractiveness of Your Solution. However, in this chapter we will perform a third pass through your Production area and take this analysis to much deeper level and we will closely examine how to produce the results you desire (i.e., the execution of detailed game plan).

Example

This chicken-or-egg syndrome and the interplay between an enterprise's Marketing & Sales and Production areas was very evident with a company that developed an automated software program for mortgage loan closings.

The owner, a very intelligent man in his late 20's, had a very strong IT background, but his development staff needed to know how they were going to market and sell the software before establishing the features they were going to program into it.

To determine the expectations that they were going to try to set in their potential customers' mind they had to make three comprehensive passes through their Production area.

As we worked together, first they conceptualized their business by defining the Vision for the company and what they wanted to produce for their customers. Then, they established what they were capable of producing as a result of their skill sets, and the overall strategy for technically delivering what their customers wanted.

Finally, they determined the detailed game plan for actually producing the software. As a result of these three successive assessments of their Production area, they were able to furnish the software for which they had set an expectation in their customers' minds.

OVERVIEW OF YOUR PRODUCTION AREA

The formula for producing the product(s) that you are going to sell to your customers is the following:

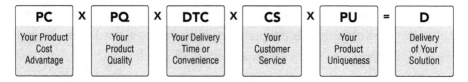

Fig. 5-3 Production Area—Overview

We will examine each of these five areas to assess the strengths, weaknesses, opportunities, and threats of them to your organization.

Please note the abbreviations at the top of each element of the formula because they will be used at the end of this chapter.

For your business to appraise its competitive advantage, lay out its overall game plan, and assess its Production capabilities, it must determine its relative strengths and weaknesses in producing and delivering its product to your marketplace. The above formula leads you through this assessment. Let's briefly review each element of the Production area formula.

- **Your Product Cost Advantage**—On a continual basis, your business can produce its product at a lower cost than your competition can.
- **Your Product Quality**—The quality of your product is consistently higher in obvious ways than your competitors' product.

- **Your Delivery Time or Convenience**—You deliver or provide your product sooner or quicker than your competition, or you are more convenient to your customers than your competition.
- **Your Customer Service**—Your customer service is dependably better than your competitions' customer service.
- **Your Product Uniqueness**—Your product possesses some desirable unique trait that your competition cannot duplicate nor obtain because of some impediment (e.g., a patent, copyright, trade secret, extreme cost to develop).
- **Delivery of Your Solution**—The delivery of your solution and advantages that you can bring to bear in the marketplace are a sum of the five above elements.

Let us apply this formula in a hypothetical example. Let's say you are the low-cost producer of your product; your product quality is greater than any of your competitors'; your delivery time or convenience is better than any of your competitors'; your customer service is better than any of your competitors'; and your product is totally unique. Then you have complete dominance of your target market because all your production factors are strengths for your business. But in reality, having all five elements as a company's strength rarely happens.

This formula serves two useful purposes in your business:

1. It can be used as a market analysis tool for you to examine a market that you are contemplating entering. You would utilize this tool to evaluate and categorize what the strengths and weaknesses are of the existing products in the market and thereby assess the opportunities for entering the new market.
2. The formula can be used as an assessment tool to evaluate how your business is doing in providing desirable and differentiated products to your current marketplace. Using the formula in this way allows you to score your business on how well it is executing and provides you with insights to understand how each one of

your products is operating. This execution tool serves as an indicator to evaluate the question, "Are we doing what we need to do to be successful today and in the future?"

Your Unique Genius

We will be examining each of these five areas listed above in detail to show you how to assess strengths of, weaknesses of, opportunities for and threats to your business in each area. However, I would like to point out that as we undertake this analysis, it is vitally important that you ask yourself, "Which of these five areas is the key to my Production area?" In other words, what is the one thing that from a Production standpoint that separates you from your competitors?

I call this one thing that separates you from your competitors your "unique genius." Once you have discerned your unique genius, it should be the basis for developing the Attractiveness of your Solution in your Marketing & Sales area.

This chapter will provide you with the tools that you will need to figure out your unique genius and integrate it into your business so that you are providing it to your customers on an unfailing basis. I will discuss how this concept relates to Marketing & Sales later in this chapter.

There are several possible ways of proceeding with your analysis of your Production area, but I recommend one of the following two:

1.   Analyze each of the target markets that you have already defined.
2.   Perform a combined analysis of all your target markets and products in one gigantic sweep.

If your business has relatively few products that are targeted at one or several markets and the markets are similar, I recommend using option two. However, if your business has a significant number of products that are targeted at multiple markets or if you have relatively few products, but they are targeted at several dissimilar markets, then I would use option one and perform this analysis separately for each target market.

DEVELOPING A SUSTAINABLE COMPETITIVE ADVANTAGE

For your business to succeed in the marketplace, you must develop a sustainable competitive advantage. What does this mean? To create a business that provides a better Win experience for your customers than your competitors, you must do something that your competitors do not—this is your competitive advantage.

By using the concepts of Win/Win with regard to developing a compelling Vision coupled with identifying your unique genius by using the above Production elements, you can create a business that has one or more competitive advantages. However, this or these competitive advantage(s) must be provided on a consistent basis. A truly successful business must meet customers' true needs virtually *all* the time, not just *part* of the time. If you only meet their needs part of the time, then you are opening the door to your competitors.

Providing a competitive advantage to your customers on a consistent basis also yields a sustainable business—and sustainability is what it is all about. Many businesses may provide a Win experience some of the time, part of the time, or even most of the time, but you should strive to provide a Win experience as close to *all the time* as is humanly possible. How you accomplish this becomes your Strategy, which will in turn provide a sustainable competitive advantage for your business.

As we will see in Chapter 13, a sustainable business has a marketable or intrinsic value, which means it is a business that can be eventually sold.

EXCEPTIONAL VERSUS GREAT VERSUS GOOD VERSUS AVERAGE

I have had discussions with many company owners who have made the statement, "I want to provide exceptional product quality and exceptional customer service." While this may be admirable and desirable, being exceptional does not happen by just wishing you were or saying you are! Use the following scale to evaluate the various areas of a business: poor, average, good, great, and excellent.

One of the crucial things to realize regarding your business's relative performance is that *it costs more and takes more effort* for your company to move up any rung on this performance ladder. In other words, it requires concentrated effort, more work, new processes, and additional costs to significantly improve an area.

For example, let's say that your business is an airline and you want to improve the customer service that your flight attendants provide. To do this you would likely have to hire more flight attendants, provide more training to them, upgrade their uniforms, implement better and more customer-focused processes, improve the ambience of the inside of your airplanes, provide additional services—all of which almost assuredly will cost more than you were spending before.

Furthermore, depending on where you were on the performance ladder when you initiated this effort, the costs will be greater between rungs the higher up the ladder you go. To improve any of the five areas of Production you cannot just say, "We will try harder" or "We will do better." This approach may work for a short period, but unless you have made systematic changes to your organization and its processes, your performance will eventually return to what it was before.

Consequently, you must keep the following three things in mind:

1. You should perform a cost-benefit analysis to determine if the benefits that you will obtain from making the changes are greater than your costs.
2. You should view the decision to improve a certain area as a strategic decision. It should be driven by input from Marketing & Sales to understand how making the change will impact how your target market perceives the Attractiveness of Your Solution.
3. To obtain sustainable results, you must systematize the changes so that you can produce the desired result consistently.

We will now examine in detail each of the five elements of your Production area. The purpose of this analysis is to assess your *strengths, weaknesses, opportunities, and threats* in each area (element) of your company.

YOUR PRODUCT COST ADVANTAGE

Do you in fact have an advantage or a disadvantage with regard to the cost of producing your product as compared to your competitors? This element being a strength means that how you utilize your raw materials, labor, processes and overhead enables you to create your product at a lower cost than your competitors.

Why is this important? If you review the formula for the Attractiveness of Your Solution, you will see that the first element is Your Price Advantage. Having a price advantage means that you sell your product at a lower price than your competitors sell their product.

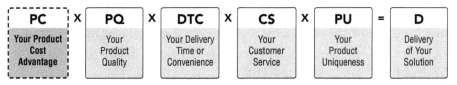

Fig. 5-4 Production Area—Your Product Cost Advantage

For your business to have a sustainable Price Advantage, you must first have a Product Cost Advantage, because unless you have a Product Cost Advantage, all you are going to do by selling your product at a lower price than your competitors is to lower your profits—which might in turn cause your business to fail!

There are two timeframes with regard to having a Product Cost Advantage or Disadvantage. The first is the present time. The second, is the future. However, the objective is to have a Product Cost Advantage now because as the saying goes, a bird in the hand is better than two in the bush. This is because if you base some or all the Attractiveness of Your Solution on a Price Advantage, and your hoped-for future Product Cost Advantage does not become a reality, then you have a major problem—

you must either raise your prices or accept the long-term prospect of lower profits.

Having higher profits from the sale of your product is always desirable. However, certain industries (commodities, standard retail items, or industries similar to commodities like toilet paper where there is little differentiation between your product and your competitors' products) are somewhat constrained in their ability to raise prices to obtain additional profits. Therefore, for these types of industries, increasing your profits by having lower production costs is fundamental if you choose to make this element the foundation of your Production area.

Example

This company, which was owned by a multi-cultural couple in their early 30's, started as the wife's interior design firm. She had an extensive interior design background, and her husband had been a purchasing manager with an international fabric company. As a result of his position, they had lived on several continents and had traveled extensively.

After she launched her company, several times she discussed with her husband that some of the fabulous fabrics they had seen and handled in India would be perfect for her high-end clients. Since he knew the sources of these materials and the producers' cost structures, they realized he would be able to negotiate great prices for them. He also thoroughly knew the import/export process, so he could get these products to her quickly and with low transport costs.

Thereafter, he decided to quit his purchasing manager position and go full time into his wife's company. The business ended up being very successful because they had a huge Cost Advantage over other high-end interior design companies. This was a result of being able procure very luxurious fabrics, materials, and furniture at very reasonable prices as a consequence of purchasing them directly from the manufacturer - which in turn produced significant profits for their company.

Complete exercise 5-1 in workbook

YOUR PRODUCT QUALITY

Next, as you examine your Production area you want to determine whether you have an advantage or a disadvantage over your competitors regarding the quality of your product. This requires an evaluation of your product's quality.

There are three ways to assess the quality of your product:

1. A subjective analysis based on your sales volume and the input from your sales personnel
2. An objective analysis based on independent survey of your customers' perception of the quality of your product
3. An independent study of the quality of your product by a third party that performs these types of product assessments

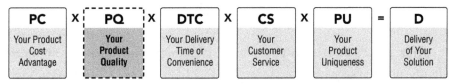

Fig. 5-5 Production Area—Your Product Quality

> If you conduct a survey and find your customer's perception of the quality of your product significantly differs from its independently verified product quality, then you may have a problem with your Marketing & Sales area that needs to be addressed.

Just as an aside, one may immediately assume that if the quality of your product is higher than your competitors, then you have a quality advantage; however, if you are not using this quality advantage as a benefit in your marketing efforts, then you may be incurring additional costs to produce a high-quality product without it translating to additional sales. This is why there is a synergistic or symbiotic relationship between Marketing & Sales and Production and why it is so important to take a holistic approach to developing and operating these areas.

Just like the Cost Advantage element, there are two timeframes with regard to having a quality advantage or disadvantage: the present and the future. Once again, if you base some or all of your Attractiveness of Your Solution on your future quality advantage, and your quality advantage does not become a reality, then you have a major problem because you will be talking a good game but not playing a good game.

Having a higher quality product than your competition is very desirable. The three industries particularly driven by higher-quality products are:

- Jewelry
- Automobiles
- Clothing

Example

This North American-based tool manufacturing company obtained significant market share because of using their Product Quality as their strategy for providing very high-end, diamond-tipped drill bits and saw blades.

The owners had been key players in other industrial tool-manufacturing companies, and when they decided to form their own entity, they had much of the know-how they needed as well already having identified the patents they had to license or acquire to make their organization a success.

They set up their production operation with both of these attributes in hand, and commensurately started their marketing and sales initiative with the stellar quality of their products as the cornerstone. This quickly led to them developing a noteworthy reputation in the very high-end, diamond-tipped drill bits and saw-blades industry. This resulted in their product's high quality setting them apart from their competition and enabling them to establish a very profitable company.

Complete exercise 5-2 in workbook

YOUR DELIVERY TIME OR CONVENIENCE

The third element to consider in Production is whether you deliver your product more quickly or whether dealing with you is more convenient than dealing with your competition. You want to determine whether you have an advantage or a disadvantage with regard to the time it takes from the point an order is placed to when it is delivered to your customer. Additionally, you need to evaluate whether you have an advantage or a disadvantage when it comes to how convenient it is for your customers to transact business with you compared to doing business with your competition.

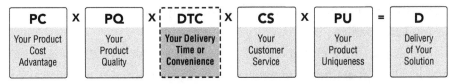

Fig. 5-6 Production Area—Your Delivery Time or Convenience

The issue of convenience comes up in two situations. First, if your customers come to your physical location, how convenient is your location to get to? Or second, if your customers order remotely via a website or by phone, how easy is that process? Keep in mind that the nature of your customer's shopping experience falls into your delivery time or convenience area and is separate from your product quality.

Delivering or providing your product sooner or more quickly than your competition or being more convenient are advantageous attributes for every business. But the three industries that are especially driven by delivery time or convenience—making it a key element—are:

- Fast food restaurants
- Dry cleaners
- Gas stations

Example

Nick and his wife Terri, an insightful couple in their mid-40's, owned an event staffing company, which they wanted to grow. Their company provided the personnel for companies that needed short-term, project-specific staffing such as people to hand out samples at stores like Costco and Sam's Club or handle special sales at car showrooms for their national sales campaigns.

Currently they only did this in the southeastern United States; therefore, they could not land larger, national contracts for event staffing. They realized if they were truly a national company, then more and larger companies would utilize their services because it would be more convenient to deal with one national event-staffing company versus numerous regional or local companies.

Therefore, they embarked on a program to purchase other regional and local event-staffing companies. Once these businesses were acquired, they unified them and expanded their operations. The strategy worked very well, and they were able to procure larger national contracts and transform their company because of making the convenience of dealing with a single company the foundation of their Production area and related marketing effort.

```
Complete exercise 5-3 in workbook
```

YOUR CUSTOMER SERVICE

As you examine your customer service area you want to determine whether you have an advantage or a disadvantage over your competitors. No matter what type of business you have, customer service is the overall experience that a customer has in dealing with you, in learning about or obtaining information about your product, or resolving problems or getting questions answered about it.

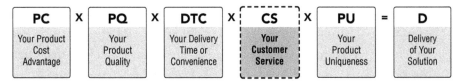

Fig. 5-7 Production Area—Your Customer Service

Customer service *does not* include your actual product or the price of it, but it does include:

- Placing an order for your product, if assistance is needed with the order
- Inquiries regarding and resolving ordering or product issues before the delivery of your product
- Post-delivery issues and problem resolution once your product has been received by your customer

Technically, your customer service area includes functions that take place in your Marketing & Sales area (i.e., the service that your potential customer receives from your sales personnel and sales operation) and your Finance & Administration area (e.g., resolving invoice problems, handling of returned products).

> Customer service is the experience that a customer has in *dealing with you,* but not their experience with your actual product.

Once again, the two timeframes regarding having a customer service advantage or disadvantage are the present and the future. One way to verify that your customer service function is operating correctly is to test it by hiring people to purchase your product and then contact your business with various issues that need to be resolved. Additionally, you or one of your staff can make phone calls to various customers to check in with them to see if your business is meeting their expectations in this area.

Having a customer service advantage over your competitors is always very desirable. However, there are certain industries where having better customer service is imperative because the customer perceives that each business's products are almost identical, or the product involves situations where the customer really does not have the knowledge to differentiate between them. Industries where customer service can be a make-or-break factor include:

- Insurance
- Accounting services
- Pharmacies

Example

An extremely high level of customer service was the key ingredient that Noel and his company ended up bringing to the market. Noel was a seasoned veteran in the Home Health industry, but since Home Health services tended to be quite generic, there were relatively few items that Noel and his management team could use to separate their company from its competition.

Once the decision to focus on improving their customer service was made, they examined every aspect of their operation to determine how they could improve it. They started with the establishment of their specially trained "Kindness Korp," which would be their front-line personnel that answered telephone calls from prospects, doctors' offices, health care facilities, patient families, etc.

Next, they provided training to all their personnel on truly understanding and being sensitive to their patients' needs and how to go the extra mile to meet their desires. They followed this up with hiring an independent company to solicit from their customers and the health care community as to what problems they experienced in dealing with Noel's company.

Then they performed an analysis of their entire company to identify and resolve all areas that did not function smoothly. This led to them developing their "No problem promise" in which they committed to doing things right one-hundred percent of the time.

As a result of these actions, their reputation for excellent Customer Service soared and provided them with the strategic competitive advantage they were seeking.

Complete exercise 5-4 in workbook

YOUR PRODUCT UNIQUENESS

Lastly, you should examine your product to determine whether you have any desirable unique characteristics or features. The Uniqueness of Your Product is not something that just happens; you must create or develop this uniqueness. While this uniqueness originates from Production, the benefit is obtained in Marketing & Sales because you can deliver a uniquely attractive solution to your customers' needs, which should generate additional revenue for your company.

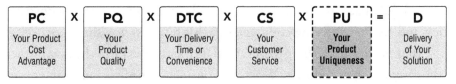

Fig. 5-8 Production Area—Your Product Uniqueness

As we discussed in Chapter 4, if your product possesses some desirable unique trait that your competition cannot duplicate nor obtain because of some impediment (a patent, a copyright, a trade secret, extreme cost to develop), you can sell your product at a higher price than your competition. In addition, you do not have to focus on your product cost, product quality, delivery time or convenience, and customer service areas as much because you are the only game in town. These factors can yield higher than normal profits.

There are three ways you can create uniqueness in your product:

1. Create the unique feature or a totally unique product as an intentional step in a research and development area. This approach may be the most expensive way of creating a unique product; however, it may be a necessary cost to create and maintain this advantage.
2. Purchase the rights for the product from someone else.
3. Create the unique feature or a totally unique product as a byproduct of your normal Production process.

While having a unique product always provides you an advantage over your competition, there are certain industries where having a unique product creates an enormous advantage such as:

* Health care
* Computer hardware and software
* Telecommunications

Example

As the owner of a civil engineering company, Roger, a bearded man in his mid-40's, had his work cut out for him because as far as heavy construction and civil engineering companies go, his business was small potatoes.

They needed something to differentiate themselves from the many other companies in their industry. When we considered the first four elements of their Production area, nothing stood out. As we discussed the Uniqueness of Their Product, Roger shared that they had developed great expertise in the testing of concrete used in various building and road projects.

Furthermore, he had invented a device to aid in this testing. As we fleshed out this unique expertise, we determined that a niche market for them would be to provide these concrete-testing and consulting services to large civil-engineering companies. Thereafter, the identification and development of this unique aspect of their Production area enabled the significant growth of Roger's company.

A Word about Research & Development (R&D)

You will not see an element titled Research and Development in the formulas for the six areas of your business. That is because it is contained inside of Production as the development arm of the Uniqueness of Your Product area. Your research and development function may be in a different building than your Production function or it may even be in a different city, state, or country than your Production function. However, from a strategic point of view, the purpose of your research and development function is to enable your delivery of the solution to be more effective.

Additionally, it is my opinion that in a correctly structured business, the research and development function operates as a joint venture between Marketing & Sales and Production. No matter who is the driving force for research and development, Marketing & Sales personnel need to be involved at a certain point so that all the factors that determine the size of your opportunity can be assessed and fully developed to ascertain the commercial viability of the product being developed.

Complete exercise 5-5 in *workbook*

DEVELOPING YOUR UNIQUE GENIUS

Now that you have examined each of the five elements of your Production area in detail and assessed your strengths, weaknesses, opportunities, and threats in each area, you want to revisit the concept of identifying your unique genius that we introduced earlier in this chapter and ask yourself which of these five areas is the key to your Production area. Think of this key as being the one or two things that, from a Production standpoint, separates you from your competitors and then make this element or combination of two elements the foundation of your entire business!

The saying, "There is wisdom in crowds, but genius in individuals" can be applied to this idea of discovering the key to your Production area. Specifically, your business will remain as only part of the crowd of competitors unless you develop the key your unique genius, which will then enable you to stand out from the crowd.

With that in mind, review the five elements of your Production area and write down which of these elements is the key to your entire business. In certain situations, your key element may be a combination of two of the elements, for example, "We will produce a low-cost product while maintaining great customer service." A two-elements unique genius is the combination of your product cost advantage and the quality of your product, which creates a product being a great value as your sustainable competitive advantage. However, the key to your Production area should never include more than two elements of your Production area.

Now that you have discerned your unique genius, it should be the basis for developing the Attractiveness of Your Solution in your Marketing & Sales area. Your next step is to return to your Marketing & Sales area and fully develop your solution based on your unique genius from your Production area. Bear in mind as you do this, if your unique genius is being a low-cost producer of your product, then in the Marketing & Sales area, a low-cost producer equates to having a price advantage.

Earlier in this chapter we discussed the chicken-or-egg syndrome between Marketing & Sales and Production. Now it becomes more obvious that to provide something that meets your customer's needs in a special way (your solution) you must first figure out how you as a business will go about producing your solution by using your unique genius as the delineator in your Production area that will set you apart from your competition. An absolute key in this process is that you always keep in mind that for an element to be your unique genius, you must provide this element 100% of the time to your customer. Your unique genius must be the bedrock of how you operate your Production area!

Example

Robert, a focused man in his mid-50's, owned a software development company that was having a difficult time competing with other companies in its marketplace.

As we examined all five elements of the company's Production area, he told me they had done several projects with County Zoning departments where they had a developed cutting-edge, on-line software that via the internet enabled any user to access zoning maps and drill down into the zoning specifics of any real estate parcel.

Their unique software was of a very high quality, and they had started to receive interest from various cities and counties regarding whether Robert's company could develop similar software for them.

As we considered what could be their Unique Genius—the thing that could be used to separate them from their competition—it became obvious that it was that they could provide unique software that would be of a very high quality. This decision facilitated them in becoming one of the leading software companies in the on-line zoning-map industry, and based on their Unique Genius, enabled them to move on to other niche markets.

Complete exercise 5-6 in workbook

CHAPTER SUMMARY

Production is the core area of any business. This is where you live up to the solution you promise to your customers. It is where your competitive advantage becomes evident—or the lack of one becomes painfully apparent. There are five elements in your production area, namely: product cost, product quality, delivery time or convenience, customer service, and uniqueness. These need to be analyzed to develop your strategic advantage. Then you want to use the above five elements to identify and fully develop your unique genius so that you can create a sustainable competitive advantage.

UPDATING YOUR CRITICAL SUCCESS FACTORS

Back in Chapter 3 you identified your Critical Success Factors, and you separated them into the six areas of your business. Now that we have worked through this chapter, please review all that we covered and determine the strengths of, weaknesses of, opportunities of, and threats to your business in your Production area. Then, if necessary, modify and/or add to the Critical Success Factors that you have already identified. Additionally, once you have done this, then add a column to your list in which you note which element of the Production area formula pertains to each Critical Success Factor.

Chapter 6

Growing Your Money Tree (Step #5)

• • • • •

In Chapters 2, 4 and 5 we analyzed the three foundational areas (Values and Vision, Marketing & Sales, and Production) on which entire your business rests. In this chapter we will examine your Finance & Administration area, the first of the three support areas that enable your three foundational areas to operate properly.

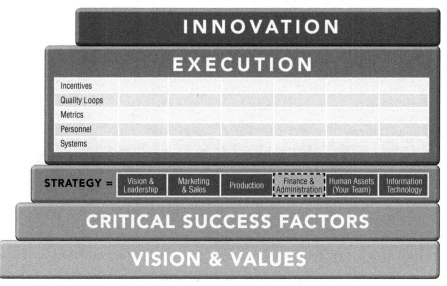

Fig. 6-1 Structure of Success—Finance and Administration Area

Why is Finance & Administration a support area? It is not as immediate and crucial a function for a business as where the business is going (Values and Vision), what the business is going to sell, how it will be marketed (Marketing & Sales), and how what is being marketed and sold will be produced (Production).

Finance & Administration is the first support area because no matter what the size of your business, you will have a Finance & Administration area. However, if you are the only employee in your company, there would be no need for a Human Assets area. Additionally, you may have a company that is completely manual, so there may be no need for an Information Technology area.

THE IMPORTANCE OF THE FINANCE & ADMINISTRATION AREA

The Finance & Administration area of a business, which includes accounting operations, can be quite boring to some people. Although some business owners may find finance unappealing, it is critical to a business; if you do not pay proper attention to this function, you may run out of money and have to close up shop. Finance & Administration provides the information to:

- Determine if you are making a profit or loss
- Manage your assets properly
- Fund your business properly
- Make strategic and tactical decisions
- Avoid operating your business in a chaotic manner

The purpose of Finance & Administration involves the scorekeeping of how your organization is doing in trying to achieve the Vision you have for it. This scorekeeping produces information that communicates what is the relative health of an enterprise.

OVERVIEW OF FINANCE & ADMINISTRATION

The formula for managing Finance & Administration is:

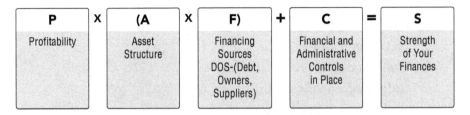

Fig. 6-2 Finance and Administration Area—Overview

Please note the abbreviations at the top of each element of the formula because they will be used at the end of this chapter.

We will examine each of these four areas to assess the strengths, weaknesses, opportunities, and threats of them to your organization.

PROFITABILITY

Profitability is almost the sole determinant of whether a company is successful, making it the most important part of your business's Finance & Administration area! Abundant profitability can cure a large number of evils throughout an enterprise. If you have a wildly profitable business, you can make a ton of mistakes in various areas and still be successful because you have a large cushion for error.

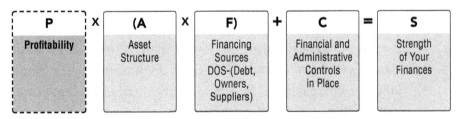

Fig. 6-3 Finance and Administration Area—Profitability

There is a difference between the terms profitability and cash flow; it is not profitability by itself that can cure a large number of evils throughout a business, but profitability coupled with a positive cash flow.

There are seven main tools that you can use to measure and gain insights into a company's profitability:

1. Gross profit analysis
2. Net income or loss calculation
3. Owner's discretionary cash flow
4. Industry comparisons and ratios
5. Budget versus actual reporting
6. Break-even analysis
7. Use of metrics

Gross Profit Analysis

The first measure of a company's profitability is your gross profit. The formula for this calculation is:

Revenue – Cost of sales = Gross profit

In the above equation, your business's cost of sales (sometimes called cost of goods sold) are those expenses of your company that are directly related to the production of your revenue as compared to overhead expenses. For example, if you were a home builder you would produce your revenue by building and selling houses; the costs that would go directly into producing a house (your product) would be:

- The wages and salaries you pay your employees to build the house
- Materials (lumber, drywall) that would go directly into the house
- Subcontractor payments for areas that your business will not complete itself (e.g., plumbing, heating, air conditioning)
- Supplies (500 lbs. of nails that you use on four different houses)
- Rental of a bulldozer to clear the land and scaffolding to put the siding on the house

All the above costs would be considered cost of sales because when you sell the house, these are the costs that were necessary to produce your product (a house). Once you subtract these direct expenses from the revenue you received from the sale of the house, you have the gross profit from the sale. What is the benefit of knowing your gross profit?

Your gross profit shows how efficient your business is at producing its revenue. It is also a measurement of the relative strength of your company's "economic engine." The greater your gross profit, the stronger your economic engine is. This information is instrumental in analyzing your cost of sales to increase your profitability. Gross profit analysis looks at the cost of sales of your business and compares that to your gross revenue in dollar terms and on a percentage basis. Additionally, you can compare your gross profit percentage to that of your competitors or industry averages to provide information to improve your profitability.

Here's an example to illustrate this point. Let us say that I was looking at buying one of the two companies below and both were in the same industry:

For the year ending December 31, 2100

	Company A	Company B
Revenue	$200,000	$200,000
Profit	$20,000	$20,000

Table 6-1

Looking only at Table 6-1, you would say that there is no difference between the two businesses because both present the same financial picture; therefore, I could purchase either of the companies. However, if I provided you with additional information, you might have a completely different opinion. For example:

For the year ending December 31, 2100

	Company A	Company B
Revenue	$200,000	$200,000
Total cost of sales	$80,000	$40,000
Gross profit	$120,000	$160,000
Profit	$20,000	$20,000

Table 6-2

What does this additional information tell you? It costs Company A double what it costs for Company B to produce the same retail sales value (i.e., revenue) of the same product. This equates to a cost-of-sales percent for Company A of 40% ($80,000/$200,000) and a cost-of-sales percent for Company B of 20% ($40,000/$200,000). The gross profit percent of Company A is 60% ($120,000/$200,000), and the gross profit percent for Company B is 80% ($160,000/$200,000). What does this mean? This means is that Company B is more efficient at producing its revenue than Company A because it has a much lower cost-of-sales percentage (lower is better) which produces a much higher gross profit percentage (higher is better).

There are two main benefits of having a high gross profit percentage. First, it means that your business is efficient in generating revenue. Second, a high gross profit percentage provides more flexibility in choosing how to operate your company. This potential flexibility affects every area of your business by providing you the freedom to make decisions and to choose options that otherwise you could not select because of having constrained finances and lack of ability to absorb expenses.

This greater ability to absorb overhead expenses can provide you with many options. For instance, you could:

- Invest more in your Marketing & Sales area to generate additional revenue

- Expand your business
- Pay your employees more or provide more fringe benefits to them to increase their satisfaction and morale
- Pay yourself more or increase your fringe benefits
- Pay off business debts
- Distribute more money to the owners of your business

With enough gross profit, you can do almost anything!

Some business owners may be thinking, "This does not apply to my business because we are a (consulting, health care, or internet marketing, …) business and not a (manufacturing, retail, or distribution) business." The gross profit analysis tool applies to all businesses because every business will incur some costs to produce its product. Keep in mind that I am using the term product in the loosest sense of the term. By properly calculating your cost of sales and gross profit, you will obtain great insights into the efficiency and true profitability of your business. In particular, gross profit analysis relates to the first element in your Production area, your product cost advantage.

The mechanics of doing the above are quite straightforward; the only problem is that many businesses do not include costs that are truly cost of sales in the cost-of-sales section of their income statement but instead treat these expenses as overhead expenses. The result of doing this is that the true operational efficiency of the business is distorted because its production costs are not being reflected in the most insightful manner. Table 6-3 shows how this distortion can take place.

For the year ending December 31, 2100

	Company C	Company D
Revenue	$100,000	$100,000
Cost of sales—labor	$25,000	$0
Cost of sales—contractors	$10,000	$0
Cost of sales—fringe benefits	$5,000	$0

Total cost of sales	$40,000	$0
Gross profit	$60,000	$100,000
Labor		$25,000
Contractors		$10,000
Fringe benefits		$5,000
Overhead wages	$10,000	$10,000
Overhead expenses	$10,000	$10,000
Owner's compensation	$20,000	$20,000
Overhead fringe benefits	$10,000	$10,000
Profit	$10,000	$10,000

Table 6-3

Using the above income statements, you would incorrectly conclude that Company D is much better run than Company C, while actually they have the same operational efficiency because the labor, contractors, and fringe benefits that appear in the overhead expense section of Company D's income statement are the exact same nature and amounts as the Company C's cost of sales—labor, cost of sales—contractors and cost of sales—fringe benefits. To solve this accounting problem, all Company D needs to do is to move these accounts to its cost-of-sales area of its accounting system. Please see the adjusted income statement in Table 6-4 below.

For the year ending December 31, 2100

	Company C	Company D
Revenue	$100,000	$100,000
Cost of sales—labor	$25,000	$25,000
Cost of sales—contractors	$10,000	$10,000
Cost of sales—fringe benefits	$5,000	$5,000
Total cost of sales	$40,000	$40,000
Gross profit	$60,000	$60,000
Labor	$0	$0

Contractors	$0	$0
Fringe benefits	$0	$0
Overhead wages	$10,000	$10,000
Overhead expenses	$10,000	$10,000
Owner's compensation	$60,000	$60,000
Overhead fringe benefits	$10,000	$10,000
Profit	$10,000	$10,000

Table 6-4

Listed below is another set of businesses (Companies E and F) in which you can properly compare their gross profit amounts.

For the year ending December 31, 2100

	Company E	Company F
Revenue	$500,000	$500,000
Cost of sales—labor	$150,000	$120,000
Cost of sales—contractors	$100,000	$75,000
Cost of sales—fringe benefits	$50,000	$30,000
Total cost of sales	$300,000	$225,000
Gross profit	$200,000	$275,000

Table 6-5

Let us assume that these two businesses' operations are comparable; therefore, we see that Company F is more efficient at producing its revenue than Company E in that Company F's total cost of sales is $225,000 as compared to Company E's total cost of sales of $300,000.

Complete exercise 6-1 in workbook

We can gain more insights in comparing these businesses by examining their financial information on a percentage basis. Listed below are Company E's and Company F's financial results reflected on a percentage basis:

For the year ending December 31, 2100

	Company E	Company F
Revenue	100%	100%
Cost of sales—labor	30%	24%
Cost of sales—contractors	20%	15%
Cost of sales—fringe benefits	10%	6%
Total cost of sales	60%	45%
Gross profit	40%	55%

Table 6-6

From the above we see that the total cost of sales percentage for Company F is 45% as compared to Company E's 60%, which means that Company F's total cost of sales is 33% better than Company E (60%-45%=15% and then take this 15% and divide in into 45%, yielding 33%). This in turn yields a gross profit percentage for Company F of 55% as compared to Company E's 40%, which is a large difference.

Complete exercise 6-2 in workbook

One issue that may need to be addressed is how to handle owner's compensation because many times officer compensation is treated as an overhead expense even when the owner is providing a significant part of the direct effort of producing the revenue of the business.

To have accurate financial statements with which to perform a correct gross profit analysis, you must allocate owner's compensation to cost of sales based on the value the owner is providing to their business from a direct revenue generation standpoint. This amount is the cost the company would have to pay someone to obtain the revenue-generating services the owner is providing. This value can be termed the fair market value (FMV) of the services the owner is providing when he/she is acting in the role as a factor of the business's production. The amount of her/his compensation over and above the production value would be treated as overhead. For instance, see Tables 6-7-1 and 6-7-2 below:

Total owner compensation— being treated as overhead	$110,000

Table 6-7-1

Total owner compensation— initially being treated as overhead	$110,000
FMV of the owner's actual production efforts	$60,000
Owner's overhead compensation (the remaining amount)	$50,000

Table 6-7-2

From an overall standpoint, by minimizing your cost of sales—which thereby maximizes your gross profit, while minimizing your overhead costs—you will improve the profitability of your business and reduce your need for financing.

Example

Ravi and Priya, a married couple in their late 50's, owned an industrial consulting company that had fallen on hard times. The market had drastically shrunken for the type of consulting their corporation provided. But Ravi just ignored this fact (he even refused to look at their financial statements) and continued to say their overhead expenses were too high and told Priya to cut them.

As we worked together, we examined a five-year analysis of their gross profit amounts and relative percentages. It showed that revenue and gross profit fell more and more each year. Furthermore, their cost-of-goods sold was barely reduced in each of the five years, which meant they had not reduced their operating expenses commensurately. Further analysis showed that even on good projects, their gross profit margins were also decreasing.

Their company's "economic engine" was in serious trouble; it was becoming less efficient at producing its revenue, and it was getting worse. When they compared their gross profit percentage to industry averages, they found the same reduced gross profit was occurring across their target market. Equipped with this information, Ravi and Priya changed the focus of their consulting, reduced staff, and embarked on a comprehensive marketing campaign in their new target market.

Net Income or Loss Calculation

The second tool that you can use to measure your profitability is the income statement for your business, which shows whether you had a profit or a loss for a certain period. Continuing from the formula that we used in the above gross profit analysis section, the formula for the calculation of your net income or loss is:

Gross profit – Overhead expenses = Net income

Simply put, your net income or loss is calculated by taking the revenue from your business and subtracting all your business expenses (cost of sales and overhead expenses). Your business's net income or loss, which is shown at the bottom of your income statement, indicates your business's overall profitability.

Your income statement shows your net income or loss for a certain period. Therefore, it is like a movie in that the movie has a start time and a finish time, and your income statement has a beginning and an ending date. You could be viewing a two-minute trailer of a movie, a short movie, or a full-length movie. In the same way, your income statement could show the revenue that your business received and your expenses for a week, month, quarter, or the entire year.

The key benefits from using your income statement are the determination of your profit or loss and the further analysis of your revenue, cost of sales, and overhead expenses so you will be able to make proper business decisions. The income statement is crucial because it the best tool for keeping score about where you are in the execution of your strategic plan for your organization. Your business's profitability or lack of profitability is the ultimate measurement of how your company is doing.

Applying this concept further in terms of revenue, the larger your business, the more profit you should have. If your business is growing or has grown in terms of revenue, but not in terms of its net income, then your business is presenting you with an increasingly risky business situation. The risk is increasing because generally the larger the business, the more things can go wrong; the more things that can go wrong, the greater the risk of operating the business.

As your business grows in terms of revenue, you should experience, in general, a commensurate increase in net income. Of course, there are economies of scale, various business growth curves, and the scaling up of an enterprise's operations. Depending on its break-even point, the business may not see the increased net income for some time. But sooner or later (ideally sooner), your revenue growth should translate to greater net income; otherwise you are increasingly putting you and your company at financial risk.

Further analysis of the components of net income from your business tells you a vast amount regarding the financial operations of your business. As you can see in the example below, while your net income shows what your business is bringing to the bottom line, you need to understand how this number was derived.

Let us now consider the purchase of either Company G or Company H. This information below shows that Company H is operating much better than Company G because it can provide more salary and fringe benefits to the business owner. If you were provided with the below information (see Table 6-8), you would have the necessary facts with which to decide which business to purchase.

For the year ending December 31, 2100

	Company G	Company H
Revenue	$500,000	$500,000
Cost of sales—labor	$150,000	$120,000
Cost of sales—contractors	$100,000	$75,000
Cost of sales—fringe benefits	$50,000	$30,000
Total cost of sales	$300,000	$225,000
Gross profit	$200,000	$275,000
Overhead wages	$10,000	$10,000
Overhead expenses	$10,000	$10,000
Overhead utilities	$5,000	$5,000
Overhead supplies	$10,000	$5,000
Overhead travel	$10,000	$5,000
Owner's compensation	$60,000	$120,000
Owner's fringe benefits	$10,000	$35,000
Profit	$85,000	$85,000

Table 6-8

Complete exercise 6-3 in workbook

Additional financial insights can be obtained regarding your operations by adding a column to your income statement showing each line item's relative percentage in comparison to your total revenue. When this column of percentages is added to your income statement, the income statement is then referred to as being a common-sized income statement.

For the year ending December 31, 2100

	Company G	Company H
Revenue	100%	100%

Cost of sales—labor	30%	24%
Cost of sales—contractors	20%	15%
Cost of sales—fringe benefits	10%	6%
Total cost of sales	60%	45%
Gross profit	40%	55%
Overhead wages	2%	2%
Overhead expenses	2%	2%
Overhead utilities	1%	1%
Overhead supplies	2%	1%
Overhead travel	2%	1%
Owner's compensation	12%	24%
Owner's fringe benefits	2%	7%
Profit	17%	17%

Table 6-9

We can see how the cost of sales and overhead expenses of Company H are proportionately lower than Company G, which in turn allows Company H to pay its owner a greater amount in salary and fringe benefits, in both absolute dollars and in percentage terms.

The next tool we will examine is owner's discretionary cash flow. However, before we can perform this analysis, we need to discuss the two ways you can calculate your business's net income: cash or accrual. What is the difference?

Complete exercise 6-4 in workbook

Cash versus Accrual Basis Accounting

Let us say that you start a business in December 2100 selling widgets, and you issue your first invoice for $10,000 on December 28, 2100. But your customer does not pay your invoice until January 15, 2101. On a cash basis, you would record the $10,000 as revenue in 2101 because that is when you received the payment for the invoice. However, on an accrual basis, you would record the $10,000 as revenue in 2100 because that is when you were legally entitled to receive the payment as a result of issuing the invoice in the year 2100.

Relatedly, when you start your business in December 2100 you purchase the widgets on December 23, 2100, that you subsequently sell to your customer. Thereafter, on December 31, 2100, you receive a bill from your vendor for $4,000 for the widgets. But you do not pay this bill until January 31, 2101. On a cash basis, you would record the $4,000 as an expense in 2101 because that is when you made the payment for the bill. However, on an accrual basis, you would record the $4,000 as an expense in 2100, because that is when you received the bill and were legally obligated to make a payment.

Furthermore, let us say that you ceased operations on January 1, 2101, except for receiving the above payment for the invoice and making the payment for the bill. On a cash basis, you would show no revenue or expenses in 2100, and the $10,000 in revenue and $4,000 in expenses would be shown in 2101 (when theoretically the business had ceased operations). However, on an accrual basis, you would show $10,000 in revenue and $4,000 in expenses in 2100 (before you had collected or spent any funds) and would show no revenue or expenses in 2101 (when you collected and spent the funds).

Neither the cash nor the accrual method is right or wrong; the difference is simply the way you are reporting what happened. The cash basis method reports the transaction when the cash (not literally—this could be a check, credit card, or electronic funds transfer transaction) either comes in or goes out of the company. Whereas, on an accrual basis, you record the revenue or expense once there is a legal entitlement or obligation for it.

The accrual basis method of financial reporting and accounting is more exact because it matches a business's revenue and expenses more accurately. Of course, in the real world, the difference between the two can become much more complex than our simple example, but this should provide enough insight into the two methods so we can proceed with examining our remaining profitability tools. If you would like to learn more about this subject, you can refer to a college-level accounting textbook or contact a local Certified Public Accountant (CPA).

Owner's Discretionary Cash Flow

Now that we understand accrual versus cash, let's examine the third tool that you can use for analyzing your business's profitability—determination of the cash value obtained from your business, or owner's discretionary cash flow.

Owner's discretionary cash flow calculates the amount of cash generated from your company's operations that is available to you as a business owner. Please note that this is a simplified definition of "cash flow from operations;" this is not intended in any way, shape, or form to cover the more complex issues that can arise in creating a Statement of Cash Flows report. We will use the term "owner's discretionary cash flow" in the loosest of ways to basically mean the owner's direct or indirect cash value obtained from the business.

Calculating your owner's discretionary cash flow is important because every business owner may take funds out of the business in his/her own unique way; therefore, it is necessary to calculate this composite amount to compare different businesses.

A question that should be answered by each company owner is, "What is the financial benefit that I am obtaining from my business?" More specifically, you want to make sure you know the cash value or financial benefit you are receiving from your business. To do this calculation, you add together the owner's salary, fringe benefits, payments made by the business for her or his personal expenses, and any other cash payments (but not business-expense reimbursements) made to or on the behalf of the business owner. To this sum, you add the net income from the business, which is calculated on a cash basis. If there are multiple business owners, you only add their own portion of the net income to the above sum. The examples below demonstrate the calculation of Company A and Company B owner's discretionary cash flow:

For the year ending December 31, 2100

	Company A	Company B
Owner's salary	$40,000	$80,000
Owner's fringe benefits	$0	$20,000
Net income	$20,000	$20,000
Owner's discretionary cash flow	$60,000	$120,000

Table 6-10

Complete exercise 6-5 in workbook

Industry Comparisons and Ratios

The fourth tool for assessing your profitability is a comparison of the dollar amounts and percentages for various line items on your income statement to averages for your industry. Ratios from your financial statements can also be calculated and compared to those of your industry. By comparing your business's dollar amounts and percentages of revenue, cost of sales, gross profit, and overhead expenses, etc. to industry averages or even the more detailed breakdowns of the quartiles of your industry averages, you will obtain concrete information regarding your business's performance compared to your competitors.

Data for industry comparison purposes is available from many industry associations or groups. Generally, they publish statistics on revenue, gross profit, overhead, net income, owner's compensation, owner's fringe benefits, and salaries paid for various levels of employees. Many times, additional expense data is also available. Some of this type of information is also available from various United States government and private companies such as Mergerstat and RMA Annual Statement Studies. Use of this tool provides additional insights to a company's operations.

Listed below is a simple income statement comparison between Company E (from Table 6-6) and its industry averages:

For the year ending December 31, 2100

	Company E	Industry average
Revenue	100%	100%
Cost of sales—labor	30%	28%
Cost of sales—contractors	20%	18%
Cost of sales—fringe benefits	10%	9%
Total cost of sales	60%	55%
Gross profit	40%	45%
Overhead wages	2%	2%
Overhead expenses	2%	1%
Overhead utilities	1%	1%
Overhead supplies	2%	2%
Overhead travel	2%	2%
Owner's compensation	12%	10%
Overhead fringe benefits	2%	2%
Net income	17%	25%

Table 6-11

This analysis shows that Company E's total cost of sales percentage of 60% was slightly higher than the industry average of 55%. The data also shows that its gross profit of 45% and net income of 17% are less than the industry averages. Percentage analyses can be done on any component of a business's total cost of sales (e.g., labor, materials, subcontractors, etc.) or any element of overhead costs. The importance of industry comparisons is that it enables you to identify areas to closely examine and improve the efficiency of your business.

Complete exercise 6-6 in workbook

Besides percentage comparisons, various financial ratios can be compared to industry averages to provide further insights into your profitability. There are many, many different ratios that can be calculated; some use only income statement data, some only balance sheet data (which we will discuss in the next section of this chapter), and some both. We will examine some income-statement-based ratios and combined ratios in this section and balance sheet ratios in the section titled Asset Structure later in this chapter.

Profit margin =	Net income
	Net revenue
Return on assets (ROA)	Net income
	Average total assets*
Return on equity (ROE)	Sales
	Average stockholders' equity**
Revenue per employee =	Revenue
	Total number of employees
Gross profit per employee =	Gross profit
	Total number of employees
Net income per employee =	Net Income
	Total number of employees

*Average total assets = (beginning total assets + ending total assets) / 2

**Average stockholders' equity = (beginning stockholders' equity + ending stockholders' equity) / 2

Table 6-12

Complete exercise 6-7 in workbook

Budget versus Actual Reporting

The fifth tool that can be employed is budget versus actual reporting, which is used to compare budget against actual revenue and expenses. This provides you with very good information regarding how your business is performing as compared to how you projected it would perform. You can generate a budget versus actual comparison on a monthly, quarterly, or an annual basis. The more frequently you produce these reports, the better you can identify and resolve problems before they become too large.

Generating the comparison is only the first step. If your actual revenue and expense amounts deviated from your budgeted amounts, the second step is to investigate why. The third step is to decide what actions to take to correct the problem. The fourth step is to put those corrective actions in place.

In Table 6-13 you will see that depending on the account, some differences are desirable while some are undesirable.

For the year ending December 31, 2100

	Actual	Budget	Difference
Revenue	$200,000	$230,000	-$30,000
Cost of Sales	$80,000	$60,000	-$20,000
Gross Profit	$120,000	$170,000	-$50,000
Marketing Expenses	$50,000	$45,000	-$5,000
Interest Expense	$10,000	$10,000	$0
Vehicle Expenses	$40,000	$65,000	$25,000
Travel Expenses	$0	$10,000	$10,000
Net income	$20,000	$40,000	-$20,000

Table 6-13

Complete exercise 6-8 in workbook

Break-Even Analysis

The next tool (once again, there are many, many other tools that are available, but I am focusing only on the major tools) to assess your profitability is a break-even analysis. To perform a break-even analysis, you need three sets of data. You can do this analysis on a monthly, quarterly, or, like most businesses, an annual basis.

First, you add up the total of your fixed costs for a given period (e.g., monthly, quarterly, or annually). Your fixed costs remain constant in the short run; for instance, your rent, insurance, utilities, etc., while variable expenses change in relation to the revenue of your company. See below for an easy way to identify your fixed expenses. The total of your fixed expenses is recorded as a horizontal line in an electronic spreadsheet.

Second, you identify the variable expenses for your business. Your variable expenses are the ones that change in a direct relationship to your revenue. These include your cost-of-sales expenses (which are the direct expenses that are related to the production of your revenue) and any of your overhead expenses that vary with your revenue, such as support staff, supplies, training, etc.

The easiest way to identify and separate your fixed costs from your variable costs is to print out your business's chart of accounts, and for the accounts in your cost of sales and expenses sections mark an F next to each account that is a fixed cost and a V next to each account that is a variable cost. Then transfer these F's and V's to the income statement you are using to create your break-even analysis. Next, total all the F accounts and the V accounts. The total of your F accounts is plotted as your fixed expenses. Lastly, determine the percentage relationship between the sum of your variable expenses and your total revenue. For instance:

For the year ending December 31, 2100

	Company F	Company G
Total Variable Expenses	$80,000	$105,000
Revenue	$200,000	$300,000
Total Expense Percentage	40%	35%

Table 6-14

Keep in mind that because of economies of scale or diseconomies of scale, the percentage relationship between your revenue and the total of your variable expenses can vary in connection with changes in your revenue. For instance, let us say that your revenue projection is $500,000 and you estimate that at $500,000 of revenue your variable expenses would be $200,000, or 40% for below revenue of $500,000. However, let's say that if your revenue projection was greater than $500,000 of revenue you estimate that your variable expenses would decrease by one percent for each additional $100,000 of revenue, to a minimum of 35% because of various economies of scale that would come into play.

Then, using the variable expense percentage that relates to your projected revenue, plot your variable expenses starting at the point your fixed expense line intercepts your Y axis and show these increasing at the slope of the percentage relationship between your revenue and variable expenses.

Third, with both your X and Y axis using the same scale, plot your revenue starting at zero and show it increasing at constant slope.

Once you have plotted these three lines, the point where your revenue line crosses your variable expenses line is your break-even point. This is the point where your business neither makes a profit nor losses money.

The differences between your revenue and your variable expenses lines at various levels of revenue to the left of your break-even point represents the loss your business would incur at various levels of revenue. Whereas the difference between your revenue and your variable expenses lines at various levels of revenue to the right of your break-even point represents the profit your business would generate at each level of revenue.

The lower is the revenue amount at which you reach your break-even point and begin to make a profit, the lower the amount of risk that your company has and the easier it will be to attract investors to your enterprise.

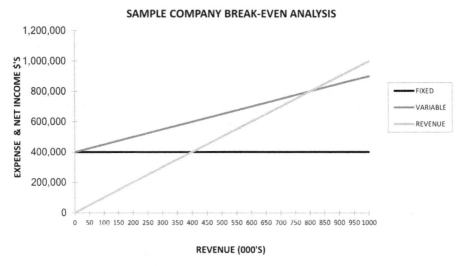

Table 6-15 Sample Break-Even Analysis

Complete exercise 6-9 in workbook

Use of Metrics

The final tool that we will examine is the use of metrics for evaluating your profitability. There are two types of metrics: financial and non-financial. In this section, we will only examine financial metrics. Financial metrics are obtained directly or indirectly from your business's accounting system.

Some people become baffled by the term *metrics*; however, metrics are straight forward; they are simply measurements of whether your business is on target or off target in a certain area.

Keep in mind that the purpose of metrics is for you to be able to gauge how your business is doing in the pursuit of your vision for your business. That is, metrics are merely another scorekeeping tool that you can utilize to create your dream business. While in this section we are concentrating on metrics that are a measurement of your profitability, you can and should have metrics that are measurements of the various items on your balance sheet. I will discuss both financial and non-financial metrics in more detail in Chapter 11.

How does a metric differ from the financial results of a business's operations? Generally, metrics are created by dividing a financial value in your business by some other value in your business. Normally, metrics are not obtained directly from your financial statements, but are a calculated figure. For instance:

- Growth per market sector
- Revenue per location
- Gross profit per store
- Market share
- Backlog amount (for manufacturing businesses)
- Average amount per sales transaction
- Number of new customers per day
- Total number of customers
- Number of lost customers per week
- Number of customer complaints per month
- Average fringe benefit expenses per employee
- Average worker's compensation expense per employee

Financial reporting generally takes place at a summary level, which means that many times very important information becomes so homogenized that you cannot effectively use it as a barometer of how your business is doing, while metrics can tell you very specifically how a system, function, or department is performing.

Because of the variations between and in departments and between each sale, each customer, each location, etc., many times looking at something at the *forest* level via an overall metric may provide better insights than at the *tree* level because you can see the entire direction in which your business is going.

You can create almost an infinite number of metrics, but you want to choose measurements that provide the most insights into what is really happening within your company and that provide you the most comprehensive analysis. As you choose your metric, you need to think about how much work it will take to create it and how reliable it is.

This evaluation is necessary because the creation and evaluation of a metric includes the work of gathering of the raw information, calculating, storing, analyzing, and providing access to the metric. You want to create a mix of metrics that present you with not only insights into how your business in operating today and has operated recently, but also metrics that indicate what is the direction of your business in the future week, month or year.

Example

This manufacturing company was owned by five men who had been friends for about 15 years, and they wanted to retire from it. It was the type of enterprise that anyone would want to own. They had come to us for succession planning for the business, so when we looked at its past and current net income, we saw a very desirable picture, with very high profits.

We also found that because the business was run very efficiently, it generated a substantial amount of owner's discretionary cash flow. When we compared their various ratios to industry averages, they were consistently above these averages. Furthermore, we constructed a break-even analysis and found that as a result of being run so well, it had a low break-even point.

Armed with these Metrics and the knowledge that its profitability indicators looked great; they began looking at the options for their exiting the company. Their favorable Metrics and high profitability gave them confidence knowing that they would be a strong point to focus on with any buyer.

Complete exercise 6-10 in workbook

ASSET STRUCTURE

The next element in your Finance & Administration area is your asset structure and along with financing sources (the following area), provide you with a snapshot that indicates the financial health of your business as of a certain date. The accounts in your Chart of Accounts that include your asset structure area and the financing sources area appear on your company's balance sheet. Your balance sheet lists the assets, liabilities, and equity of your business. Your balance sheet shows the relative health of your enterprise's finances, and it functions somewhat like a lab-work report that is part of a periodic "physical" for your company.

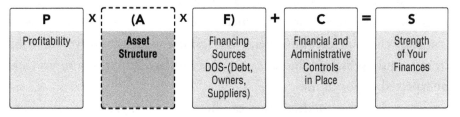

Fig. 6-4 Finance and Administration Area—Asset Structure

The overall health of your business is determined by the amount of your profit or loss, the amount and type of assets your business possesses, the liabilities you have, and the amount of equity in your company. In this section, we will examine the structure of the assets of your business, how they are deployed, and determine whether the structure of their distribution is a strength or a weakness. Listed below are the things that might be part of a business's assets:

- Checking, savings, and money market accounts

- Investments by your business
- Accounts receivable
- Other receivables (e.g., employee advances, officer loans)
- Inventory
- Prepaid expenses
- Equipment and similar assets

As you can see from the above list, assets are good things for your business to have; however, everything is relative, including assets. For instance, you might assume that having a large amount of money sitting in your checking account would be very positive, and you might be right in making that assessment. However, if the money is earning very little or nothing, instead it might be better invested in inventory and equipment that is being used to produce revenue. With this kind of investment, you would be earning a much greater return on those funds, and therefore your business would be healthier.

Conversely, if all your funds are tied up (invested in) in accounts receivable, inventory, and equipment and you have very little in your company checking account, then your business would not be very healthy from a liquidity standpoint, and you wouldn't have funds to jump on any unexpected opportunities.

There are three methods that can be used to analyze the deployment of your business's assets:

1. Direct observation of and analysis of your asset items on your balance sheet.
2. Metrics that focus on your asset area
3. Ratio analysis

Listed below is a sample of asset-based ratios.

For the year ending December 31, 2100

Current ratio =	Current assets
	Current liabilities
Quick ratio =	Quick assets*
	Current liabilities
Net working capital ratio =	Net working capital**
	Total assets
Asset turnover ratio =	Net revenue
	Average total assets***
Accounts receivable turnover ratio =	Net revenue
	Average accounts receivable++
Inventory turnover ratio =	Cost of sales
	Average inventory+++

*Quick assets = current assets-inventory

**Net working capital = current assets-current liabilities

***Average total assets = (beginning total assets + ending total assets) / 2

++Average accounts receivable = (beginning accounts receivable + ending accounts receivable) / 2

+++ Average inventory = (beginning inventory + ending inventory) / 2

Table 6-16

Example

Getting its asset structure corrected was critical for this furniture importer/wholesaler that was owned by Doug, a powerfully built, outgoing man in his mid-40's. Doug came to us because his wife, who was doing the bookkeeping for the company, was complaining that it was continually running out of funds.

As we reviewed its balance sheet, we found its checking account balance was close to zero, its accounts receivable was very high, and its inventory was extremely high. Upon further examination and discussions, we discovered that some of the company's largest customers were not paying their invoices, and over the past year they had strung out their invoice payments to 120 days.

Even worse, some of these large customers were making Doug's company carry more and more inventory. While this made the customer's balance sheet look great because of having lower inventory, it was consuming all the profits of Doug's company by forcing it to plow them back into purchasing much greater inventory than it should be carrying.

Armed with this information, Doug had meetings with officials from these customers to resolve these problems they were creating.

Complete exercise 6-11 in workbook

FINANCING SOURCES

Financing sources and their associated risks, along with your asset structure, reveal the financial health of your business. The liabilities and equity section of the Chart of Accounts in your general ledger comprise your financing sources. Just like your assets area, your liabilities and equity accounts are shown on your balance sheet, and they provide a key snapshot about how healthy your business is at a certain point in time regarding how you are funding your business's operations.

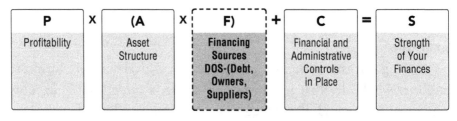

P	x	(A	x	F)	+	C	=	S
Profitability		Asset Structure		**Financing Sources DOS-(Debt, Owners, Suppliers)**		Financial and Administrative Controls in Place		Strength of Your Finances

Fig. 6-5 Finance and Administration Area—Financing Sources

Financing sources include the following general categories:

- Accounts payable
- Credit card, sales taxes, and other payables
- Payroll tax liabilities
- Unpaid payroll and fringe benefit liabilities
- Other liabilities
- Loans, mortgages and notes payable
- Investments in your business by its owners
- Retained earnings of your company

All but the last two are business debt owed to third parties.

You need to examine the inherent risks of how you are funding your business. Is the funding structure a strength or a weakness? Debt is double-edged sword; in profitable times it can be leveraged and used to magnify your net income, but in unprofitable circumstances debt can amplify your losses.

As we have discussed, everything is relative, and nothing is absolute. Since the first five funding sources above are classified as liabilities of your business on your balance sheet, they inherently present a hazard if you do not use debt wisely and manage it properly. Misuse of your funding sources can lead to enormous problems for your business.

There are three methods that can be used to analyze the structure of your business's financing sources:

1. Direct observation and analysis of your financing sources on your balance sheet.
2. Metrics which include financing sources data to monitor the health of your balance sheet.
3. Use ratio analysis to scrutinize the financial condition of your business's liabilities. By comparing your ratio results to industry ratios, you can obtain insights into your company.

Below is a sample of ratios involving your financing sources.

For the year ending December 31, 2100

Debt ratio =	Total liabilities
	Total assets
Interest coverage ratio =	Net income before interest and income tax expenses
	Interest expense
Debt to equity ratio =	Total liabilities
	Total stockholders' equity

Table 6-17

Example

Jimmy, a driven man in his 40's, owned a company that grew and sold sod, but it was having significant problems as a result of how he and his wife Carol were operating it. The business had a steady stream of customers and because of a housing boom, its profits were beginning to increase.

However, in the sod business there is a large outlay of money to either purchase or lease the land to grow the sod, sow the seed, fertilize it, water it regularly, as well as maintain all of the expensive equipment necessary to start, maintain, harvest, and transport the sod. This cash outflow was incurred months before any revenue from the sod sales was received.

A compounding difficulty was that Jimmy and Carol were dealing with was that historically their profits had been sub-standard, so they could not get loans for financing needs from traditional sources like banks. Therefore, they had to turn to individuals who charged them very high interest rates with very unfavorable loan terms. The high interest rates further reduced their profit margins, which in turn made them less attractive to traditional lenders.

We worked with them to reduce their expenses, sell off unused equipment, and contract out some work for which they maintained expensive equipment. These actions increased their profits enough that a bank was willing to offer them a line of credit at a very reasonable interest rate. The flexibility of the line of credit was perfect for handling their sod growing cycle, and the lower interest charges provided them the increased profitability that enabled them to eliminate the prior high interest financing they had been saddled with.

> **Complete exercise 6-12 in workbook**

FINANCIAL AND ADMINISTRATIVE CONTROLS

The last component for determining the strength of your finances are the financial and administrative controls you have in place. These permit all three of the previous areas (your profitability, asset structure, and financing sources) to function properly and accurately. They also include internal and external communications systems and internal work-flow processes.

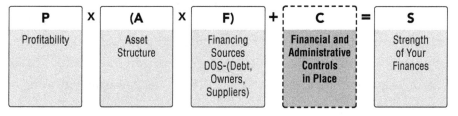

Fig. 6-6 Finance and Administration Area—Financial and Administrative Controls in Place

Proper financial and administrative controls and procedures ensure your business is operating correctly and smoothly, avoiding chaos, and crisis management that can so easily beset a business. Having proper financial and administrative controls produces an efficient business that can be easily operated by the owners or managers on an exception basis.

The key to having the proper financial and administrative controls in place is the use of systems or processes across all six areas of your business. The topic of systems, processes and controls will be discussed in more detail in Chapter 11.

Example

A residential home building company owned by Bernardo, a pleasant but self-absorbed man in his late 30's, had a problem. Bernardo loved the construction end of his business and preferred to stay out of the office and at construction sites as much as possible.

He had come to us for help because while the business had continued to grow in terms of the number of houses built, its profits were decreasing. As we worked with him and his management team, we learned that much of the company operated in an uncontrolled fashion because Bernardo had abdicated control to his personnel.

While there were many matters that needed to be addressed, one crucial area was its the company's lack of financial and administrative controls because, as we soon discovered, his main accounting person was embezzling significant amounts from his company.

Once this person was terminated (and subsequently prosecuted) and proper financial and administrative controls were enacted, Bernardo became properly engaged in all facets of the company. Relatedly, effective processes were put in place which enabled Bernardo to easily and properly manage the company. That in turn led to the company returning to profitability.

> **Complete exercise 6-13 in workbook**

CHAPTER SUMMARY

Although Finance & Administration is one of a business's three support areas, it is an important area on which to keep close tabs. Profitably is a key factor in determining the success of your company, for which we examined a number of tools to utilize. We also analyzed your asset structure and financing sources areas. Lastly, we considered your financial and administrative controls. Also, throughout the chapter, we reviewed proper systems and metrics to put in place to track and monitor your finance & administration area.

UPDATING YOUR CRITICAL SUCCESS FACTORS

Back in Chapter 3 you identified your Critical Success Factors, and you separated your Critical Success Factors into the six areas of your business. Now that we have worked through this chapter, please review all that we covered and determine the strengths of, weaknesses of, opportunities of, and threats to your business in your Finance & Administration area. Then, if necessary, modify and/or add to the Critical Success Factors that you have already identified. Additionally, once you have done this, then add a column to your list in which you note which element of the Finance & Administration area formula pertains to each Critical Success Factor.

Chapter 7

You Can't Do It Alone (Step #6)

• • • • •

We are now ready to focus on the second of the three support functions of your business—your Human Assets area—which is a critical area for an organization of any significant size.

I use the term *Human Assets* instead of *Human Resources* because the term *Human Resources* often makes people think of a someone sitting in the corner going through a policies and procedure manual, or worse yet, someone pointing to one of those government regulations posters that scare business owners half to death.

Instead what should come to mind when you consider Human Assets is the personnel in your business, the *team* that you have assembled to achieve the Vision for your company. The members of this team are truly your business's Human Assets. Your traditional Human Resources function should be thought of as a subset of your Human Assets area—the members of your team who deal specifically with personnel matters.

How does Human Assets function as a support area? Motivating, training, and managing your employees is instrumental in accomplishing your business's goals. In Chapter 2, we discussed that besides providing a Win/ Win experience for your customer, the second most important ingredient in creating the business of your dreams is to have fully engaged employees who feel your business is presenting them with a Win/Win experience.

Human Assets is critical because it supports all the other areas of your business—Vision and Leadership, Marketing & Sales, Production, Finance and Administration, and Information Technology. Unless you are going to do everything yourself, you are going to need other people in your organization to accomplish your Vision.

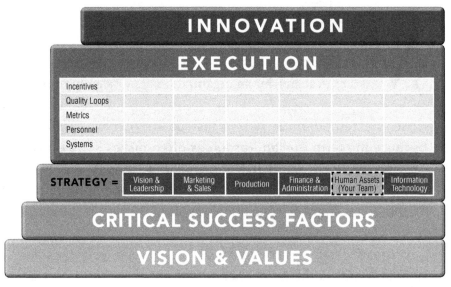

Fig. 7-1 Structure of Success—Human Assets Area

THE SIGNIFICANCE OF YOUR HUMAN ASSETS AREA

However, despite considering the above perspective regarding the true value of your Human Assets area, you may still be thinking, "Human Assets means Human Resources, which means personnel which equals pernicious rules and regulations, a minutia of detailed paperwork, and government and union intervention." While these may be things that may have to be dealt with, we will be examining your Human Assets at a much more strategic level. We will analyze your Human Assets area to make sure that you have the proper personnel and systems in place. To do this, it will help to answer the following questions:

- What are your personnel needs?
- What will be your recruiting strategy?
- What will be your selection and hiring process?
- What salaries and benefits will you offer?
- How do you properly build a team environment?
- How do you create a positive work environment, so you have great employee morale?
- What are your current employees' duties, and are these duties clearly defined?
- What are your current employees' strengths and weaknesses?
- What will be your training processes?
- What are your personnel policies?
- Do you have the correct managers in place?
- How effective are your current managers?
- Are you doing what you need to be doing to properly lead your personnel?

In general, studies have shown that there are four factors that provide for happy and productive employees:

1. Employees must feel *competent*—this translates to proper hiring, correct job descriptions, and ongoing training.
2. Employees need to know *what is expected* of them—this is produced by good management that is focused on outcomes.
3. Employees need to function in a *positive and team-oriented* work environment—this results in job satisfaction and high morale.
4. Employees need confidence in the *leadership* of their business—this means leadership knows where they are going and communicates regularly with employees.

As you will see in this chapter, these four factors span the six elements of your Human Assets area.

OVERVIEW OF YOUR HUMAN ASSETS AREA

The formula for managing your business's Human Assets is the following:

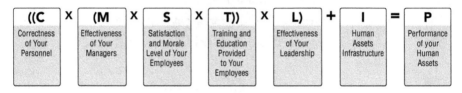

Fig. 7-2 Human Assets Area—Overview

Please note the abbreviations at the top of each element of the formula because they will be used at the end of this chapter.

We will examine each of these six areas in this formula to help you assess strengths and weaknesses of, and opportunities or threats to your business with regard to your Human Assets area.

As we examine this area keep in mind that the same Win/Win foundation to operating your business that has been stressed throughout this book also applies to this area. A business gets the Win of having a productive employee and the employee gets three possible Wins:

1. Their employment, income, and their sense of belonging needs being met;
2. By providing a solution to customers that they could not do on their own;
3. They are making the world a better place.

CORRECTNESS OF YOUR PERSONNEL

The starting point for analyzing your Human Assets area is to determine if you have the correct quantity and quality of personnel in terms of their skill sets, level of experience, personal characteristics, and work ethic?

Having the correct personnel in place is like preparing a dish by using the very best ingredients. Just as you cannot create great food with insufficient or poor-quality ingredients, you cannot build a great business with an insufficient number of employees, or ill-suited or poor-quality ones.

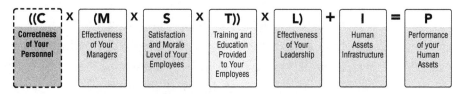

Fig. 7-3 Human Assets Area—Correctness of Your Personnel

As you determine the correctness of your personnel, avoid three mistakes that can occur in your personnel area:

The first mistake is making the assumption that you need incredible personnel throughout your organization to have a great company. That is not true; some areas of your business can do fine with just average personnel and other areas need above average or exceptional personnel. You as a business owner need to determine these areas. For instance, if you are a manufacturing business that needs to be driven by innovation, then your research and development function needs top-notch personnel, but it may be perfectly fine to use average personnel in your actual production area.

Second is ignoring the fact that the cost of hiring above average or exceptional personnel is greater than hiring average personnel. Their salary costs will be higher, mostly likely their ongoing training and education costs may be higher, and their fringe benefit costs may be higher because they may have greater expectations than an average person. Hire above average or exceptional personnel where they are beneficial to your business but be aware of spending more than you need without receiving any incremental benefit to your organization.

The third mistake is not realizing that if you have very good processes in place, you can accomplish the same or more with lower-quality personnel in place than if you have higher-quality personnel but poorer processes. We must all keep in mind that by and large the world is made up of average people. Using accepted statistical analysis techniques, the maximum number of people who are above average is about 14 percent, and the maximum number of people who are exceptional is about two percent.

Therefore, if all businesses are trying to hire this 16 percent, who is going to employ the other 84 percent of people? The great news is that by having excellent processes in place, an average employee can perform at an above-average level and an above-average employee can perform at an exceptional level, all with a lower cost to the business!

The two important things to keep in mind are: hire personnel at the appropriate level of qualifications based on what level is needed for each area and use desirable processes to improve all your personnel's performance to reduce your overall personnel costs.

There are many facets to having the correct personnel for your business. Namely:

- Determining the correct quantity of personnel
- Determining the correct level of education and training that is needed in your personnel
- Determining the correct skill sets that are required in your personnel
- Having the correct recruiting, selection, and hiring processes
- Making certain that your personnel possess the correct personal characteristics for your business
- Making sure that you have the correct quality of personnel
- Ensuring your personnel have the adequate level of experience
- Ensuring your personnel have the correct demographics and geographical distribution you need for your business
- Making certain that the correct personnel diversity is present in your business

Once you have ascertained the specifics listed above, the recruitment of the appropriate personnel takes place as part of this function. This element also includes the ongoing monitoring of this area to ensure that your enterprise continues to maintain the appropriate mix of personnel.

Example

Jacob, a seasoned Information Technology professional, owned an e-commerce company, and he and his leadership team wanted to take their company to the next level. They had a great "product" and the company was very profitable. But they knew they needed additional personnel to add various features to their e-commerce website and put the infrastructure in place necessary to grow the company.

As we worked with Jacob and his management team regarding the performance of their human assets, the first area we analyzed was whether or not they had the correct personnel into place to accomplish what they needed to do. To determine this, they performed a comprehensive skills inventory of their current employees and matched that with what they felt would be required to take the company to the next level.

They discovered a number of areas in which their current staff fell short. Using the skills-inventory information and their projected manpower requirements, they aggressively pursued adding the personnel they would require, retrained some of their current employees, as well as putting the proper management in place to effectively train and supervise the additional staff.

Complete exercise 7-1 in workbook

EFFECTIVENESS OF YOUR MANAGERS

How effective are your managers at motivating, leading, and managing their personnel so that you can achieve your Vision? Having effective managers is like preparing a dish using ordinary ingredients and then immersing those ingredients in a marinade that will transform them into something extraordinary.

Fig. 7-4 Human Assets—Effectiveness of Your Managers

> When I use the term *managers,* I am referring to everyone in your business who supervises personnel from the lowest level up to the top of your organization.

Highly effective managers bring out the best in employees. Conversely, ineffective managers can inhibit the productivity, contentment, and the stability of your workforce.

Most of us have worked for a great boss, someone for whom you would break through a concrete wall just to please. Many of us have also worked for bad bosses for whom you wanted to do nothing at all because of how they mismanaged their area. What is the benefit of having effective managers? You will be able to achieve the Vision for your company.

An effective manager turns an employee's talent into demonstrated performance. For a manager to achieve this, they must first find out the unique things about each of their employees and then capitalize on these attributes.

> To be a great manager, you must know your personnel and how they are wired. The use of various personnel tests can be very beneficial in trying to understand and properly manage your personnel, such as the DISC Assessment. Please contact me at Fountainhead Consulting Group, Inc. (George.Horrigan@ FountainheadConsultingGroup.com) for this and other personnel assessment tools.

To be an effective manager, you need to know each employee's:

1. Strengths and weaknesses
2. Motivators
3. Style of learning (analyzing, doing, or watching)
4. Preference for receiving recognition (be honored by their boss, be honored by fellow employees, honored by customers, awards, certificates)

Example

This large, integrated design/build construction company, which was owned by Diego and his wife Denise, was being stymied by personnel problems. The company had been founded about 20 years before and had grown into a formidable company, building both commercial and multi-family dwellings.

However, because of their significant size, turf wars were occurring between various departments, and cooperation between various areas had degenerated into competition. Additionally, completely opposite management styles were being employed by various managers, personnel in various departments were being evaluated differently, and the skills to effectively manage their employees was clearly lacking in some of the supervisors.

Therefore, a comprehensive training program was put in place to train their current managers on how to properly and effectively oversee their team members. Additionally, all the managers starting meeting once a week so that they could get to know each other, break down departmental barriers, and start to cooperate on cross-departmental efforts. Finally, employees who management thought had great manager potential were given training to speed them along in their advancement within the company.

These actions greatly improved the performance of the managers of Diego and Denise's business and its personnel.

Checklist for an Effective Manager

To assist you with the analysis of your Human Assets, below please find a list we developed of the attributes of an effective manager. You can use this list as a quick checklist for how your business is doing in this area.

An effective manager:

1. Is loyal to the business and clearly communicates the business's vision, management's decisions, tasks and goals
2. Can motivate employees
3. Creates a team environment that is safe and free from politics
4. Has sufficient knowledge of the area he/she manages
5. Has earned respect of all her/his employees and is respectful of others
6. Demonstrates leadership to employees, can implement changes, and leads by example
7. Manages in a positive and supportive manner
8. Makes his/her employees feel appreciated and valued, recognizes employees for their contributions, and is a cheerleader for the personnel under his/her supervision
9. Empathizes easily with others and can put him/herself in the other person's shoes
10. Is decisive and makes clear-thinking personnel decisions
11. Treats all employees in a fair and compassionate manner and does not let personnel problems persist
12. Is a good listener, tries to understand what her/his employees are saying, and acts upon the input received
13. Can delegate activities to others
14. Possesses good people skills and is approachable
15. Is an effective communicator either by writing, verbally or both
16. Is proactive, adaptable, and flexible
17. Is results- and goal-oriented and delivers what she/he promises to deliver
18. Is organized, reliable, and is a good time manager
19. Provides opportunities for growth for his/her employees
20. Displays high integrity
21. Is a positive role model and mentors others

Complete exercise 7-2 in workbook

SATISFACTION AND MORALE LEVEL OF YOUR EMPLOYEES

A key question that every business owner or leader should ask themselves is, "What is the morale level of my employees and how satisfied are they with their employment situation?" Having a high level of morale and employee satisfaction may very well determine whether your business achieves its Vision. The satisfaction level and morale of a business's workforce is an often-overlooked area.

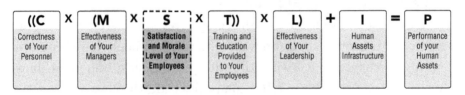

Fig. 7-5 Human Assets—Satisfaction and Morale Level of Your Employees

Employees Are the Problem, Employees Are the Solution

I have had countless discussions with business owners and leaders regarding the challenging area of Human Assets, often a pet peeve of many them. Some business owners wish they could get along without any employees. Others feel that if they are paying a fair wage, what more could employees want? This type of thinking will not give employers the high employee morale they wish for.

Sometimes when this topic comes up and they have voiced their frustrations I ask them, "Well, what is the solution?" After a moment to reflect, they have to admit, employees are the solution to their employee problem! If a business is going to get beyond the one-person fruit stand, it needs employees; having satisfied employees results in productive employees and a profitable company.

The best way to determine the satisfaction and morale of your employees and whether you have an enjoyable environment is to do anonymous employee surveys. However, you can obtain an initial feel regarding whether you have a rewarding, fun and enjoyable place to work by asking yourself if you would you want to work with and for you?

For your response to be somewhat realistic, you need to put yourself in your employees' shoes and answer this question totally honestly. Many business owners have a difficult time mentally and emotionally putting themselves in the shoes of their employees to do this self-analysis because they say to themselves that their employees "should be thankful for their job because they get a paycheck." They do not look at the full picture of what it means to have an engaged and contented work force in place.

Achieving Employee Satisfaction

What is necessary to have satisfied employees with high morale? I won't try to cover this entire topic (on which thousands of books have been written) in this chapter, but I will share with you the most important things that have come up with the 1,200 companies with which we have worked.

First, we must separate *motivators* from *non-motivators* in the workplace. Motivators are things that will increase an employee's performance over their normal base line on a continuing basis. The presence of motivators puts your staff in the zone. The absence of motivators becomes an impediment to having a content and productive employee. A non-motivator is a given, something that is expected as part of the employee-employer relationship. Let's examine four motivators and four non-motivators.

Motivators

A team atmosphere—Many studies have shown that employees want to work in a truly collaborative team environment. This includes getting constructive input, support and encouragement from other team members. In settings like this they are more content and productive than in a non-team environment. Just like the players on a football team where there is mutual commitment to the other team members, employees feel bonded to fellow employees and to the business that is creating the team environment.

The development of a team environment is the single most influential step in optimizing your Human Assets and creating a successful business. A key element of creating a team atmosphere is to communicate and practice the concept that "we all depend on each other, and we are all working toward a common and shared goal."

Making a difference in their customers' lives—Employees find it extremely gratifying to know they are positively impacting their customers' lives by enabling them to achieve the goals related to your product. Environments that share customer testimonials with their staff and tie this to their employees' actions produce a high level of morale and satisfaction. It is critical to celebrate the positive results your workforce is providing to your customers on a regular basis. This should include sharing both individual and group recognition of the difference your personnel are making in your customer's lives.

Employee's opinions are being solicited, valued, and used in the business—By nature, people want to be able to influence, effect, or change their future in a positive way. When an organization invites employees to provide input on various issues impacting their work environment and your business in general, they appropriately feel this is *my* business because they had a say in its operations. This sense of quasi ownership causes most people to work harder, go the extra mile, and look out for the enterprises' good. This results in people thinking outside the box to try to make the company better. These actions translate into two things: first, the business performs better and financially operates better; second, employees are more motivated, which results in the organization achieving its Vision and overall goals.

> How can you utilize your employee's opinions
> to improve your systems?

> One way to help improve a system in your business is to bring all of people who are involved in the system together in one room. As facilitator, ask: "How do you do . . . ?" or "What tips could you share with the group that you have found in doing . . . ?" Then go around the room and let each employee answer. In every work place this exercise will bring out the superstar, the average, and the laggard employees.

Business is impacting the world in a positive way—Various surveys have shown that people are happiest when they feel they are part of something bigger than themselves. Most people realize that there is relatively little that they can do on their own to positively impact the world. If employees share a vision to impact the world in the same way as their employer, they may even work for an organization for free (e.g., Peace Corps), or at a compensation level that is less than a market level. They will work long, hard hours and be extremely productive because they believe in what they are doing—it is more than a job.

Non-Motivators

Continued employment—Depending on how credible their evidence is and how troubled they feel, if people feel that their jobs are at risk, their performance may deteriorate. If you address their concerns and thereafter the employees have no reason to feel that their jobs are at risk, their performance should return to normal. Conversely, if you guaranteed their employment for life, you would not get better performance from them. In fact, you might get worse performance because they would know that they could do whatever they wanted, and they would still have a job. Therefore, you need to address the issue of continued employment at a satisfactory level; doing more than that will not get you better performance.

Personal safety—If employees feel at risk for their personal safety (e.g., machinery that does not have proper safety features, working along a roadway without flaggers, inadequate safety measures when cutting down trees), they will feel that you do not value their lives and safety. They may feel that you are willing to compromise their wellbeing just to make an extra buck. This will adversely affect their performance. Once you have adequately corrected the issues, their performance should return to normal. Once again, going above and beyond that level will not accomplish much for you.

Fringe benefits—Studies have shown once basic benefits are being provided, additional ones cease to be a significant motivating factor. Not having an adequate level of health care insurance, life insurance, vacation, sick leave, etc. can make personnel feel unprotected, at risk, and may lead them to look for work elsewhere. But beyond those basic benefits, others that you may choose to provide will not significantly improve their performance.

Reasonable compensation—A lack of reasonable compensation leaves employees feeling unappreciated, taken advantage of, and unfairly treated and their performance will definitely suffer. The use of compensation surveys is a very useful tool with regard to ensuring you provide reasonable compensation. However, there is little payback from excess compensation. For instance, you will not get double a person's production by doubling their compensation.

In summary, a non-motivator is something that is expected by your employees and providing these things is the entrance fee to get in the gate of having them as your employee. By providing these non-motivators you are making the work environment neutral (not exceptionally desirable, but not undesirable), however by not providing these minimum requirements, the work environment becomes negative. Therefore, you must provide an adequate level of non-motivators to have the foundation that can lead to a high level of employee morale and employee satisfaction.

The important thing to remember is that while providing an adequate level of non-motivators is necessary for happy and contented employees, a business will accomplish more by ensuring that motivators are present in the workplace. This is because motivators are the key to improving your employees' performance over the base line you would expect from the employee in a normal situation. By concentrating on providing motivators in your work environment, you can provide a stimulating, fulfilling, and rewarding work experience for your employees.

Example

A great job ended up being done by this residential painting company in building their employee morale and job satisfaction. The company was owned by three brothers in their 30's, but they were having difficulty finding painters because of a construction boom.

In the course of addressing their staffing shortage, we examined their entire human-assets area. As a result of the examination, numerous actions were taken, including the following steps to improve their employee morale and engagement.

One of the brothers, who was very good with people, spearheaded this effort. Daily "all hands on deck" meetings were initiated with all the painting crews, where each day's projects were reviewed, and "at-a-boys" were regularly being handed out for jobs well done. During the meetings, employees' opinions were solicited and implemented regarding how the jobs could be done better.

Feedback was obtained from the homeowners on a daily basis and was communicated to the team members during the meetings, so they realized they were making a difference in their homeowners' lives. This led to awarding of an "employee of the day" based on customer input.

Additionally, incentive cash payments were handed out to individuals for exceptional work, and bonuses were paid to crews based on a review of the completed job by another one of the brothers. These and various other actions resulted in a growing team atmosphere, which led to a huge jump in the satisfaction of their employees.

Checklist for the Satisfaction and Morale Level of Your Employees

To assist your analysis of your employee environment, please find below a short list of the characteristics that generally must be present in a business to have a high level of employee satisfaction. Use this as a quick checklist to ensure your organization has the essentials in place to create satisfied and engaged employees.

1. A people-oriented business with a friendly, upbeat, and positive team environment where people get along with each other
2. Adequate compensation is provided
3. Adequate benefits, perks, and amenities are provided
4. Engaging and effective managers who have the respect of their employees, are good role models, led by example, and are willing to work alongside employees when necessary
5. A business that regularly communicates its Vision and is an employer of which the employees can be proud
6. Job activities are accomplishing the goals of the task at hand and/ or the Vision of the business, and their skills are being used effectively
7. Employee input is solicited, valued, reviewed, and implemented
8. Employees feel challenged in their positions including possible future growth and advancement opportunities
9. Employees are recognized for their work, their contributions, and for taking initiative
10. Employees are valued and treated fairly as individuals, they feel the business cares about them, their employer is sensitive to employee emergencies, and their special needs and personal lives are valued and respected
11. Respect is shown to employees, customers, and vendors; and employees are supported by their managers and management

12. Management communicates openly with their employees, there is effective two-way communication, reasonable goals are set, and work expectations are fully communicated

13. Located in an easily accessible work location, flexible work schedule, and desirable physical work environment are provided

14. Job security is present, employees have some control over their future, and they work for a business that is financially stable

15. The presence of good working conditions and safety of employees is provided

16. Their employer has provided the proper tools, education, and training for completing the employee's job responsibilities

17. The employee's manager and business management display integrity in their actions

Complete exercise 7-3 in workbook

TRAINING AND EDUCATION PROVIDED TO YOUR EMPLOYEES

The next element of the Human Assets formula is the training and education provided to your employees. Unless you provide the appropriate level of ongoing training and education to your employees, you will not be able to achieve the full benefit from them.

Fig. 7-6 Human Assets—Training and Education Provided to Your Employees

> The terms "training" and "education," while very similar, are different. I view training as targeted at a particular function or desired outcome (more skill-set oriented) and education as more general in nature. Education may not have any immediate benefits to the employer but should result in more long-term benefits to both the employee and employer.

Just like seasonings enhance and bring out the best flavor in food, so does proper training bring out the best in your employees.

As was discussed earlier in this chapter, for employees to be satisfied and engaged they must feel *competent* in their positions and being adequately trained and educated is a key.

There are several ways to determine what training is necessary. First, you can analyze and assess your personnel situation to figure out what additional training would be beneficial for them. Second, employees can be surveyed to determine what areas they feel is lacking in their training. Third, you can interview your top-performing personnel to see if they possess certain knowledge and training that is lacking in the remainder of your employees. Fourth, you can hire outside training experts to analyze your situation and make recommendations as to what additional training would be advisable.

Example

Husband and wife, Ricardo and Celeste, were both engineers, and they jointly owned a consulting engineering company. But they had a unique problem. Their employees did not work at their location. In fact, they had no "location." It was a virtual company because they were working at the clients' locations and embedded with their staff.

Therefore, Ricardo and Celeste had very little interaction with their personnel, and many times their staff felt they were employees of the clients, more than ones of Ricardo and Celeste. In working with Ricardo and Celeste on growing their company, this sore subject came up.

However, a great solution to this dilemma was unearthed in the form of providing additional employee training and education. The initiative was given the prestigious name of the Advanced Engineering Program, and since both Ricardo and Celeste had a Master's Degree in Engineering, they could teach some of the classes. Additional classes would be taught by a college professor. The classes would take place virtually once a month for four hours and in person, once a quarter for a full day.

This was a win/win/win for everyone. By their staff getting additional training, it boosted their skill sets and confidence. The customer also obtained more highly trained personnel. The company received two benefits: the employee felt more allegiance to Ricardo and Celeste's company, and they could in turn charge the customer more for the personnel because of the advanced training.

> **Complete exercise 7-4 in workbook**

EFFECTIVENESS OF YOUR LEADERSHIP

This fifth element of the Human Assets formula—the effectiveness of your leadership—is different from the prior element about the effectiveness of your managers because it is focused exclusively on you as the business owner and how you lead your personnel.

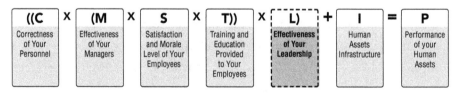

Fig. 7-7 Human Assets—Effectiveness of Your Leadership

> The term *leadership* has three aspects to it. First, a leader
> has clearly laid out and communicated the Vision for
> the business. Second, a leader inspires and motivates
> employees, so they see, believe in, and work toward
> the business's Vision. Third, they oversee and direct the
> execution of the plan to achieve their Vision.

Proper leadership is like the chef guiding, leading, and inspiring the entire restaurant staff to produce the best meals—time after time after time—from the raw ingredients they have at hand. Since your employees are one of the raw ingredients of your business, a business owner who is properly leading his/her business will bring out the best in this raw ingredient—employees.

Effective leadership is similar to being a football coach. Successful ones first create the detailed game plan for winning the game (this game plan would be equivalent to the overall Structure of Success™ methodology). Then they oversee the execution of the game plan from sidelines. That is, they do not try to guide the team from the press box, but instead are on the sidelines of the field and in the locker-room encouraging and directing their players. Your role as the leader of your company is very similar.

Likewise, soldiers want a commander that walks among the troops (like U.S. General Omar Bradley did in WW II). Additionally, in a smaller armed force, the commander knows all his/her troops by name. Therefore, depending on the size of the organization, you should try to personally connect with your employees and periodically encourage with your presence.

What Does an Effective Leader Look Like?

There have been countless books written of the subject of leadership, and the concept of leadership has almost taken on a life of its own. Many business owners I have talked to are perplexed by, intimidated by, and overwhelmed with the thought of being a leader. Before we go any further, I have some great news for you—this whole leadership thing is not nearly as complex as you might think! While we obviously have neither the time nor space to take a deep dive into the concepts that are discussed in this book, there are three important foundational thoughts related to leadership.

First, back in Chapter 2 we discussed the five roles of a leader:

1. Develop and cast a compelling Vision for your organization
2. Develop a strategy for achieving your Vision
3. Create the organization to accomplish your Vision
4. Oversee your business's execution and manage it via metrics
5. Apply transformational innovation to your entire organization

Now that is very doable, isn't it?

Second, there is no one leadership style that you must possess to be a great leader. Your leadership style needs to reflect your personality and temperament. There are several books that delve into the concept of assessing and understanding your personality and temperament and how they affect your leadership style. If you have questions regarding this area, please consult one of these books for more specific information so that you do not try to be or become someone who you are not. However, keep in mind that no matter what leadership style suits you best, you must accomplish the five things above to be a successful leader.

Third, leadership is a skill set that can be acquired and used in virtually any setting. If you concentrate on developing your leadership skill set, you can become a world-class leader of your own business!

The rallying of and cheering on of your employees starts with the realization to which any good leader comes: Your employees are your business! If you do not value your employees, empower them, and fully develop them as an asset, you are doomed to never creating the business of your dreams. Therefore, you want to communicate to your employees that they are the company. Encouraging your employees should occur *every time you have an opportunity*. This can be verbally one on one, in writing, in speeches, with posters, etc. This encouragement should include celebrating the successes of your business with your employees on a daily, weekly, and monthly basis.

> One small action that is very commonly overlooked but can be very meaningful to an employee: Send a card or email on an employee's anniversary date. This will say to the employee, "I am very glad you are here. The company and I value you as a person and your efforts on behalf of our business."

A chief responsibility you have as the leader of your business is to develop and cast the Vision for your business to your employees, so they perceive the Win for your customers and, if applicable, the world in general. Therefore, they believe in the purpose of and Vision for your business, which becomes a motivator. This responsibility also includes ensuring and communicating that your company practices good ethics, and it has admirable values and principles by which it operates.

These two concepts of truly meeting your customers' needs by putting them first and trying to make the world a better place become a shared goal for you and your employees that also strengthens the team atmosphere of your business. In this entire discussion, it is an absolute given that you must be truthful, honest, and completely above board in crafting and casting your business's Vision to your employees—dishonesty or manipulation will backfire.

What we see very often is that the business owners have never really thought about the altruistic benefits that they are trying to provide to their customers and the world in general. By missing this, they devalue the gravitas of their company.

Examples of Companies Benefiting Society

Let's look at seven seemingly ordinary businesses and see how they are positively affecting their community, society, and the world:

Junk Yards—By providing recycled parts, these businesses allow people to maintain their vehicles in a cost-effective manner, allowing drivers to make a living, provide for their families, visit friends and family, and be a functioning part of society. Furthermore, by recycling parts for vehicles, they promote a green earth and contribute to a more sustainable economic system.

Telecommunications Companies—These businesses have become an absolute necessity to mankind. They allow friends and loved ones to stay in touch with each other in an easier fashion, thereby fostering a healthy society. Their services permit improved functioning of businesses and the civilization in which they operate.

Building Materials Companies—Provide the materials necessary for the construction of homes and other buildings, thereby allowing for the proper shelter for people. This enables the development of family units, which is the foundation of any society.

Transportation Businesses—Allow people to travel to see loved ones, friends, or for business purposes. Seeing people in person enables individuals to form deeper relationships, which in turn helps to accomplish desirable social goals.

Clothing Retailers—By providing clothing so people are properly and attractively dressed, these businesses provide for the health, well-being, and self-esteem of its customers, which ultimately enables them to reach their overall goals in life.

Civil Engineering Businesses—By providing engineering services, these businesses allow the construction of buildings, bridges, roads, waterways, etc. that enable civilizations to function and thrive. These services provide for the well-being of society and the safety of its members.

Monitor Manufacturers—By providing monitors used to view data, these businesses enable the functioning of modern civilization. They empower people all over the world to be able to do, learn, and know more. By manufacturing monitors with functions like reducing eye strain, these businesses are improving the health for all the users of their monitors and help make the information age possible.

We could go on forever looking at examples of how businesses improve the lives of its customers and positively impact society. It is just a matter of perspective. Too often business owners and people in general fail to look at the big picture with regard to what they mean to society? This leads them to incorrectly and unfortunately getting stuck in the thinking that "the purpose of this business is to make profits for the business owner" when there is a whole lot more to their enterprise than just that.

The bottom line is that you as a business owner need to analyze what the total value (i.e., its Vision) of your organization is providing to your customers and society in general. As the leader of your company, use this information to inspire and motivate your personnel.

Example

Nicholas, the CEO of this health care company, needed to make some changes in his business to continue to grow. He had built a very profitable company and had a great and seasoned management team in place, but he was not someone that most employees related to—which was detrimental to the organization.

He realized that he needed to be the face of the company and tell personnel where he and his leadership team wanted to take the company. Therefore, he started to share with their employees the Vision he had for the company and the strategy for achieving the Vision. That way, the staff could get on board with and also influence the game plan for accomplishing the Vision.

He also concluded that he had led the company "from the press box," instead of being in the "locker-room" encouraging and directing the staff and being a commander that "walks among the troops."

He determined he needed to do two specific things. First, he started regularly walking around the office and greeting people and talking to them about what they were doing. Second, he held a monthly "press briefing" where he would answer questions from his personnel. These actions significantly increased the effectiveness of his leadership and brought him and his employees closer together.

Checklist for an Effective Leader

To assist you with your analysis, shown below is a short list of the attributes of an effective leader that my business has developed as a result of working with our clients. This list can be used as a quick checklist on how your business is doing in this area.

An effective leader:

1. Develops, cultivates, and refines the Vision for his/her business, clearly communicates the values and Vision of the business, and represents the business favorably
2. Focuses on the big picture and does not get lost in the details
3. Leads the business in a positive and supportive manner and leads by example
4. Displays passion, creativity, adaptability, flexibility, innovation, and is not afraid to take chances; also thinks outside the box
5. Is decisive and results-oriented
6. Shows respect for and values all people and therefore has earned the respect of her/his personnel
7. Creates a team environment where people feel safe and employees feel appreciated and valued
8. Is reliable, delivers what is promised and is accountable for the results of the business
9. Is approachable, listens to and understands what personnel are saying, identifies with and connects well with employees
10. Can motivate and inspire the organization and is a cheerleader
11. Communicates well with his/her staff either in writing or verbally, including fully communicating expectations
12. Can effectively delegate duties to others
13. Has a thorough knowledge of the business and its issues

14. Takes initiative, is a self-starter, is proactive and able to implement changes
15. Creates a fair environment where realistic goals and expectations are set and rewarded
16. Displays honesty and high integrity in all her/his actions, has the best interest of all customers, employees, and suppliers in mind, and therefore earns their trust
17. Handles pressure well and demonstrates confidence
18. Is a good manager and supportive of his/her direct reports
19. Displays humility and is not detrimentally ego-driven

> **Complete exercise 7-5 in workbook**

HUMAN ASSETS INFRASTRUCTURE

For the correctness of your personnel, effectiveness of your managers, satisfaction and morale level of your employees, training and education provided to your employees, and effectiveness of your leadership to operate correctly, your business will need to have an adequate Human Assets Infrastructure in place. The larger the number of people you have in your company, the more important this infrastructure will be.

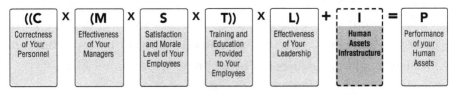

Fig. 7-8 Human Assets—Human Assets Infrastructure

A properly functioning organization is required to make sure that personnel-related actions and processes operate correctly and are not done randomly and haphazardly. If a proper infrastructure is not in place, it reflects poorly on all the Human Assets areas and makes it difficult to have a high satisfaction and morale level of your employees.

Listed below are the main areas that a business may need to address in its Human Assets support area:

Human Assets Administration—General administration of your entire Human Assets area.

Human Assets Policies and Procedures—Having written policies and procedures for the various functions that take place involving your personnel.

Hiring and Termination Procedures—To avoid potential lawsuits, it is highly desirable to have specific written personnel hiring and termination procedures.

Job Descriptions—So that your staff knows what is expected of them and upon what criteria they will be evaluated, written, accurate job descriptions are a must.

Performance Reviews—The procedures for and forms necessary for periodic performance reviews should be in place.

Employee Handbook—Having an Employee Handbook that is provided to your staff when they are hired—and which is updated when required—eliminates confusion and potential ill-will that can arise from your policies and procedures not being properly communicated.

Government Rules and Regulations Compliance—A business must comply with various federal, state, and local employee rules and regulations. To run afoul of government regulations can wreak havoc on any business and lead to discord in your personnel.

Fringe Benefits—The selection of various fringe benefits and regular re-evaluation of them is necessary to ensure that your employees remain happy and engaged.

Fringe Benefits Administration—Administering your fringe benefits is a must to make sure that you and your personnel are in compliance with the government and non-government regulations involving your fringe benefits.

Compensation Compliance—The larger your business is, the more important it complies with your internal rules and guidelines regarding employee compensation

Sufficient Human Assets Personnel—To properly handle all the above, you must have sufficient Human Assets personnel in place.

Example

The result of tightening up the human assets infrastructure of this very large electrical contractor was that they created employee goodwill and avoided any possible discord or legal action. During the prior 15 years, the company had grown from 20 employees to over 300. However, from a human resources perspective, it was still being operated as a small company.

As a result of several employee disagreements, the leadership team realized that they needed to solidify and clearly define their employee policies and procedures. This included hiring and termination procedures, job descriptions, compensation guidelines, and how performance reviews should occur.

They also determined they needed to publish an employee handbook that documented fringe benefits and how they would be administered. Lastly, they invested the time to ensure that they were in compliance with all relevant government rules and regulations, and they had the proper Human Resources personnel in place to properly handle the above responsibilities.

These steps proved to be invaluable in maintaining a great work environment.

Complete exercise 7-6 in workbook

CHAPTER SUMMARY

Managing, motivating, and training your employees is instrumental for your business to accomplish its goals. This starts with ensuring you have the correct personnel with appropriate skill sets in place. Next, managers need to be carefully hired and trained to understand how to motivate and reward employees.

Third, the ingredients that provide for the satisfaction and morale of employees, which are critical to achieving your Vision, need to be present in the workplace. Fourth, your personnel must be properly trained so they feel competent in their roles. Fifth, you as the leader of your company need to be visible and engaged with your employees for them to feel happy and satisfied. Finally, the Human Assets department of your business needs to be structured appropriately for the number of the size of your organization.

UPDATING YOUR CRITICAL SUCCESS FACTORS

Back in Chapter 3 you identified your Critical Success Factors and separated them into the six areas of your business. Now that we have worked through this chapter, please review all that we covered and determine the strengths of, weaknesses of, opportunities of, and threats to your business in the Human Assets area. Then if necessary, modify and/or add to the Critical Success Factors that you have already identified. Once you have done this, add a column to your list in which you note which element of the Human Assets area formula pertains to each Critical Success Factor.

Chapter 8
Technology to the Rescue (Step #7)

• • • • •

e have now arrived at the final of the three support functions of your business, the Information Technology area, which should be providing the information, tools, data infrastructure, and automated technology that allows the other five areas of your business to operate properly. Unless your company is very small, in our modern society no business can operate without appropriate Information Technology functions and processes.

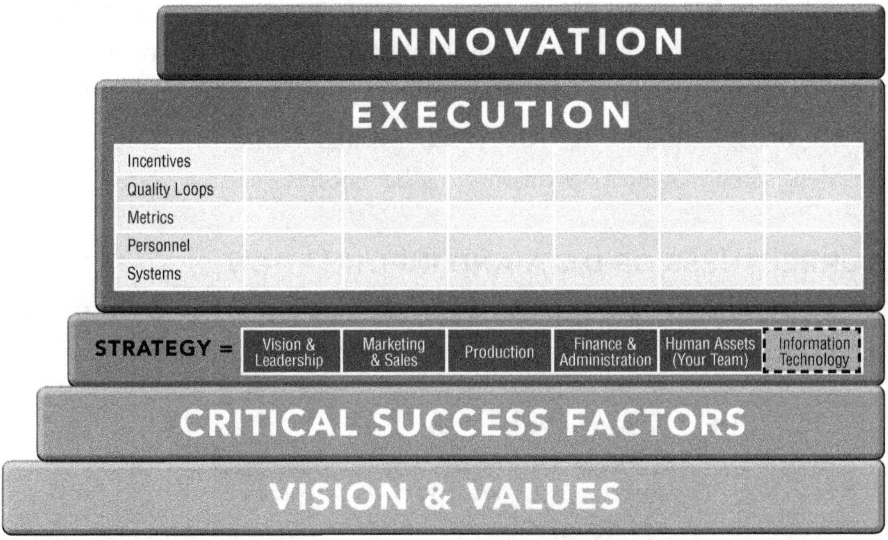

Fig. 8-1 Structure of Success—Information Technology Area

OVERVIEW OF YOUR INFORMATION TECHNOLOGY AREA

The formula for managing your business's Information Technology area is the following:

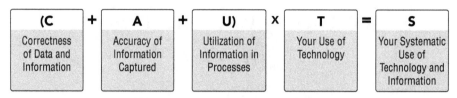

Fig. 8-2 Information Technology Area—Overview

Please note the abbreviations at the top of each element of the formula because they will be used at the end of this chapter.

We will examine each of these four areas to assess the strengths, weaknesses, opportunities, and threats to your organization.

Please note that many times when people think of Information Technology, only computer hardware and software come to mind. There are two important items to note in this formula. First, sometimes the quest for the latest technology, newest equipment, or glitziest gadgets may become an end in itself, instead of a means to an end. If you examine the formula you will see that technology is multiplied by the sum of correctness of data and information, accuracy of information captured, and utilization of information in processes. Therefore, if someone throws technology at a problem, they may end up wasting his/her money.

CORRECTNESS OF DATA AND INFORMATION

Information Technology should provide you with correct data and information regarding your business and the environment in which it operates.

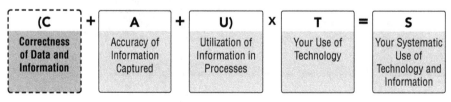

Fig. 8-3 Information Technology Area—Correctness of Data and Information

It is impossible to manage any organization of any appreciable size without having the information to control and monitor its operations. To find out if you have the *correct* information, first ask yourself if the information you need to operate your company is available? This means that your business must be capturing the data itself or the data is available to you from some outside source.

Second, is the available data in fact the correct data you need for your operations and management? There may be a huge amount of data available, but if it is not the correct data then it is next to worthless to you.

The question you want to ask regarding each of six areas we examined of your business so far is: "Do I have the correct data available to properly operate and monitor my business?" For instance, you may have volumes of inventory consumption data, but if that data does not also tell you which of your customers are buying your products that have the highest profit margins, then you are missing some vital information.

To perform this analysis, you want to examine each of the six areas of your business and create a wish list of the information you would like to have in each area. This analysis should include examining your Information Technology area itself to determine if you have the correct information to manage it. For instance, what database are you using, which operating system runs it, what software is installed on each PC? Having this information assists you in supporting your Information Technology infrastructure.

Example

Alex and Kitty, a couple in their late 40's, owned a software development company, and they were looking to sell it so they could concentrate on another of their businesses. They came to us to ensure their company was in ship-shape to be sold.

In the course of implementing the Structure of Success™ methodology in their company, we had worked through the various areas of it and we were now focusing on their internal Information Technology area. While Information Technology in the form of the software they created for their customers was their product, we were considering their internal Information Technology area, as a support for the other aspects of their organization.

As we examined their Information Technology function as a support for the various areas of their company, including their Marketing & Sales and Finance & Administration areas, we determined they had the correct information for running and selling their enterprise.

However, in the Production and Human Assets areas, they were missing some key information, such as how productive each programmer was, the average time it took to design a software module, and software defect statistics? Once the missing information was identified, they were able to design the systems to collect the needed information, which in turn was very beneficial in the marketing of their company related to its eventual sale.

Complete exercise 8-1 in workbook

ACCURACY OF INFORMATION CAPTURED

The next element to examine is how accurate, timely, and consistently reliable is the data you have at your disposal? That is, what is the quality of the data and information available to you?

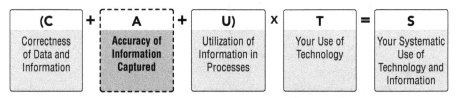

Fig. 8-4 Information Technology Area—Accuracy of Information Captured

Not only does a business need precise, *correct* data, it must be available to you on a timely basis for it to be of use. Any time the data you get is inaccurate or untimely, you need to ignore it. While inaccurate data is worthless, it may also cause you to ignore other related data that is accurate and useful, which ends up compounding the problem.

Once you have considered the accuracy of the information available in the six areas of your business, look at what you recorded in the prior analysis of the correctness of your data and information and consider if any items from that area spawn additional thoughts related to the accuracy of your information.

Example

This health care research and marketing firm was owned by Susan and Betty, who were both in their late 20's, and they had big plans for the company. In fact, a major investor had approached them about purchasing part of it.

Related to this occurring, we were progressing through the Structure of Success™ methodology in preparation for this capital infusion. Susan and Betty had a number of Project Managers on board who would oversee three to five projects at time.

While the data and information they provided to their clients was very accurate, as we analyzed their operations, we found that some of their internal Finance & Administration and Human Assets areas information was suspect.

Therefore, an internal project was initiated to validate all of their internal, online and hard copy information. The results of this effort was that they ended up being comfortable with their internal information, which in turn eased their concerns related to the possible investor's upcoming due-diligence inquiries.

Complete exercise 8-2 in workbook

UTILIZATION OF INFORMATION IN PROCESSES

Once you have the correct information and it is accurate, you need to evaluate your processes for utilizing the information. Even if you have a great amount of high-quality information, if you do not have the processes for transforming it into practical and actionable knowledge, your efforts will not provide you with many tangible advantages. This element is called your *utilization of information in processes.*

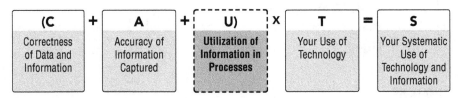

Fig. 8-5 Information Technology Area—Utilization of Information in Processes

The objective is to have the processes in place to convert your data and information into actionable knowledge you can use to manage and direct your business. Without the proper systems in place to utilize the information, your data collection effort won't get beyond the potential of having a benefit to your business.

To assess this element, review the six areas of your business and create a wish list of the processes you would like to have to properly utilize the information and knowledge you do or could have at your disposal.

Once you have completed the above, consider what you recorded in the prior analysis of the correctness of your data and information and accuracy of your information captured, and access if any items from those areas generate any additional thoughts related to the utilization of information in processes.

Example

Ensuring they had the correct processes in place for utilizing the substantial amount of information they produced was critical for this chain of Chiropractic offices. In the seven years since they started, they had grown to five locations, and they wanted to double their size over the next couple of years. But they had seen other businesses grow too fast and end up failing.

Therefore, they wanted to ensure they had the processes in place for producing practical and actionable knowledge. With this in mind, they embarked on a comprehensive review of both their Chiropractic offices and Corporate office to verify they had the correct processes so their data collection effort would truly generate a benefit to their company.

To accomplish this, they reviewed the six areas of their operation and looked at each information technology related process to see if it provided the information they needed, whether it needed to be revised, or if a new process was required to be created. As a result of this effort, they felt ready to pursue their desired expansion.

Complete exercise 8-3 in workbook

YOUR USE OF TECHNOLOGY

The last of these four elements, *your use of technology*, has two aspects to it: First, how technology is utilized to automate and optimize the processes in each of the other five functional areas of your business:

1. Vision and Leadership
2. Marketing & Sales
3. Production
4. Finance and Administration
5. Human Assets

Second, how technology is used to provide the correct and accurate information for you to know what is going on within your business.

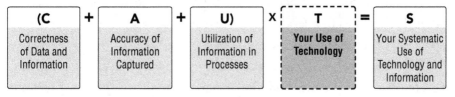

Fig. 8-6 Information Technology Area—Your Use of Technology

Technology is a tool to augment and automate the systems throughout your business. The proper use of technology assists with the collection, validation, and automated utilization of information and knowledge. While technology is not an end in itself, the proper use of technology can enhance all the other areas of your Information Technology area and enable all the other five areas of your business to operate that much better.

However, if you only throw technology at a situation without having the other three elements already identified or in place, you could be going nowhere fast.

Likewise, if you only toss technology at various areas of your operations without fully analyzing and understanding your company' systems and desired outcome, you may end up with a technological nightmare. Unproven technology or too complex of a technological solution can result in disaster. Technology should never be used just for the sake of technology.

If you have identified or have your *correctness of your data and information, accuracy of the information captured,* and *utilization of information in processes* in place, then by applying the proper use of technology, you will multiply the benefit of these other elements of your Information Technology area.

When you look at the big picture of Information Technology it is not merely the availability of data that's important, it is the use of this data in terms of what knowledge you can obtain about your operations, customers, markets, competition, production, finances, employees, etc. By gaining and applying this knowledge, you can manage your operations most effectively, beat your competition, and plan and prepare for the future.

In the formula, the sum of the other three factors is multiplied by your use of technology because, properly used, technology enables the other three factors to operate in a more beneficial manner than they would operate without the proper technology.

Information technology is a tool that can be used to enable your business to operate in a better and more efficient manner. Your use of technology reflects how skilled your business is in using this tool.

The proper use of technology can improve your overall Information Technology area and enable all the other five areas of your business to function that much better. By using technology correctly, you can automate your operations and data collection capabilities. It can also increase the accuracy of and provide for a systematic utilization of information and knowledge.

Staying Current with Information Technology Developments

As you no doubt are aware, information technology and technology in general is always changing. These two areas are complex, constantly moving targets. Therefore, you must stay abreast of new technologies and how they may impact your business.

One way to do this is regularly engage a consultant who specializes in information technology as it applies to your industry. This would involve meeting with the consultant several times a year to learn what new and relevant technological developments are occurring. The consultant must be someone who stays fully aware of new technologies that are being developed and how they may impact your specific industry. The consultant should act as a counselor to share what technologies are either emerging, proven and reliable or have become obsolete.

As the final step, review what you recorded in the prior analysis of the *correctness of your data and information, accuracy of the information captured,* and *utilization of information in processes* to determine if any items from those areas generate any additional items that need to be considered pertaining to your use of technology.

Example

Brandon was a stout man in his mid-40's who owned a cattle ranch that he bought from his cattle ranching father. While Brandon proclaimed, he was not a "techie," he realized that cattle ranching was changing and that he needed to move into the Twenty-First Century.

He had a son and daughter who were starting to work on the ranch, and they kept introducing their father to various technologies they used. So, he decided to make the plunge into using current technology to manage and grow his ranch. First, he did the fun stuff. He bought a couple of drones to watch and track where his cattle were. Then he got his tractors set up with GPS so they could drive themselves.

Next, he went high tech with an automated feeding and nutri-tion-monitoring system. He also got connected to online information sys-tems that would keep him abreast, in real time, of farm commodity prices.

Finally, he put in a wi-fi system across his ranch that enabled these and the other technologies that he implemented to seamlessly communicate with each other. Both he and his children were proud that he had moved into the Twenty-First Century with an advantageous use of technology.

Complete exercise 8-4 in workbook

CHAPTER SUMMARY

Information Technology is a useful tool but one to be utilized prop-erly and effectively. Just because data is highly available in this informa-tion age, doesn't mean that all data is equal. Be sure the data you collect and information you use in your business is accurate and that it is correct data you need for your organization to operate properly. Then ensure that you have the processes in place for the proper utilization of the informa-tion you are capturing. Next, make sure you are using the most appro-priate technology to process and utilize the above-mentioned data and information. Finally, consider hiring a consultant whose job is to keep you informed of new technology as it pertains to your industry.

UPDATING YOUR CRITICAL SUCCESS FACTORS

Back in Chapter 3 you identified your Critical Success Factors and you them into the six areas of your business. Now that we have worked through this chapter, please review all that we covered and determine the strengths of, weaknesses of, opportunities of, and threats to your business in your Information Technology area. Then if necessary, modify and/or add to the Critical Success Factors that you have already identified. Addi-tionally, once you have done this, then add a column to your list in which you note which element of the Information Technology area formula per-tains to each Critical Success Factor.

Chapter 9

Double Checking Your Compass (Step #8)

• • • • •

In Chapter 2 we first examined the concept of developing a compelling Vision for your business. In the preceding chapters, we examined five of the six strategic areas of your business:

- Marketing & Sales
- Production
- Finance and Administration
- Human Assets
- Information Technology

YOUR ROLE AS A CHIEF VISIONARY OFFICER

Now it is time to revisit and build upon the first and most important part of your company, the Vision you have for it and your role as your business's Chief Visionary Officer (CVO). From a strategic standpoint, we will also consider how visioning and leadership should drive the strategy and execution of the above five areas of your business.

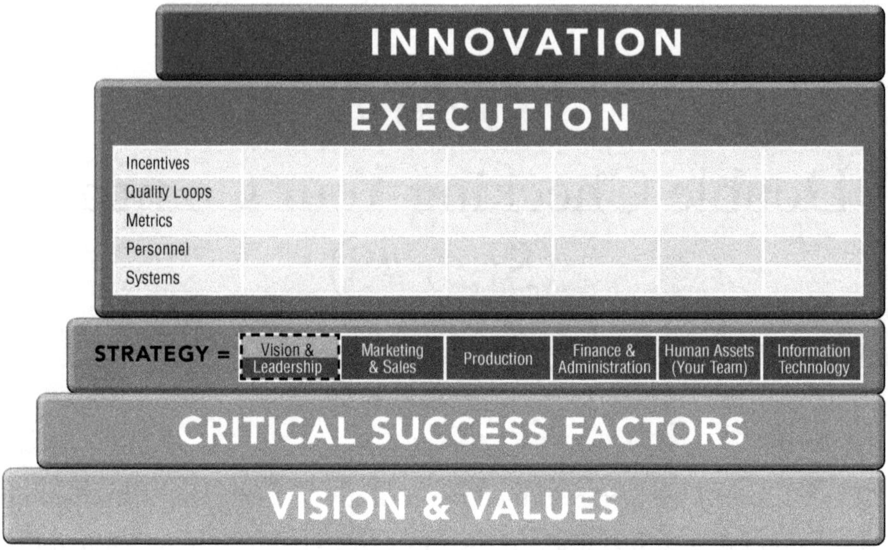

INNOVATION					
EXECUTION					

Incentives
Quality Loops
Metrics
Personnel
Systems

STRATEGY =	Vision & Leadership	Marketing & Sales	Production	Finance & Administration	Human Assets (Your Team)	Information Technology

CRITICAL SUCCESS FACTORS

VISION & VALUES

Fig. 9-1 Structure of Success—Vision Area

Directly related to your responsibilities as Chief Visionary Officer is the role you play as the leader of your business. This includes looking at where you should spend your time as a leader. In this chapter we will examine the task of being the Chief Visionary Officer of your business so you can take your company to the "next level." Then, in Chapter 10, we will build upon these concepts and delve into the how-to of becoming a world-class leader.

If you recall, in Chapters 2 and 3 we discussed how you develop an initial compelling Vision for your company and how to create an executable strategy to accomplish that Vision. We will now take those concepts and systematize them so that the compelling Vision and strategy you have for your organization stay current. So, let's dig into this all-important area.

I feel there are two things you as the leader of your business should be doing in and for your business:

- Living, eating, and breathing Vision and Leadership
- Overseeing your business's execution and managing it via metrics

We'll get into metrics more in Chapter 11, but let's begin by focusing on Vision and Leadership.

> **Please note**—Throughout this chapter and the remainder of this book we will use the term *Owner* for the person who oversees the operation of an entire business. While Owner is an appropriate term with respect to smaller businesses, for larger businesses the more appropriate term is *Leadership Team or Officers* who, in a larger business, are functioning in the role of a business owner.

SCOUTING FOR YOUR COMPANY

The Vision you have for your company and the leadership you are providing to drive your organization into that Vision will determine your business's ultimate success or failure! So, what should you be spending your time on? The first thing is figuring out where you want to take your business, the direction of, the destination for your company. In other words, what does a successful and thriving business look like to you? This is what I call "living, eating, and breathing Vision and Leadership."

Let me give you an analogy of what this should look like.

In classic American Western movies, you might see the captain of the U.S. Calvary send a scout out before the troop breaks camp. The scout would ride out to a certain destination, say a broad valley, where he might look through binoculars and observe that there were hostile Indians to the west, a wide river that cannot be forded to the south, and a tall mountain range that cannot be crossed to the north. Then the scout would return to the camp and report to the captain that they must go to the east.

In the same way, a company owner should be the scout for the organization. A business owner should be out there with "Vision" binoculars considering the future. In doing this they might see intensified competition and market threats to the south, cost pressures to the east, increased government regulations to the west, or new market or business opportunities in front of them. This analysis of what an owner sees should lead to creating an updated Vision of where he/she wants to take the company. Once this reconnaissance work is done and a *renewed* Vision has been laid out, the company owner should use her/his leadership skills to drive the business into this revised Vision.

Why is renewing your Vision so important? Over time the world has a curious tendency to wipe the slate clean and equalize the playing field for the businesses in a particular market. This is because companies can innovate and catch up to each other. This leveling of the playing field means that many organizations end up innovating past their competition.

Renewing your Vision is a necessary response to your changing business environment because even if you are currently ahead of your competition, without taking concrete, definite, and purposeful steps, your competition will eventually catch up to you. Unless you expend effort and specifically take actions to maintain a leading position in your market, you will eventually fall behind your competition. We see this demonstrated all around us in the natural world: weeds take over your garden unless you continue to arduously work on it; ocean waves wipe out sandcastles you have built without a fortification; fine houses deteriorate into dilapidated structures without maintenance. Likewise, in the business world, today's cutting-edge technology becomes tomorrow's obsolete know-how, and your position as current leader in your industry disappears.

Conversely, this concept of the playing field being leveled over time for businesses also works to your advantage if you are behind your competition; you can see what does and does not work for your competition and then through this Visioning process and innovation, leapfrog your competition.

Example

Charlene was a soft-spoken woman in her late 50's who owned a chain of wedding and prom dress stores. When she came to us, it almost was too late to save her stores. Over the prior 10 years she had grown and expanded her stores. During the first five of these years, her profits had increased, however, during the second five years, the profits had plummeted.

What happened?

As we discovered, she had been so busy working in her company she had not looked around to assess what was happening in her industry's overall environment. She had not been acting as a scout for her business.

She had missed three seismic changes that devastated her company: first, the huge growth of online shopping for wedding and prom dresses; second, the renting of dresses versus the purchase of them; and third, the use of "pop-up" stores that would only occupy space for two or three months, and therefore would avoid the nine or so months of little revenue that hamstringed stores like hers.

Armed with this information, she and her leadership team plunged into these areas and began to turn the company around. But just as importantly, Charlene learned that as part of her job as the CEO of her company, she needed to constantly be functioning as a scout for her business so it does not get caught off guard again by changes in her market that could impact her company.

SCALING YOUR BUSINESS

A key component of determining where you want to take your business and what you ultimately want to do with it is the scaling, or growing of your enterprise so it can progress to the "next level."

Once a business has gotten to the point where it is viable and successful you want to determine the strategy for taking it to the eventual destination you desire for your company.

I realize that for some business owners once they have achieved a certain level of success, they may not want to grow their company past that point. If this is your line of thought, please note that because your operating environment is always changing and your competition continually gunning for your customers that just trying to stay where your company is currently at most likely means that in reality it is going backwards in terms of its competitive advantage.

Conversely, if you have a good business, why not expand it and allow it to meet the needs and wants of other people who have not had the opportunity to benefit from your company?

Scaling or growing your enterprise can include any of the following strategies:

- Organic business growth
- Additional products/services
- Adding locations
- Multiple delivery channels
- Franchising it
- Overseas expansion
- Vertical or horizontal integration

The above growth options can be key components of the process of renewing and reconceptualizing your Vision that will be introduced in the remaining part of this chapter.

As you proceed through the topics in this chapter remember to think about how they may apply to your possible desire to scale your company using the above options, or any other growth strategy.

Complete exercise 9-1 in workbook

VISION AND LEADERSHIP

Let us now delve into what renewing a comprehensive Vision for an organization looks like. If you recall from Chapter 2, there are five stakeholders of a business:

- Customers
- Employees
- Owners and Investors
- Suppliers
- Society

The key question to ask is, "How engaging and attractive is my company's overall purpose to my five stakeholders?" The answer is that the appeal of your Vision and the effectiveness of your leadership determine this attractiveness.

The figure below illustrates this concept by identifying each element of the Vision and Leadership of a business.

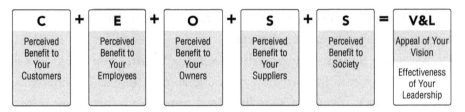

Fig. 9-2 Vision Area—Overview

If you notice the letters associated with each one of the above elements spells out the acronym CEOS'S. Therefore, you want to have a CEOS'S Vision for your organization. We will examine each of these five elements in detail to help you assess your overall Vision and Leadership by evaluating your company's strengths, weaknesses, opportunities, and threats in each area. Once we have laid the proper foundation, we will discuss how to dramatically increase your organization's perceived benefit to each of your stakeholders.

Please note the abbreviations at the top of each element of the formula because they will be used at the end of this chapter.

PERCEIVED BENEFIT TO YOUR CUSTOMERS

More than any other factor, your business's success is ultimately tied to its perceived benefit to your customers (i.e. creating a Win/Win experience). From my experience with over 1,200 businesses, an organization that truly provides a Win/Win experience to their customers has about an 85% success ratio!

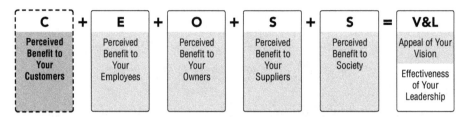

Fig. 9-3 Vision Area—Perceived Benefit to Your Customers

There are three different indicators of the impact that your perceived benefit will have on your customers.

1. **Sales figures and growth**—Your sales figures and sales growth track record indicate how desirable your customers consider your product. If your sales are flat, decreasing, or not increasing at least at the growth level of your industry, then your market is giving you a big warning message regarding your product.

2. **Competitor analysis**—Your competitor analysis and the percentage you have of your target market tells you a lot about whether your product's value proposition is resonating with your customers. Your competitor analysis is an assessment of how convincing your brand message is to your customers.

3. **Results of surveys and similar customers analyses**—Surveys and similar analyses of your customers and target market tell you whether your message is getting through and what is the perceived value of your business/product to your customers. *Perceived* value is the key because your message reflects the casting of your Vision to your customers as well as their perception of your leadership to accomplish that Vision. This assessment includes your past record of leadership and delivering on your communicated Vision.

Keep in mind that it is your customer's perception of your Vision and Leadership that really matters, not how *you* think you are doing in communicating your Vision to your target audience and the Leadership that you are displaying.

Complete exercise 9-2 in workbook

PERCEIVED BENEFIT TO YOUR EMPLOYEES

Successfully convincing your employees that your business's success is instrumental and foundational to the achievement of their personal goals is the essence of fully developing the perceived benefit of your organization to your employees. In Chapters 2 and 7 we discussed how to create a business that produces a desirable employee/employer relationship by developing a Win/Win connection for your company and employees. You must regularly evaluate this relationship to verify that the perceived benefit to your employees is both real and relevant to them.

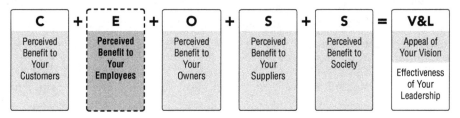

C	+	E	+	O	+	S	+	S	=	V&L
Perceived Benefit to Your Customers		Perceived Benefit to Your Employees		Perceived Benefit to Your Owners		Perceived Benefit to Your Suppliers		Perceived Benefit to Society		Appeal of Your Vision Effectiveness of Your Leadership

Fig. 9-4 Vision Area—Perceived Benefit to Your Employees

There are three different indicators of the status of your perceived benefit to your employees.

1. **Employee productivity**—If productivity is low, then you need to use the various tools in Chapters 7 to identify then rectify their disengagement.
2. **Employee turnover**—Low turnover says that employees are aligned with your Vision for them as an employee and your Vision for your customer. The various tools in Chapters 2 and 7 can be used to resolve any turnover issues you may have.
3. **Results of surveys and similar employee analysis tools**—These analyses will provide you the specific information regarding your company's perceived benefit to your employees. Remember, per-

ceived benefit is the key because your message reflects not only the casting of your Vision to your employees but also their perception of your leadership to accomplish that Vision.

Complete exercise 9-3 in workbook

PERCEIVED BENEFIT TO YOUR OWNERS

Obviously paramount in your mind is the benefit you and any other owner/investors perceive is being obtained from the operation of your company. Company owners who regularly work in the business observe these benefits on a daily basis. However, if you have other owners or investors who do not work in your business on a regular basis, you need to treat them much like a customer and have a communication system in place to keep them abreast on how you are doing in the pursuit of your Vision in a way that appeals to them. Remember, your message reflects not only the casting of and actual delivery of your Vision to your owner/investor but also their perception of the effectiveness of your leadership in driving your business into its Vision.

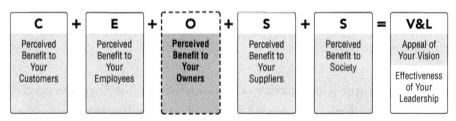

Fig. 9-5 Vision Area—Perceived Benefit to Your Owners

There are three different indicators of your perceived benefit to your owners/investors.

1. **Stock price**—If your company is publicly traded, stock market analysts and your stock price will indicate how your owners/investors view your company and your Vision for it.

2. **Owner discussions**—If you have a limited number of owners, you should be able to talk with them directly to get a sense of how they view your organization and your Vision for it.

3. **Surveys and similar analyses**—Surveys and similar analyses of your owners/investors will indicate their perceived benefit of your business.

Complete exercise 9-4 in workbook

PERCEIVED BENEFIT TO YOUR SUPPLIERS

The next element is the perceived benefit to your suppliers, which only applies to any strategic vendor relationships you may have. This is because if your company is insignificant to your vendor or supplier as a result of your size, then this element has no importance to your business.

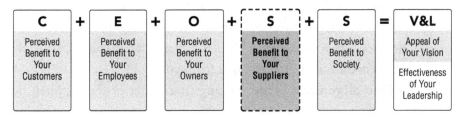

Fig. 9-6 Vision Area—Perceived Benefit to Your Suppliers

A few examples will help illustrate this. If your business was a local sign shop, then you don't have a strategic relationship with your natural gas supplier. However, if you were a large steel manufacturer that uses very significant amounts of natural gas in its production process, then there would be a strategic relationship between the companies. When I use the term *strategic,* I mean there is symbiotic relationship between the companies so that if they work in concert, both will win.

Another example is a tree service that has a strategic relationship with their dumpster supplier and their equipment repair vendor, because if the dumpsters are not dropped off and picked up on time, then logs and branches sit on their customer's lawn and no matter how good job they do, their customers will be unhappy. Similarly, tree service equipment regularly breaks down and needs to be repaired, so they need to foster a Win/Win relationship with their repair company.

The process of conceptualizing, creating, and casting a compelling Vision for your business to your suppliers is similar to doing so for your employees. However, depending on the nature of your company, the perceived benefit to your suppliers may not be as crucial to your business as its perceived benefit to your employees.

There are three different questions to ask that indicate your perceived benefit to your suppliers (you only do this with strategic supplier relationships).

1. **Supplier performance**—Are you getting the performance and cooperation from your key suppliers you need for your organization to thrive? If not, this indicates that they do not view your business strategically as a Win for them but instead are merely interested in obtaining revenue from you.
2. **Vision alignment**—From talking to a leader of the supplier, do you see evidence they understand and are aligned with your Vision for your company?
3. **Surveys and similar analyses**—Do surveys and similar analyses of your key suppliers indicate that they perceive a benefit from working with your company?

Complete exercise 9-5 in workbook

PERCEIVED BENEFIT TO SOCIETY

The final element is a business's perceived benefit to society. Many company owners overlook how society perceives a benefit from your organization and your Vision for it. Businesses intrinsically exist to improve the lives of the members of the society in which it operates. If it is failing to accomplish this, public opinion may turn against a business in the form of falling sales, boycotts, or even legal actions.

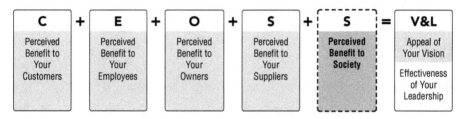

Fig. 9-7 Vision Area—Perceived Benefit to Society

While most societies sanction the existence of a business purely for the financial gain of the owner, larger businesses must communicate the reason for their existence, the benefits their company provides to society, and the Vision they have for their organization as it pertains to society.

Listed below are some of ways society forms its perception of a business's benefit to society. Does it:

- Provide a valuable product to society?
- Provide desired employment to society members?
- Improve the lot of its employees' lives?
- Function as a good corporate citizen?
- Give back to the community?
- Act in socially responsible ways?
- Try to make the world a better place?
- Get involved in desirable social causes?
- Avoid damaging the environment?

There are three indicators of your perceived benefit to society.

1. **Evaluating your current activities**—Perform an honest evaluation of what you are currently doing to improve society and determine if you should do more.

2. **Press coverage**—Is the press coverage you are receiving positive or negative with regard to your company's standing in the community?
3. **Social media**—What response is your company receiving on social media pertaining to how the public feels about it as a member of society?

Example

This heavy manufacturing company was owned by Herb, a hefty, driven man in his early 50's. He had worked for other companies as a General Manager and finally had saved up enough money to purchase his own business.

He had operated it for several years, and while it did okay, he had not had the profits nor the growth in revenue he had expected. So, he enlisted our services to assist him to take the company where he wanted it to go.

As we analyzed his business, it became clear there was a sought-after benefit to him (greater profits and wealth, the lifestyle he desired, the prestige of owning a successful company) and some perceived benefit to his customers. But that is where it stopped.

It turned out that he was hard on his employees, and there was a lot of turnover. He was also overbearing to his suppliers and gave nothing back to society. As he started to see the big picture and how he needed to change as a person and a business owner, he began to reshape the company, provide incentives for good work to his employees, and include them in decisions so they felt like part of a team.

He also took the time to get to know each of his customers and how he could make them more successful through meeting their needs. Likewise, he started being cooperative with his suppliers, instead of castigating them for any and everything that did not meet his expectations.

Lastly, he adopted several social causes his employees chose and started to get involved in helping with these efforts and giving back to society. These actions changed his company into one that was truly benefiting its Customers, Employees, Owners, Suppliers, and Society.

Complete exercise 9-6 in workbook

THE FIRST STEP IN RENEWING THE VISION FOR YOUR BUSINESS

This entire chapter is all about renewing, updating, and recalibrating your Vision for your business. Surprisingly, this can for the most part be systematized! You can orchestrate the renewing of your Vision by doing two things:

1. Make a commitment to regularly attend or participate in conferences, seminars, workshops, etc. that will expose you to the latest information, challenging ideas, concepts, and developments that could affect your company, customer, or market. Alternatively, or additionally you could avail yourself of CDs DVDs, tapes, and books that would provide these things. How frequently you engage in these activities is up to you, but the more often you do so will enable you to better fulfill the role of being a *scout* for your organization.

2. Set aside time to ponder and possibility-think about the direction of your business and consider the information with which you are being exposed and presented by doing step #1. During these pondering sessions, consider how this information may affect what your company could look like in the future.

Here are some specific tips regarding pondering and possibility thinking about your business:

- The desired outcome should be that you end up fanning the flame of your Vision.

- Always have some business-related reading material in your car or in your brief case or backpack to take advantage of even small amounts of free time to plant seeds in your mind.
- Use your commuting time and lunch hours for planning, thinking and dreaming about your business. Turn off your radio and play CDs that will expose you to new information, ideas, or concepts that can help you achieve your Vision—or simply think!
- Think about, ponder, "noodle," and incubate the idea, issue, or situation. *Incubate* is a key word. Sometimes you simply need to mull something over, examine it from several directions, and consider as many options or ideas as possible regarding a certain area of your business or issue to have these seeds germinate in beneficial ways.

THE THREE STAGES OF VISIONING

With regard to the above information, as you start to ponder, possibility-think, and work through the process of updating the Vision for and the reconceptualizing of your business, there are two very important things to keep in mind:

1. There are three stages a business goes through in developing and refining its Vision: the start-up stage, the solidification stage, and the reconceptualizing stage.
2. Visioning is a progressive process; you should always and continuously be working on the Vision for your business.

Let me further define these three stages in developing the Vision for your business:

Start-Up

This first stage initially takes place even before your business is operating. This stage occurs as you:

- Dream about what your business will look like
- Begin to understand your five stakeholders
- Develop your Win/Win paradigm for each of your stakeholders
- Craft your Vision statement
- Begin to cast your Vision statement to your target audiences
- Develop your strategy for achieving your vision
- Begin business operations

When you are in the start-up stage of Visioning, you should be open to experimenting to try to understand your customers' needs and wants, their short-term and long-term goals related to your product, and what will motivate them to purchase your product.

Depending on how well you really knew your initial target market and how detailed were your initial Vision, Vision statement, and business model, they may be revised one or several times.

This first stage usually lasts six months to one year, however for some businesses, it could take up to three years. If you are still trying to figure out the business after three years, you are doing something wrong; the information in this book and my previous book, *Creating a Thriving Business,* will be invaluable to you in getting your business model figured out.

Solidification

Once you have been operating your business for six months to a year you should have moved into the second stage of developing the Vision for your organization: Solidifying your Vision. This stage involves the testing of your Vision in your marketplace, resulting in the development of a very concrete direction for your company. Your business will remain in this second stage until it purposely and intentionally moves into the third stage of Visioning.

Reconceptualizing

After you have progressed to the above solidification phase, the next step is to ask the question "Does the Vision for my business need to change?" Once you start doing this, you are in the third stage of Visioning. In this third stage, you should be assessing your Vision based on input that you are receiving from the five stakeholders of your organization and deciding if you need to update the Vision. The resetting of your Vision is all about trying to improve your company. I recommend that every six months to a year you re-examine your Vision and update it if necessary.

Once you have solidified your Vision (as occurs in step two), your Vision should not change very often unless you feel that there is a need for your business to change its fundamental direction. During the business planning retreats that we will discuss later in this chapter you should re-examine your business, Vision, Critical Success Factors (which rarely change), and strategy for achieving your Vision. You need to be open to the possibility that because of these meetings the Vision and strategy for achieving your Vision will need to be adjusted by going through the reconceptualization process.

Visioning Is a Progressive Process

You do not develop your final Vision the first time you work on the Vision for your business. The Visioning process is progressive and as you take each subsequent step, the next step becomes clearer.

Proper Visioning is an incremental process because the world, your market, and your customers are always changing. This needs to be a thoughtful process compared to what I call "Vision churning" where a business owner continuously changes the direction of the business based on the latest seminar they attended, article reviewed, book read, television show watched, etc.

Example

Understanding the three stages of Visioning was very reassuring to Jeremy, the owner of this unique business, and to his leadership team. Jeremy's company had been providing services associated with the exterior of commercial buildings and skyscrapers for almost 20 years. But during this time the business grew and shrank, had changed direction several times, and had started and spun-off several related operations.

He now felt his company was ready to go to the next level, but he was plagued with self- doubt. When he started his company, it had focused on commercial window washing. Then it pivoted to both the interior and exterior cleaning of buildings. Recently, he started to solidify his long-term Vision for the company and formed a sister company to manufacture chemical cleaning products he had invented.

Now he was involved in large scale projects involving the refurbishment and restoration of exteriors of commercial buildings and skyscrapers. This would require a complete reconceptualization of the company and the reorganization of its leadership's team. Using the sequential steps incorporated in the Structure of Success™, Jeremy was able work though the progressive process involved in updating the Vision for his company to meet this new chapter in its life.

THE PROCESS OF RECONCEPTUALIZING YOUR VISION

I introduced the concept of reconceptualizing in the previous section. Now let's explore how to do that. We use the same process to revise your Vision (reconceptualize it) as we used to develop your original Vision. Back in Chapter 2 we discussed the concept that everything related to your business (this is also true for other things in life) should be created three times: first in your mind, then on paper as you record your thoughts, and finally, it is created in the real world.

In Chapter 2 we also discussed that there are three steps in the creation of a compelling Vision for your business; we called these the three C's of Visioning:

- Conceptualizing what your business is all about
- Creation of or crafting a compelling Vision
- Casting your Vision

To continually renew your Vision, we need to turn these three prior steps into a systematic process. Let us now take the above three C's of Visioning and apply them to the renewal process.

The process we are about to explore involves the assessment and determination of how you can change your business from its current state to the state in which you desire it to be. I use the term *process* because this is a systematic way of periodically questioning everything regarding your business and being open to reinventing it to serve your five stakeholders better. Jack Welch, former CEO of General Electric, said, "An organization's ability to learn and translate that learning into action rapidly is the ultimate competitive advantage."

Reconceptualizing Should Produce a Competitive Advantage

The goal of the process of reconceptualizing your Vision is that you obtain a competitive advantage in the marketplace by staying ahead of your competition!

As you move through this progression you want to be looking for trends, not fads. What is the difference?

Trends are movements that are most likely to continue because of huge underlying changes in your market or the world. For instance, things like "green" products, LEED building construction, concern for the environment, energy conservation initiatives, and diversity in the workplace are trends that almost assuredly will continue. Beanie babies, pet rocks, brown plants, and certain clothing styles were fads and when they disappeared so did their impact on society. Focus on trends; you want to fulfill a need that will still be there once your organization is fully developed.

Keep in mind as you regularly work on comparing where your business currently is and what it would look like if it was providing the solution to your customers that will be needed in the future, there is a state of tension between your current reality and your future solution that will never be fully abated. The desired outcome from this process is that a compelling, motivating, and captivating plan (i.e., your Vision and strategy) is developed to move you closer to the desired solution for your customer. The gap between what you want (your Vision for your business) and what your current company looks like should decrease over time.

Recreating or Recrafting a Compelling Vision

The next step in completing this re-examination of your Vision is to incorporate the updates in your actual Vision statement. This involves two steps:

1. Updating your General Vision statement
2. Updating your Time-Sequenced Vision Statements as discussed in Chapter 3

If you have updated your Vision statement as a result of the above, you also need to review your mission statement to determine if you need to make any changes to it to reflect the current Vision for your business.

Another important step is to review your unique selling proposition (discussed in Chapter 4) in light of your recrafted Vision statement to see if it needs to be updated so that your recreated Vision statement is properly reflected in your unique selling proposition.

Next you want to re-examine your Critical Success Factors to determine if any of them require updating. If your reconceptualized Vision is basically going in the same direction as your previous Vision, then it's unlikely you will have much to revise. However, if you are making any substantial change in direction, then you will need to modify your Critical Success Factors accordingly.

> Finally, almost invariably as a result of your reconceptualized Vision, you will need to go back and review and revise your strategy because where you want to take your company has changed.

Recasting Your Vision

Once you have completed the above two steps and have produced a revised Vision Statement, you are now ready to put your compelling Vision Statement to work! The objective of this final step, as was the creation of your original Vision Statement, is to communicate, discuss, and promote your Vision to each possible stakeholder with whom you come in contact. Your Vision Statement should be so motivating and compelling to you and your employees that it continually burns inside of you because you think about it regularly. You can taste it, you can see it, and you just *have* to talk about it.

Your Vision Statement and the underlying concepts should be like a volcano erupting inside of you—you simply cannot hold it back; it is uncontrollable because it is so powerful. Because you fully and completely believe in your business and its Vision it will be shared with your target audience so naturally because it is a part of you. It should roll off your tongue like you were telling someone about your children or your favorite hobby.

> It is important to note that studies have shown that to fully grasp something we must hear it seven times, so communicating the Vision for your business multiple times is appropriate. If the listener (e.g., a customer or potential customer) has never heard your Vision Statement before, then sharing the Vision for your business by telling your unique selling proposition verbatim is perfectly acceptable since it reflects the Vision for your organization.

Example

Peter owned a large manufacturing support business, but his industry had run into rough times because he and his direct competitors concentrated on working with Fortune 1000 companies in a niche telecommunications segment, and those companies were in an economic downturn. This meant two things; there was a lot less work that needed to be done for these companies, and the profit margins were being drastically cut.

In fact, Peter's company was on life support, and they had already laid off 70% of their staff. He came to us looking for assistance in turning the company around. As we progressed though the Structure of Success™ methodology, we came to the area of reconceptualizing his business and the Vision for it. As we moved through the topic, he realized he needed to be looking for trends in the marketplace that could impact his business over the long haul, and he had noticed one.

Next, as we analyzed his company's expertise, the new target industry looked like a perfect fit for his enterprise. Therefore, he and his leadership team recreated a compelling Vision, updated their Critical Success Factors, and then began casting this Vision (i.e. Marketing & Sales effort) to companies in this market. These companies bit big time, and Peter's business began to get one customer after another. As they developed their knowledge of the new industry, they quickly became a market leader and grew his enterprise into something much larger than it had ever been before the economic downturn.

Complete exercise 9-7 in workbook

CHAPTER SUMMARY

In this chapter we revisited the visioning process and considered how your Vision and Leadership are viewed by the five stakeholders of your company. We then went through the steps required to reconceptualize your Vision and recast it to your target audiences.

UPDATING YOUR CRITICAL SUCCESS FACTORS

Back in Chapter 3 you identified your Critical Success Factors and you separated them into the six areas of your business. Now that you have worked through this chapter, please review all that we covered and determine the strengths of, weaknesses of, opportunities of, and threats to your business in your Vision area. Then, if necessary, modify and/or add to the Critical Success Factors that you have already identified. Additionally, once you have done this, then add a column to your list in which you note which element of the Vision area formula pertains to each Critical Success Factor.

Chapter 10

Effectively Calling the Shots (Step #9)

• • • • •

We are now ready to examine the second part of the Vision and Leadership area of your company, your Leadership. Many people have a hard time seeing themselves as a great leader of their business. If you are one of them, I have good news for you—being a leader is a lot less complicated than you imagined.

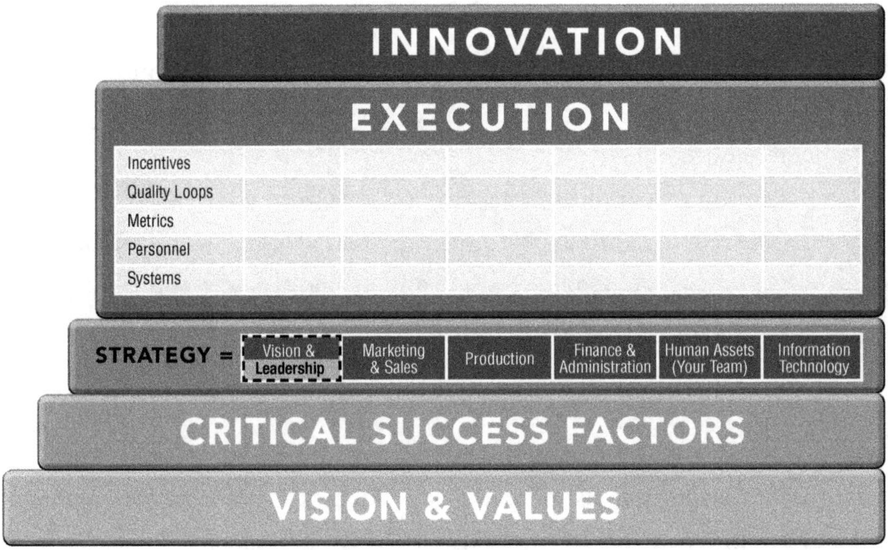

Fig. 10-1 Structure of Success—Leadership Area

BECOMING AN EFFECTIVE LEADER

There are countless seminars, thousands of books, endless discussions around the water cooler on what leadership is, but what does leadership look like in action?

My view on leadership is a little different from most of what you might read in the current business literature. I believe leadership is a skill set that can be acquired and used in virtually any setting. A person could use their leadership skill set to organize a pick-up baseball game, for a volunteer group for the United Way, lead a project for their church, organize a disaster relief project, or lead their business.

The collection of leadership skills that are necessary in a business situation include:

- Focusing on the big picture and not getting lost in the details
- Displaying passion, vision, creativity, flexibility, innovation, fearlessness, and thinking outside the box
- Providing guidance, being positive and supportive, and being a role model
- Taking responsibility for both positive and negative outcomes
- Being decisive, results-oriented and effectively producing desirable outcomes
- Valuing all people and earning respect from all employees
- Creating a team environment which is in synch with the business culture where people feel safe and employees feel appreciated and valued

If you are thinking, "How can I model these traits?", don't worry, we will now flesh out what effective leadership looks like. If you recall, in Chapter 7 an extensive list of leadership skills was presented. As we focus on developing your leadership skills in this chapter and how to apply them in your company, you may want to refer to that section.

The main problem with leadership is the almost cult-like focus on "leadership principles," "becoming a leader," and "being a leader" when all leadership really is a person practicing their leadership skill set. People are left with the impression that either you are endowed with the mantel of leadership or not. This leads to the leadership bar being set so high that company owners try to emulate Jack Welsh, Jeff Bezos or Richard Branson in their small businesses. Therefore, if you choose to read any of the many books written on leadership, keep in mind that the real issue is how are you going to *use* the leadership skills about which you are reading?

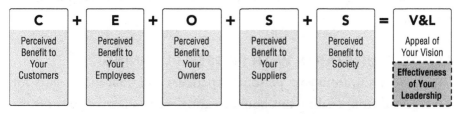

Fig. 10-2 Leadership Area—Overview

DEMYSTIFYING LEADERSHIP

Leadership is *what you do not who you are!* That is, if you do the things that a leader needs to do (which are outlined in the rest of this chapter) then you will be a successful leader!

A leader is not someone who stands up and says, "I am the leader." A leader is a person who is looked to as the official or unofficial guide of a business. A leader is the person who provides direction, whether it is in an official role (the business owner, an officer, or director of the business) or not. An unofficial leader is a person to whom employees talk to get opinions and interpretations on various things regarding the company. These individuals are the thought and opinion leaders within a business, sometimes called the "back channel" leaders.

A key role of a leader of a business is to provide information on and insights into what is happening within the business to the affected parties. If the leader doesn't directly address issues, problems, and situations, to fill the vacuum or void people will ask each other what their reading is on what is happening. The back-channel communication system will fill the void. There will always be some gossip in any organization, but the more clearly the actual leader of a business communicates, shares information, and provides insights, the less influential the unofficial leaders of your organization will be.

If your business has a vacuum of leadership, we will discuss the remedy in this chapter.

The central consideration in this discussion of leadership is the concept of "possibility thinking", how you can lead your company to where you want it to go. Let's cover some ways this possibility thinking can happen.

LEADERSHIP STARTS WITH PROPER PLANNING

As you know from your personal experience and from the insights you have gained from reading this book, creating the business of your dreams does not just happen; it is accomplished as the result of planning, execution, and evaluation. Planning and evaluation require concentrated time to be done effectively—business owners need to set aside specific time for doing these in their company.

In working with over 1,200 companies, I have found the most effective way to do this is by utilizing business planning retreats. The old analogy "You can't see the forest through the trees" is applicable here. You need time to take a step back and take a much broader perspective of your organization and the environment overall in which it operates (the forest).

There are four levels of *stepping back* to utilize in your business:

1. Quick thinking about your business time
2. Designated business pondering time
3. Individual business owner planning time
4. Group business management time

Quick Thinking about Your Business Time

This is where you listen to an educational CD while driving or you are review some information you have with you, where you think about your business for 15 minutes, maybe an hour. There is no formal agenda for these times, and there may be no outcome, but you are simply musing about some aspect of your business.

I suggest you do this almost anywhere—in your car, sitting in a doctor's waiting room, going for walk, etc.

You do not want to be the type of business owner who makes little or no progress year after year in having your dreams for your business come to fruition because you never quite get around to fully focusing on your company.

Complete exercise 10-1 in workbook

Designated Business Pondering Time

This is a longer period where you have an issue or problem that you are trying to solve, and therefore you have some specific information you are thinking about. Generally, the outcome from this type of *stepping back* is a decision or a course of action that you choose.

I suggest doing this any place you like to go simply to think without interruptions.

Complete exercise 10-2 in workbook

Individual Business Owner Planning Time

This is formal planning time for which you ideally have created some type of an agenda. Depending on how complex your operations are and the issues with which you are dealing, this designated planning time could be several hours to several days long. If this session is a day or longer, it is in effect a periodic personal retreat that takes place away from your business.

A desirable setting for this activity is your favorite place to go to think and process: the beach, the mountains, a state park, a resort—anywhere you feel relaxed and peaceful. These are excellent locations for this extended time of planning and evaluation.

Whether you have your retreat over a two- or three-day weekend or during the week, do not do it any less often than once a year; every six months is even better. You need to recalibrate your Vision for your business regularly—which will in turn enable you to lead it most effectively.

The two things you want to accomplish in these retreats are:

1. Contemplate specifics related to your business. For instance, consider market factors, customer status, and your employee situation. These items are closely tied to the various areas we have covered so far. Evaluate how your business is doing now and what should be done in the future in these areas.
2. Consider issues driven by what you want to do with your life—personal goals, what is important to you, what brings you pleasure and enjoyment, succession planning, your financial situation, etc. Just ponder what you want to do with your life and how your business fits into your overall desires and plan for your life.

> Please see the companion workbook for this book for a detailed agenda for an individual planning retreat.

> **Complete exercise 10-3 in workbook**

Group Business Management Time

These are formal planning sessions that include your business management team and for which a detailed agenda is required. Depending on the various issues you are addressing, this planning time could be several hours to one or more days long.

For these group meetings, I suggest a venue where the participants feel relaxed and emotionally positive so that you can delve into potentially complex issues with a proper frame of mind. Choose wisely because the wrong locale can cause your meeting to go awry. Business conference centers, business retreat centers, resorts and vacation homes are conducive to these types of retreats.

Almost every business owner would agree that they need the first two types of processing time described above. Likewise, owners of larger businesses generally realize that they need formal time for them and their management team to specifically work on planning for their business (the fourth category). However, if you have a smaller company you may be wondering if you really need this third type of time for evaluating, assessing, and planning for your organization.

I feel very strongly that any company owner needs periodic planning retreat times for many reasons. First, you need time to evaluate what is happening in your organization at both the macro and micro level and assess the state of your business now. This includes taking time to gauge how you are doing in achieving the goals and objectives that make up your Time-Sequenced Vision including evaluating how you are doing financially.

Second, these tree and forest types evaluations open your mind to big-picture questions like "What is the Vision for my business?", "Is my current strategy appropriate?" and "What is the direction for my business?"

Third, these questions lead to even more global questions like, "What is the dream for my business?" "Where do I want to take my business?" "Am I truly providing a Win/Win experience for my customer?" "How ought the world work for the customers obtaining my product?" Clearly, these questions and many others like them should be considered. To reflect on these topics requires specific time spent away from your work location in contemplation of these issues and topics.

Example

Ralph owned a mid-sized water-products sales company he had started five years before. After he created the company and it began to grow, he realized there were several different directions in which he could take the business. He sold products to end consumers as well as to distributors in the water-products industry. So, he realized he needed to decide what he wanted to focus on, either consumer sales or becoming a company entirely in the wholesale market. To make this choice, he set time aside to determine which path he thought was most attractive.

In his mind, he wrestled with these options time and time again, so much so that he started taking a pad of paper with him whenever he was driving in his truck so he could write down thoughts that arose related to this decision. Once he chose the path he wanted to proceed with his company, he had found the note pad so beneficial, he continued to use it.

After the decision related to the direction of his organization was made, the opportunity arose to start manufacturing some of the items they were selling, as well as items he had invented. He set up a three-day planning event away from the office, for him and his entire management team to work through the pros and cons of doing this. Thereafter, he decided to start a manufacturing operation, which in turn fueled the business's subsequent growth. He had such good results from quick thinking about his business's time, designated business pondering time, and individual and group business management time, he continued to use them throughout his company.

GROUP BUSINESS MANAGEMENT TEAM RETREATS

As we just discussed, businesses are a team effort, so group management retreats are necessary. If your business is large enough to require a management team (the group of people who ultimately will determine your business's success or failure) then it is paramount that your management team meets for group retreats to get the entire team on the same page and working together.

Group business management retreats center on specifics that are related to your operations not on the owner as an individual. Areas of focus during the retreats include:

- Consideration of market factors
- The conditions of your customer universe

- Marketing & Sales results
- Operations
- Financial results
- Personnel issues and decisions

These are items that are very closely tied to the various areas of your business that we have covered in this book. The principal things that take place during these meetings are:

- An assessment of the current state of your business
- Evaluation of various possible courses of action
- Deciding on a go-forward game plan

Two additional things that should take place during the group business management retreats that do not necessarily take place during your individual planning retreats are:

1. A celebration of the successes of your business since the previous group business management retreat. This is a key activity since one of your chief responsibilities as the leader is to rally and encourage your employees, and that starts with your management team!
2. Plan some fun and relaxation time into each retreat. This may be a game of golf, a trip to an amusement park, a massage therapist coming in, or a fancy, relaxed dinner. Keep in mind that you should do things to make the event something to which everyone looks forward instead of dreading the next grueling, 10-hour-a-day stressful planning "retreat."

Having had the benefit of peering inside many, many businesses, I feel that there are two main ingredients for having a successful and rewarding group planning retreat:

1. The meeting or retreat should take place away from your work location.
2. It should have a written, detailed agenda.

Whenever comprehensive planning sessions take place at your regular work location three problems occur:

- The participants have a difficult time disconnecting from the urgent work that is waiting for them on the other side of the wall.
- Interruptions occur because employees break into the meeting with things that simply could not wait, which in turn causes the entire planning process to be less than optimal.
- The participants, for some mysterious reason, end up being limited in their thinking. and they wind up *not* thinking outside of the box.

Generally, the retreat will last for two or three days, however if you have a larger business, it may take longer. While having your individual planning retreat over a weekend may personally work well for you, your management team may consider it an incursion into their personal time, so these planning events should take place during the normal work week.

If your business is large enough to require a group business management retreat, about one month before the group meeting, you should prepare and review in detail an agenda for the retreat. You want to do this beforehand to make sure you have not missed any items on the agenda and to mentally plan for issues and discussions that most likely will occur. Please see the companion workbook for this book for a detailed agenda for a group planning retreat.

Meeting Frequency

In-depth evaluation, revisioning, and planning can take place too often. Think of a relay race. While you have the baton, you must be totally focused on running the race—not looking at other runners, the spectators or the stadium. However, when you do not have the baton is when you can take the time to look around you.

In the same way, you need enough time in between the planning retreats to run a "leg of the race" with the baton in your hand as you execute the plan. While you have the baton, you totally focus on executing the plan for the race ahead of you and concentrate on your immediate next step. At the end of your leg of the race you can look around and consider everything else.

If you end up doing detailed business planning so frequently that you do not have enough observable data with which to evaluate your current plans, you end up doing yourself and your business is disservice. Please note that I am not referring to tactical weekly, bi-weekly, monthly, or even quarterly status meetings; these meetings oversee the execution of your strategy, not the creation of a new strategy.

From my experience I recommend that these planning retreats take place every six months or year. The least often you want them to take place is once a year.

Catastrophic Events

Unfortunately, there are unforeseen events, maybe even catastrophic events that may happen in between your semi-annual or annual planning retreats. How do you handle these types of events, especially ones that directly impact your plan? First, keep in mind that most of these events are not truly catastrophic—with 20/20 hindsight you could have seen them coming. I recommend, for all but the truly *catastrophic* events, that you continue executing your current plan until your next regularly scheduled business planning retreat.

In between your planning times, if a truly catastrophic event happens that dramatically affects your company (i.e., September 11, 2001) you may want to have an emergency planning retreat to recalibrate your Vision and to reexamine your strategy for achieving your Vision. Otherwise, you should stay totally focused on your current plan until your next regularly scheduled retreat.

Example

This integrated dog care, grooming, training, and boarding business was owned by Ivana and Igor, who were in their late 30's and had a ten-year-old son. They had started the company about 12 years before, and it had grown into a large operation with nearly 75 people working in the company.

However, as they grew, they found that many areas of their company were not working as well together as they did when they were smaller. Battles for control, placing blame, competition for the best employees, and criticizing other departments had become frequent. This all was affecting Ivana and Igor's family life with their son.

As we were completing the Structure of Success™ process with Ivana and Igor and their management team, the topic of management team retreats came up and everyone thought they were sorely needed.

Therefore, off site, semi-annual meetings were instituted. The first one took place at a lake house, and it included time to relax together as a team and have fun playing on the water. During the retreat, they examined the entire company and its overall operating environment. This included what was happening in its customer area, Marketing & Sales results, operational issues, financial results, and personnel issues.

The retreat also included time to celebrate the recent successes in their company. The semi-annual business-planning retreats became a crucial tool for getting and keeping its management team working together as well as reducing stress in Ivana and Igor's family life.

Complete exercise 10-4 in workbook

DEVELOPING YOUR LEADERSHIP SKILL SET

Now let's pull together the ideas about leadership we have discussed in the past several chapters. I view leadership as the possession of a set of skills and developing your leadership skill set is a three-step process.

First, you want to find something about which you feel passionate and then develop a Vision for the entity that embodies this passion. It could be little league baseball, your church or synagogue, a social cause or a subject in this book about your business. As you implement and practice these concepts, you will automatically develop your leadership skill set because I assume that your business is something that you feel passionately about.

Second, use the list of leadership skills presented in the section on leadership in Chapter 7 as a self-assessment tool and grade yourself on where you stand with regard to these attributes. Alternatively, you can have others who know you well provide you with feedback regarding how you stack up regarding these characteristics.

Third, you could read some of the many books on leadership. However here are two things you should consider as you choose which of these you should spend time reading:

- Some leadership books advocate an autocratic, Machiavellian, intimidating, aloof, or despotic style of leadership. Those—or leadership philosophies like them—run completely counter to mine; using these approaches to develop your leadership skill set would be incompatible with the concepts I have been presented in this book.
- In his book, *Good to Great,* Jim Collins talks about a concept he calls "Level 5 Leadership" referring to a five-level hierarchy of leadership where a leader takes fundamental leadership one level beyond the norm. This Level 5 Leadership philosophy is compatible with the ideas advocated in this book. Look for books on leadership that advocate being approachable, engaged, a "general that walks among the troops" and talks to your employees eye to eye and heart to heart.

Keep in mind that it is impossible to be perfect; depending on our temperament and personality, each of us has certain strengths and, unfortunately, weaknesses. Therefore, you as a leader will want to hire people who will fill those weaknesses present in your leadership type. Look for people who disagree with you slightly or even moderately—but not totally—on a regular basis.

You want people on your leadership team who will hold up the mirror of reality to you, not just agree with everything that comes out of your mouth. You want people who will say, "This does not make sense to me" or "Have you taken . . . into account?" or "I think that we should consider . . . ."

Conversely, you do not want people in your business who will regularly totally disagree with you; this would quickly gridlock your company and cause your work atmosphere to degenerate rapidly. The bottom line is that by fully developing your leadership skill set and surrounding yourself with great people who will complement your leadership, you can create an effective leadership team ("team" is the key word here). You will then end up a better leader of your business because of functioning as a team.

Complete exercise 10-5 in workbook

WORKING *IN* VERSUS *ON* YOUR BUSINESS

No doubt you have heard the saying, "You should work *on*, not *in* your business." But what does that adage truly mean?

Working *On* Your Business

No matter what the size of the business is, I feel working *on* your business involves two tasks a business owner must do on an ongoing basis.

First, live, eat, and breathe Vision and Leadership for your business. This task encompasses all that we have covered with regard to guiding and directing your business. Always be a scout considering the future of your company so you can guide and lead it.

Second, manage the operations of your business using metrics. Business owners and leaders who use metrics correctly can sit on a beach far away and still effectively manage their companies because they are getting the daily, weekly, and monthly information that tells them whether the systems are operating correctly that they worked so hard to put into place. I will cover this topic more in Chapters 11 and 13.

These two tasks fall clearly within the realm of working on the business. Whether you are the leader of a start-up, small, medium, or large organization, a portion of your time should be spent working on your business.

If your business is of a smaller size (less than $20,000,000 or so in annual revenue), then most likely besides working *on* the business you are also going to work *in* the business. I have found if your company is over $20,000,000 or so in annual revenues, most business owners or leaders do not work *in* the business because their responsibilities of working *on* the business takes all their time.

If a company is under the above threshold, listed below are several scenarios for a company owner or leader to work *in* a business.

Working *In* Your Marketing & Sales Area

The most important area a business owner can work *in* is the Marketing & Sales area. Marketing & Sales is the lifeblood of every organization—if you produce the best product but you haven't convinced anyone to buy your product, then you really don't have a business. Marketing & Sales drives everything in your company because without sales you have no revenue, and without revenue you do not have a business.

You are your business's most effective salesperson because no one will have as much passion for or knowledge of your product as you. Another tremendous benefit of working in your Marketing & Sales area is that you can see firsthand what does and does not work in its processes. Then you can change, refine, and fully systematize your business's Marketing & Sales operations.

A side benefit of being involved in your Marketing & Sales operations is that you get unique feedback from your customers and prospects about what they like and do not like about your product, what improvements can be made, and what the new products are in which they would be interested. This benefit ties back to your unique role of being the scout for your company.

However, there is one huge challenge for you if you regularly have customer or prospect interaction while working in your Marketing & Sales area: Customers or prospects will view you personally as the Marketing & Sales operation of your business and will only want to deal with you. Also, they may perceive your business as more the fruit stand model where *you* are the business as compared to the factory model where you are overseeing your operations.

There is a way to avoid this: Be sure to regularly take other Marketing & Sales personnel with you on sales calls, operate your sales function like a team where you regularly hand the ball off to someone else, and have someone else take over as soon as the sale is made. These will demonstrate to the customer that you are only a part of the Marketing & Sales area, that others can do your job, and things can and do operate perfectly fine without your direct involvement.

Working *In* Your Production Area

Some people are not comfortable in a Marketing & Sales role. If that is you, and you have tried but you cannot get over that hurdle, then the second-best place to work *in* the business is your Production area, where you deal primarily with operations. Sales could be going through the roof, but if you cannot provide the product that meets or exceeds your customers' expectations, then your business will quickly fail.

All aspects of Production are critical to your business. You as owner know your products better than anyone else, so you will be in a unique position to ensure that your product is of the quality that you desire. However, despite choosing Production over Marketing & Sales to work *in* your business, keep in mind that you never really stop selling because you will always be casting your business's compelling Vision to someone, which is a type of selling.

Working *in* your business in Production means you should be looking for new ways to innovate your Production processes, systematize its operations, and perhaps develop new products, which leads to increasing your business's attractiveness to a potential buyer. Optionally, if your company is small enough, you could split your time between both Marketing & Sales and Production.

Working *In* Various-sized Businesses

If you are still in the start-up phase of your company (and, therefore, most likely still operating as a fruit stand), I feel you should spend two-thirds of your time in Marketing & Sales and the majority of the rest of your time in Production ensuring that the product is being made and delivered properly. Of course, you still need to spend sufficient time in your Finance and Administration, Human Assets, and Information Technology areas to ensure that they are running properly, but they are the proverbial tail of the dog—so don't misplace your priorities and let the tail wag the dog instead of vice versa.

If you have grown to the $20,000,000 or so revenue point where you have delegated (but not abdicated) these areas to others, you need to oversee the Marketing & Sales, Production, Finance and Administration, Human Assets, and Information Technology areas using metrics that we have mentioned and will discuss in Chapters 11 and 13.

The important thing to keep in mind is that you need to systematize all areas of your organization so you can move your business into operating as a factory. If you fail to properly systematize your business, then by default you will end up staying in the daily operations of your business, and most likely your business will stay in some aspect of operating as a fruit stand mode instead of moving to a factory model.

Example

Finding the proper place to *work in* the business, as well as be *working on* the company was instrumental to Todd, the mid-50's cerebral owner of an electronics manufacturing company. We were finishing up working with him and his key personnel in getting everything in place a for a large expansion they had planned, so it was imperative to solidify Todd's future role in his business.

Todd was a quiet electrical engineer who did not enjoy anything related to sales. Therefore, the normal place, (Marketing & Sales) in which a business owner operates in a small company was not an option for him. This meant that for him, working in the Production area of his enterprise was the next-best option. This way he could use his engineering background to develop new products and improve his company's internal production processes.

Armed with a new plan to stay in touch with their customers, he would meet with his sales personnel once a month to discuss what they were hearing from their prospects and customers. This briefing would include both issues and problems customers were having with the company's current product, as well as new products in which they might be interested. This new operational structure ended up working out fine, and Todd was able to keep a pulse on their customers' needs, as well as oversee their Production area.

> **Complete exercise 10-6 in workbook**

LEADING YOUR TEAM

As you apply your leadership skill set to your business, keep in mind that one of your chief roles is to lead your personnel, encourage them, and be the cheerleader who makes your employees feel good about their efforts to achieve the Vision of your business.

Celebrate Successes

One of the most important aspects of encouraging your personnel is to share with them that progress is being made toward the business's Vision. People need to feel that it is worthwhile to keep plugging away at the goal in front of them. Having one-on-one discussions, group meetings, and companywide events where mile markers (your Time-Sequenced Vision on the road to your Vision) are celebrated is key to keeping morale high.

A wise company owner takes advantage of every opportunity to celebrate an organization's successes as it applies to encouraging your employees.

> Consider this analogy: Imagine that you are enduring the strenuous work of hiking up a rocky, tall mountain, and in order not to trip and fall, you keep looking at the path immediately in front of you. You are so focused on each next step that you miss looking around to enjoy the beautiful view nor take the time to stop and congratulate yourself on all the progress you have made. Similarly, to reach your goals, you must focus on the business tasks in front of you and not stumble and fall in dealing the complexities of your company. But you also need to stop and celebrate your organization's successes with your employees by taking the time to enjoy and appreciate reaching milestones along the way.

A business owner who does not regularly and sincerely encourage employees is missing the mark badly. Employees will get burned out, jaded, and discouraged, which leads to them not giving their best efforts in pursuit of your business's Vision.

Empower Your Personnel

Effective leadership definitely involves empowering your employees in a way that helps keep their morale high. There are four steps to empowering employees (and contractors):

- Cast your Vision to your personnel
- Create the organization that is required to achieve your Vision
- Provide the resources (e.g., equipment, Information Technology, personnel . . .) required to achieve your Vision
- Unleash your employees by not micro-managing them but giving them the freedom and flexibility to pursue the company's Vision

Be Approachable

Employees must not be intimidated by you or your behavior. If you are intimidating and unapproachable, the process of encouraging your personnel will come off as forced, artificial, and purely a show that you are trying to put on. If you do not have the trait of being approachable, then you should consider getting some training or coaching. If you do not know if you are approachable or not, ask someone who will give you a straight answer!

Be a Good Communicator

As was seen in the list of Attributes of an Effective Leader, to encourage your personnel and be their cheerleader, you must be a good communicator. If you cannot or will not communicate with them, your personnel will not view you as an effective leader. One of the worst things a business owner or leader can do is to keep people in the dark about things that impact their jobs, their employment, and their lives. As the saying goes, "Nature abhors a vacuum"; if you are not regularly communicating with employees, then the rumor mill will fill the vacuum, your employee's morale will suffer, productivity will drop, and their level of worry and anxiety will increase.

Additionally, if your communication is unclear, you change your mind on a regular basis, or avoid issues, then your personnel will start to disregard you as a leader and will look to someone to provide leadership. Even if you are saying things that are not particularly positive, it is better to be clear to your personnel, even if it's not necessarily encouraging, than to lead them along with false communication and then go back on your word on an issue or situation.

Insatiable Drive to Know More

An important quality that should be present in any leader is an insatiable drive to know more about your business, its market, and how to make your business more successful.

To create an organization which provides a solution that enables its customers to achieve their goals related to your product, you should be on a continual quest to know more about your customers' needs, goals, and wishes, and what can be done to better meet these.

This pursuit to know more is part of using your Vision binoculars as the scout of your company. You as a business owner or leader should be energized by your business. If you were not previously excited about your business, I'm confident that after reading this book, you see all the thrilling opportunities in front of you and your organization.

Desire to Make Changes

An essential attribute of a leader should be a strong desire to make changes in the business to improve its performance. If you are not making changes to your business, chances are that you are *not* effectively leading your company! No business is perfect, and if you are not working on improving it and moving it closer to your Vision by making changes, then most likely your organization is drifting in the sea with the threat that the waves from your competition could someday overwhelm it. However, you don't want to make changes just for the sake of change, but the changes should be necessary to move your company closer to your Vision for it.

You Must Be Optimistic

An intrinsic part of moving your business toward its Vision is that you as a business owner or leader must be optimistic! If you are pessimistic by nature, then it will be a big challenge to be an effective leader, because great leaders are always optimists. If you are pessimistic because of the state of your business or its market, then implementing what has been covered in this book will move you from your current pessimistic state of mind to an optimistic one as you see your Vision come into view and become a reality.

Self-assurance and Self-confidence

Along with being optimistic, leaders must have the self-confidence to want to be at the helm and oversee a business. This could originate from the personality of the business owner; however, it can be nurtured and cultivated by developing a compelling Vision, which in turn causes business owners to move closer to their goals by motivating them as they see the progress being achieved. It is very important that in building your self-confidence, you pick the right role models to emulate as the leader of your business. If you choose the right leadership role models, then you will develop a desirable leadership style.

```
Complete exercise 10-7 in workbook
```

MENTORING AND LEADERSHIP ROLE MODELS

While I do not think having a business mentor is necessary, I do think that a carefully chosen mentor can save you time, enable you to avoid frustration, help you avoid dead ends, and alert you to upcoming issues and situations. A carefully chosen mentor has been down the path you are traveling. A good mentor will say to you, "Don't be surprised when . . . happens" or "Have you looked at your situation from this angle?" or "You know when I was where you are at, I . . . ."

Individual Mentors

The problem is trying to find a suitable mentor. There are various federal, state, and local government programs where you can start your search. For instance, the Service Core of Retired Executives (SCORE) is administered through the Small Business Administration and is a good place to look for a mentor.

Another approach is to look around you for someone who has operated a successful company and seems to have the leadership traits discussed in this chapter. Then try to start to develop a relationship with them. If the relationship clicks, the only remaining decisions are how often you should meet and for how long.

Or you could look for a business consultant, business planner, or Certified Public Accountant who appears to have business acumen, have counseled many companies, and is willing to share his/her experiences and insights.

Meeting once a month is typical. However, you may find meeting once a quarter is enough. Normally meetings are one to two hours, perhaps over a long meal. The most important thing in any mentoring relationship is that the person does not lead you astray in your business and that their advice and counsel is sound and practical.

I strongly suggest that you ask any mentor you are considering to read this book, and then you and your mentor have several initial discussions regarding the concepts presented in this book to assure yourself that both you and she/he are on the same page. If it seems appropriate, you could even use this book and the companion workbook exercises as the basis for your mentoring relationship.

Leadership Support Groups

An alternative to finding an individual mentor is to find a support group for you and your company. Let me emphasize that this should be a support group, *not* a group that was formed only for obtaining marketing leads. Here are a few things to keep in mind when looking for a support group.

First, the other businesses in the group should be similar to yours in both size and complexity. While it would be nice to have the other members come from business sectors that are related to yours, that is not necessary or even desirable. Of course, you do not want your competitors in your group! Also, having one of your customers in the support group can be risky; some things that might be discussed in the group could jeopardize your relationship with your customer. You want to be free to talk about whatever is on your mind without worrying about your customer's reactions.

Second, the support group should have members that can truly provide insight into issues with which you are currently dealing or ones you will need to address in the near future. To evaluate the group's ability to help you and your business, I would recommend the same thing as I mentioned above regarding finding a mentor: Ask the group to read this book and then have several discussions regarding the concepts presented or ask them to use this book and the companion exercises as the basis for your discussions. This way you can be assured that you are all on the same page.

Please keep in mind that the knowledge base you will possess by the time you finish reading this book is far greater than many business owners enjoy; therefore, you should avoid groups that may take you backwards from operating your business in methodical, effective, and structured manner.

With regard to meeting the above need, please feel free to visit our website at FountainheadConsultingGroup.com for information on our network of consultants and supports groups for leadership support that have been specifically trained in the methodology presented in this book and my previous book, *Creating a Thriving Business*.

Complete exercise 10-8 in workbook

CHAPTER SUMMARY

Strong leadership is critical for any business. Leadership skills can and should be learned. You want to apply your leadership skills to motivate your employees and create a team atmosphere where everyone works toward a common goal. The result of this is that you will be working *on* your business rather than *in* your business.

We looked at several things in this chapter:

- Business planning activities
- Developing your leadership skill set
- Working *on* versus working *in* your business

- Leading your team
- Mentoring and leadership role models

The bottom line is that to create the business of which you have always dreamed, you must use your leadership skills to move your business from where it is today to where you want it to go. This requires that you do not rest on past successes—yesterday is history and since you have not yet arrived at fully realizing the business of your dreams, you need to make a difference today in moving your company forward. In the process of doing this, you will be transformed into a world-class leader.

Chapter 11

Proper Execution Will Win the Day (Step #10)

• • • • •

We are now ready to delve into the fourth building block of the Structure of Success™, the systematic execution of the strategy for creating the business of your dreams! This building block is imperative because it is not enough to have a comprehensive strategy; you must execute it in a logical, systematic way—what we call Structured Execution.

In Chapter 1 we discussed the five roles of a leader, namely to:

1. Develop and cast a compelling Vision for your organization
2. Develop a strategy for achieving your Vision
3. Create the organization to accomplish your Vision
4. Oversee your business's execution and manage it via metrics
5. Apply transformational Innovation to your entire organization

In Chapters 2 through 10, I laid out how to fulfill the first two roles of a leader. We are now ready to cover the third and fourth roles of a leader.

In this chapter, we embark on the task of executing all that we have discussed so far in this book—the execution of your strategy throughout your business. Early in this book I shared studies showing that 55% to 70% of a business's success is tied directly to proper execution.

As we have discussed several times, you create your business three times: first in your mind, second on paper (your blueprint), and the third time in the real world. Creating a business in the real world is execution. The steps we will discuss in this chapter will determine whether you only have a blueprint for a business or a real business!

THE *BUSYNESS* METHOD OF EXECUTION

From one standpoint, execution is easy; you just do it (whatever "it" is). However, there are two different types or methods of execution. The first is to simply get busy doing various activities. I call this the *busyness* method. The activities engaged in the busyness method may or may not be productive activities. The underlying problem with the busyness method is the majority of activities are tactical actions, which are not necessarily tied to the strategic plan.

Just like the paraphrase from *Alice in Wonderland*, "The faster you go, the behinder you get," the busyness method can lead to activity for the sake of activity. Its mantra is "get busy doing something."

In the absolute, the busyness execution approach can lead to operating in the envelope of the ill-fated "tyranny of the urgent," where a company spends so much of its time in crisis management that it loses sight of the big picture—what it should be trying to accomplish—and thereby sees little or no progress toward its long-term goals. The organization then starts to operate primarily in a reactive mode with the concept of planning being nothing more than the solution to today's crisis du jour.

LEADERSHIP BURN OUT

The bottom line of the busyness approach to execution is that it is an unstructured method that is not tied to an overall strategic plan. This unstructured method of execution does not fully utilize systems that are intentionally tied to the business's overall Vision and strategy. In the end, this approach can lead to the endless fatigue of a fruit stand-type business where the owner becomes burned out with the business. The business is overly dependent upon the owner, and the owner ends up doing the same things day after day, week after week, month after month, year after year—the perfect recipe for burnout.

STRUCTURED EXECUTION

The second approach to execution within a business, and the one I recommend, is *structured execution*, which uses a systematic methodology based on the overall Vision, Critical Success Factors, and strategy of the business. The key to structured execution is that it is an *intentional* method of executing the company's overall game plan in a disciplined manner. Here is a break down the three key factors of structured execution:

1. **Intentionality**—The execution does not take place haphazardly, but there is a definite train of thought behind each action. The visible execution is a result of a comprehensive game plan that has been laid out clearly behind the scenes.
2. **Systems**—Structured systems have been developed, implemented, and are being monitored so that the correct actions take on a consistent basis. Actions are not left up to individuals to do as they see fit, but the steps a person or team takes to accomplish a given task have been identified beforehand and optimized to get the desired outcome on a predictable basis.
3. **Discipline**—A disciplined atmosphere exists throughout the organization to ensure that the optimized systems that are in place are followed explicitly, and adherence to the systems are rewarded, and deviation from the systems are penalized. The discipline to adhere to the systems in place is not mindless but is an acknowledgment that the best systems are being used to produce the desired results. Additionally, the execution plan is reviewed regularly with an eye to whether the systems can be improved.

By using a structured approach to execution, you gain the benefit of having an actual execution plan instead of execution by the busyness methodology. One of the hidden benefits of operating with a structured execution plan is that it operates like a gleaming, efficient economic factory that is an enjoyable place to work, where things just hum along.

This results in the company owner or leader avoiding burnout because the business is executing based on an overall strategy, not haphazardly, which in turn moves it closer to its goals. The freedom inherent in the factory model is enduring (as much as anything in this life is enduring) because a systematic approach is being used for achieving the enterprise's Vision.

This topic of burnout regularly comes up when we work with a business leader or owner. The key to avoiding burnout is maintaining enthusiasm and keeping a positive mental attitude regarding your company. We touched on some of this topic in Chapters 2 and 3, but let us delve into a more detailed answer at this juncture.

In working with various business leaders, I have found there are five key steps that will help you avoid burnout and maintain an optimistic mental attitude:

1. Making tangible progress in achieving your Vision
2. Renewing your Vision with outside input/guidance
3. Maintaining a proper work/leisure harmony to recharge your batteries and ensure that you *own* your business, not vice versa
4. Surrounding yourself with a like-minded team; a business is a team sport, not an individual one
5. Operating your company in a systematic, structured way so you avoid functioning in a "tyranny of the urgent" syndrome

With that in mind, let us examine how to operate your company in a systematic, structured manner.

Complete exercise 11-1 in workbook

THE FIVE COMPONENTS OF STRUCTURED EXECUTION

There are five sequential steps to having a structured execution plan that is intentional, systematic, and disciplined:

1. **Systems**—Your systems encompass both your overall plans and detailed processes, which are the blueprints for how you want to operate each of the six areas of your business. No two businesses would have the exact same systems because they are unique to each business.

2. **Personnel**—This is the determination of the people whom you will require to execute your systems.

3. **Metrics**—These are the measurements that indicate if your processes are working correctly or not.

4. **Quality loops**—These are mechanisms which ensure that if a process stops functioning properly, the individual or team that is executing it can self-correct without the business owner needing to get involved. Quality loops also involve a process-redefinition step that can be used if something has changed in your business's overall environment that necessitates a redesign of the entire process.

5. **Incentives**—These are financial and non-financial rewards to the employees, suppliers or business owner for adhering to processes and executing them correctly. Incentives are necessary to reinforce the performance that in the end leads to your business achieving its Vision.

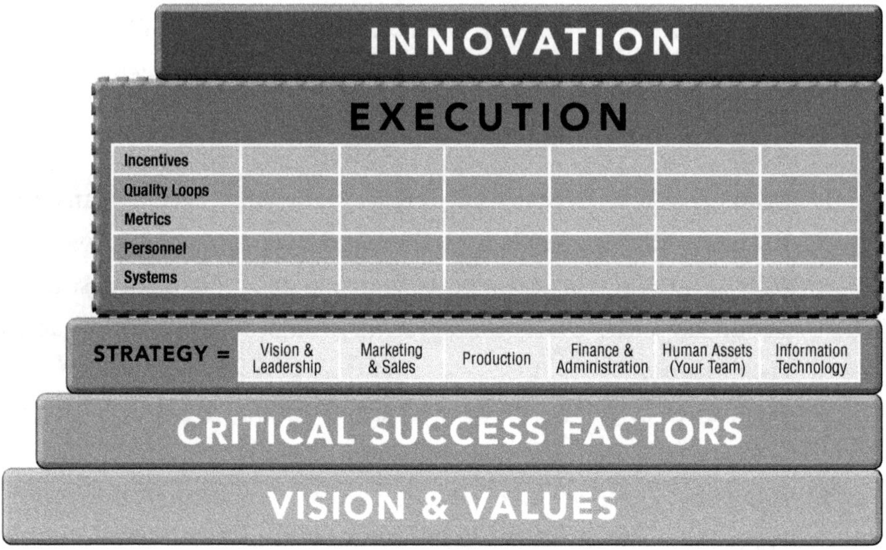

INNOVATION

EXECUTION

Incentives					
Quality Loops					
Metrics					
Personnel					
Systems					

| STRATEGY = | Vision & Leadership | Marketing & Sales | Production | Finance & Administration | Human Assets (Your Team) | Information Technology |

CRITICAL SUCCESS FACTORS

VISION & VALUES

Fig. 11-1 Structure of Success—Execution Area

Before we get into the details of these five components, let's look at why proper execution is an absolute must in any business. A business's success is tied directly to proper execution, and relatedly your level of customer satisfaction will ultimately determine the success or failure of your business. When a customer (or an employee or supplier) interacts with your business, they interact at the execution level of your business.

If you have successfully done your job of communicating your Vision through sharing your Unique Selling Proposition and setting an expectation of your brand experience, then at a general level they will understand the Vision for your company, but they will not interact with your Vision. Likewise, a customer does not see or interact with your Critical Success Factors or strategy, only with your execution. To your customer, Vision casting is part of *talking* a good game; Execution is *playing* a good game. So, to your customers as well as your employees and suppliers, execution is the bottom line!

As we know from everything in this book, you cannot get to the step of structured execution without first knowing your Vision, Critical Success Factors, and strategy. Therefore, the final benefit of defining these is that you now have the foundation in place to develop a nearly flawless structured execution plan. Furthermore, in a structured execution plan, the little things done right can change the world!

SYSTEMS

Your systems are comprised of your overall and general plans and your specific and detailed processes.

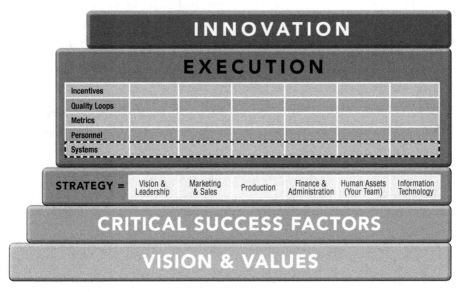

Fig. 11-2 Execution Area—Systems

Plans

Your plans state how you want things to operate within your business at the general level. They are specific to each of the six areas of your organization, and they state from an overall standpoint what your methodology will be for accomplishing things within your company.

The philosophy from your values we discussed in Chapter 2 determines from a conceptual standpoint how you would like your business to operate (your plans); therefore, your plans are developed with your values, philosophy, and principles in mind. Your plans lay out the blueprints for the operations of each of your six areas; therefore, they are general in nature, while the exact details of your plans are specified in your processes, which reside beneath your plans.

Processes

Processes are the detailed procedures and courses of action that are necessary to carry out your overall plans. These are written documents that identify the necessary steps to follow to produce effective and consistent performance in each area. Processes need to be completely in synch with your plans and are the executable portion of your systems, which specify how everything is done within your business and who does it.

A process should eventually be developed and documented for literally everything in your business. For example, processes include opening your business in the morning and closing it at night, the details of your sales efforts, how you: develop your product, close the books at month end, do performance reviews, carry out planning retreats, upgrade the software on your network, etc.

Systems and their detailed processes are key for your business. There are three steps that must be completed with regard to your processes:

1. Identify your processes
2. Optimize your processes
3. Fully document your processes

We will dig into these steps in the remainder of this section on systems.

> Processes are critical to fully satisfying your customer 100% of the time. Without the correct processes in place, you will end up with inconsistent results. This can lead to customer dissatisfaction, which leads to inability to reach your Vision for your company. Systematizing your organization using optimized and documented processes ensures that as your business's volume grows while your product quality does not decrease—which can easily happen as you scale up your operations.

Development of Your Processes

There are three fundamental keys to defining the processes for your business. First, optimized systems are developed for *all* the activities, actions, and procedures that take place within your business.

Second, each step of every process is fully documented in writing; nothing is left to chance for the executers of the process to figure it out on their own.

Third, personnel are fully trained on them. Processes are used by personnel consistently. Written processes are available to the personnel executing the process. Keep in mind that the execution of processes leads to outcomes which are measured in upcoming metrics component. Also, these processes are the foundation of the upcoming quality loops segment of your structured execution area.

In trying to gain a full understanding of this concept of processes, let's go back to the fruit stand versus factory analogy. Most businesses start out by going through the normal phase of being a fruit stand during which the company owner is trying to figure out the business. A pattern of trial-and-error is typical during this phase; it leads to discovering what works and what does not work. Therefore, an indicator that your organization is moving from the fruit stand to a factory mode of operating is when you move beyond trial-and-error and start to solidify the processes for your business.

After this initial phase of systemizing your business, you want to continue figuring out the best processes for your company to optimize your systems. When you are first solidifying your processes or if you have no written processes in place, an excellent way to developing optimal processes is to gather all the persons who are involved with a particular function and as a team figure out the best processes.

For instance, let us say that you have five salespersons. Up to now you have let them fulfill their sales responsibilities as they saw fit. You have one superstar salesperson, one very good salesperson, two average salespeople, and one below-average salesperson. If you and all five of your salespeople get together in one room and share in detail how each executes his/her sales activities, you can jointly determine the optimal sales process. You also obtain buy in from each of the salespeople, since they are participating in the formulation of the optimal sales process.

A key benefit of doing this is that it increases the percentage of users who will adhere to the process because they have been included in defining the process and it ends up being *their* process.

Periodically the team that defined the process or a group of people who represent all the users of the subject process should meet to discuss any suggestions about the process. However, only an authorized group or individual can approve actual changes to the process.

A key part of documenting the final optimized process is to record *why* the process was solidified as it was so that all future users of the process understand the analysis and logic used to develop the current process.

Example

Mark, an affable, but technologically exacting man in his early 30's, owned a large company that performed business valuations. They had recently made a change about which market they were focusing on, and because of this, the company was poised for large growth.

In preparation for this growth, he and his team members realized they needed to improve the systems their field personnel used for obtaining the information necessary for performing business valuations. Besides streamlining the processes for obtaining the information, they needed to improve the systems for validating and verifying the information and performing the actual business valuation.

These changes required examining their overall business valuation and data capture methodology. It also required customizing their general business valuation plans and processes to the new specific market on which they were going to focus.

While doing this, they realized the need for new data capture tools as well as for improving various work-flow processes. The result of reviewing and revising their Systems was so successful they were able to reduce the hours it took to perform a business valuation, which in turn, improved their gross profit margin.

> **Complete exercise 11-2 in workbook**

PERSONNEL

While the plans and processes that comprise your systems—what will be done and how it will be accomplished—a certain amount of people are required to execute the systems. No matter how automated yours is, you will still need to determine the people resources you will require to execute and monitor your systems.

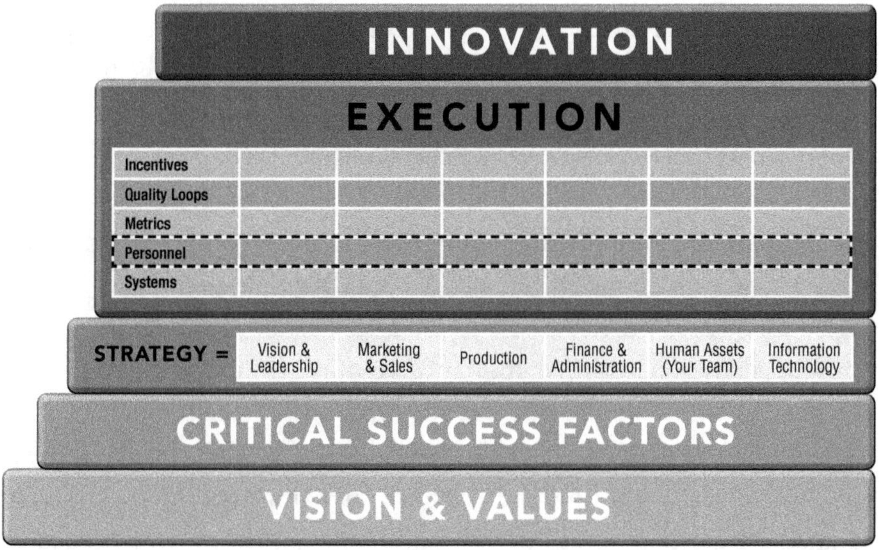

INNOVATION					
EXECUTION					
Incentives					
Quality Loops					
Metrics					
Personnel					
Systems					

STRATEGY =	Vision & Leadership	Marketing & Sales	Production	Finance & Administration	Human Assets (Your Team)	Information Technology

CRITICAL SUCCESS FACTORS

VISION & VALUES

Fig. 11-3 Execution Area—Personnel

This personnel component is different from and unrelated to your Human Assets area that we covered in Chapter 7. Borrowing a term from college management textbooks, your personnel component of structured execution is like a "line function" in that it is a core function of your business, while your Human Assets function or area which supports your personnel segment fulfills a support role, much like a staff function plays in an organization.

This personnel component involves four basic tasks:

1. Defining the role each person will play and his/her job responsibilities
2. Determining how many people you will require for each process
3. Ascertaining the skill sets or employee profiles you will require for each process
4. Establishing what pay, fringe benefits, and other employment benefits you will offer employees

Example

This industrial compressor manufacturer and distributor was owned by Abe, a hard-charging industrial engineer in his late 0's. Abe had spent his entire career working for other large industrial compressor and related-items companies, so he was an expert in this industry.

Five years before, he started his own company, which was now beginning to grow significantly. His enterprise was undergoing a change from various tasks being done by him and a couple of employees to him entrusting entire areas to others.

This alteration required him to determine each new person's role, the number of personnel each area required, and the delineation of their job responsibilities. This effort also required him to ascertain the skill set required for each position and establish its compensation level. Lastly, to facilitate his company's big step up in the marketplace, he needed to reassess the fringe benefits and other benefits they would offer employees.

As a result of these changes, he was able to add the personnel he required, and after a break-in time period, the new team members started to perform admirably. As a result of the transformation of his Personnel area, he was able to grow significantly and decrease his personal involvement with the nitty-gritty details of the business.

Complete exercise 11-3 in workbook

METRICS

Metrics are measurements that effectively track your performance in various areas of your company or monitor your progress on key issues. In this section, metrics refer to the measurements that are used to determine whether your systems are working correctly. As we discussed in the context of measuring your Time-Sequenced Vision in Chapter 3, measurements are crucial because:

- What gets measured gets managed and improved
- You cannot improve what you do not measure
- In the end, what you measure is what you get

Let us examine these three statements a little more thoroughly. First, if you do not measure something, there is no way to determine how well you are managing it. Without an ongoing measurement, it would be like a person wanting to lose weight, but never stepping on a scale to see how he/she is doing.

Second, you cannot determine if your actions to improve a process or an area of your business are successful unless you monitor them through an effective indicator (a metric).

Third, if measurements are the key to ascertaining if your actions improve your operations and if you correctly use these measurements to continue to improve your processes, then you can infer that what you measure ends up determining what you get from your company.

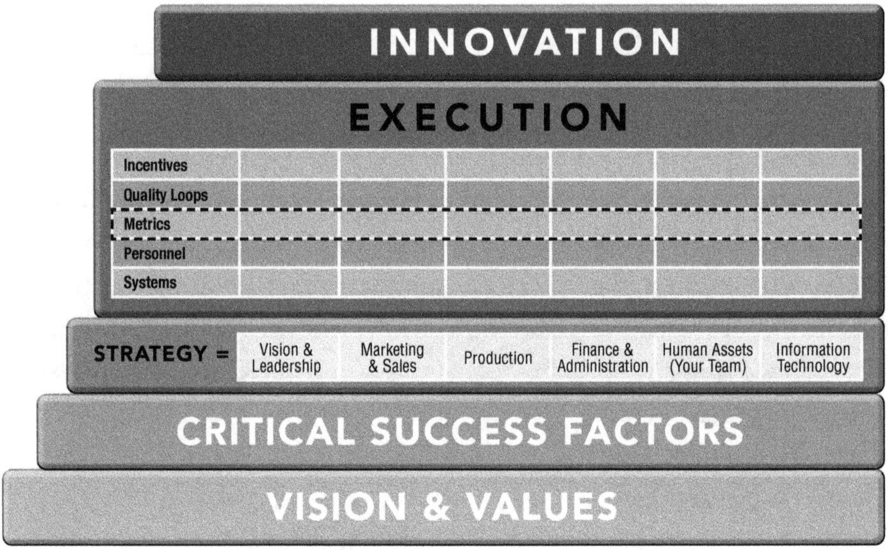

Fig. 11-4 Execution Area—Metrics

> Processes are critical to a business because the target is to fully satisfy your customers 100% of the time. Metrics are the barometers used to ensure that your processes function as designed.

To determine your metrics, you closely examine the process that you are trying to measure and ask yourself, "What is the key measurement that indicates whether the process is operating correctly, and the desired outcome is being achieved?" If more than one measurement could be used as an indicator for a process, choose the measurement that is the most comprehensive gauge of the process. Additionally, as you choose your metric, keep in mind how easy it is to obtain the metric and how reliable the metric is. This means that if it is at possible you want to select a metric that is a consistent indicator and that does not cost significantly to collect.

Metrics fall into two categories—financial and non-financial. Financial metrics are obtained directly from your business's accounting system—daily collections from your Accounts Receivable, daily sales amounts, or gross profit on each sale, for example. Non-financial metrics must be obtained from some other source such as customer surveys, direct mail response rate, defect rates from product inspections, employee turnover statistics, or the number of customer service calls regarding product quality issues.

Additionally, metrics can either be historical or predictive. Historical metrics reveal past performance—how your business did today or this week or last month. Predictive metrics predict future performance—how your business should do next week or next month or later this year; for instance, the amount of your unfilled sales orders, the number of prospects in your sales funnel or government forecasts for your industry.

Therefore, while historical metrics are of great value, you want to obtain as many predictive metrics as possible so that you can plan for the future.

Maximizing the Benefit of Your Metrics

There are three main steps that must be completed to fully benefit from the use of your metrics. The first step is to identify your metrics, which we just dealt with. The second step is to calibrate your metrics. This involves determining the acceptable and unacceptable range of values for each metric including identifying the point when you as a business owner need to get personally involved in dealing with a metric that is out of the acceptable range. We will discuss the calibration of your metric values later in the section titled quality loops.

The third step is the interpretation of the metric. This involves gaining a full understanding of the cause-and-effect factors that affect the metric and then deciding what action must take place based on the various favorable or unfavorable values of each metric.

How Many Metrics Should You Have?

The last issue regarding metrics is trying to find—if at all possible—one overall metric or "core score" of how your entire business is doing. In Jim Collins' book *Good to Great*, all the companies he examined that transitioned themselves from good to great developed an easy-to-assess economic denominator metric, such as profit per customer visit or profit per ton of finished steel they used as the overall defining measurement of how their organization was operating. An overall metric is a very good tool but not a necessity. If you choose to define an overall metric, please keep in mind that this is *in addition to* the detailed metrics that you establish throughout your business.

This leads to the question, "What metrics should you have?" Theoretically, you should have a metric for each one of your processes. As you will see in the next section, the benefit of having a metric for each process is that this enables your quality loops to function correctly. However, if you do not want to define that many metrics, you should at least have a metric for each of your major processes, and you absolutely need to have metrics for each one of your crucial Critical Success Factors.

The next question is, "Who should review, monitor, and act upon a metric?" For crucial processes, it should be you the business owner. For metrics related to each of your other processes, it should be the person in charge of an area. All metrics (including the above two types), should also be provided, in real-time, to the individual or team executing the process, so they can self-correct or have the assurance and satisfaction they are achieving the target metric.

The above discussion of metrics leads us directly to the topic of finding and using a tool that allows for easy monitoring of your key metrics. This tool is a thing called a *digital dashboard*. A digital dashboard is a computer program that utilizes things like gauges, charts, and indicators to automate the monitoring of your key metrics—just like looking at the visual displays on the dashboard of your car. The digital dashboard allows you to very quickly ascertain if you have a problem or if the process is operating.

Example

Putting the proper Metrics in place was instrumental for this X-ray equipment repair and maintenance company owned by Michelle, a single mother of two in her mid-40's. Michelle had been an X-ray equipment technician all her adult life, so she was mechanically very skilled, but she had a hard time managing people.

She had difficulty with determining the proper amount of authority and autonomy she needed to grant to each of her field service personnel. First, she started out micro-managing everything they did and "running up their backs." This caused a number of them to resign. Then, she gave them so much freedom, they ended up doing the work for customers any way they saw fit, disregarding her instructions, and eventually stealing the company's inventory and doing work on the side.

However, when she was introduced to the concept of Metrics, how to set them, and properly hold people accountable to them, she began to regain control of her company. Over time, she was able to utilize both financial and non-financial Metrics to manage the work being performed and appropriately reward her employees for their part in achieving various company goals.

Complete exercise 11-4 in workbook

QUALITY LOOPS

Quality loops are written documents that function as a key tool in ensuring that your business's processes continue to operate as they are designed by including a self-correcting mechanism within your structured execution plan. If a process stops functioning properly, the individual or team that is executing the process can rectify the problem by use of a quality loop without the company owner needing to get involved. The quality loops assist your business in functioning on auto pilot as much as possible, which in turn fosters a factory approach to your business.

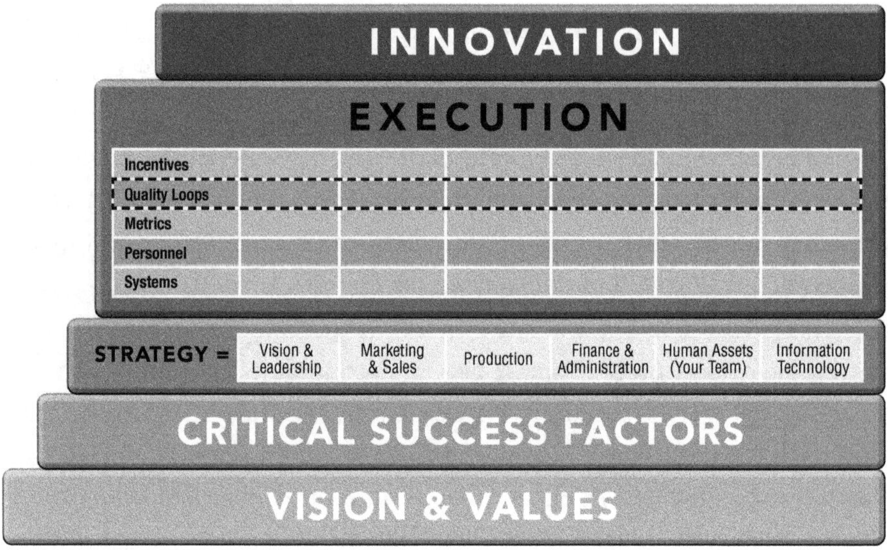

INNOVATION

EXECUTION

Incentives						
Quality Loops						
Metrics						
Personnel						
Systems						

STRATEGY =	Vision & Leadership	Marketing & Sales	Production	Finance & Administration	Human Assets (Your Team)	Information Technology

CRITICAL SUCCESS FACTORS

VISION & VALUES

Fig. 11-5 Execution Area—Quality Loops

The use of quality loops also empowers and releases your personnel by giving them the freedom and flexibility to resolve problems and issues themselves and not be micro-managed. Relatedly, increasingly we are seeing telephone support personnel being given the power and authority to try to resolve a customer's problem themselves. This has resulted in both tremendously increased customer satisfaction and employee morale.

A quality loop integrates and combines problem determination, accountability, and coaching to maintain and improve the quality of and the output from each of your processes.

There are five steps in creating a quality loop:

1. Identify where you need to define a quality loop. Initially, you may decide not to define a quality loop for each of your processes, but eventually as you observe their benefit you may include them in all your processes.
2. Use the metric for the related process to determine if the measurement is within or outside of the acceptable range of the metric.

In this way the metric functions as a barometer for determining whether or not the process is operating correctly.

3. If the actual metric value is outside of the acceptable range, you then need to define the steps that should be taken to correct the improperly functioning process. This set of steps (or remedial system) may include many diagnostic steps. This self-diagnosis will likely include directions to review the documents that define how the process is supposed to be executed to determine if a step is being omitted or executed incorrectly.

4. Thereafter, the analysis of the results from executing the diagnostic steps should guide the individual or team executing the process to a range of actions to undertake, which are correlated to metric value and diagnostic results. The actions that each person takes who is involved with the quality loop must be stated in such a way that there is accountability for each person's actions.

5. Determine when company management must get involved. The quality loop must also include directions stating when management needs to be apprised of the problem situation.

The accuracy and reliability of the metric is paramount to the quality loop process to ensure that incorrect information is not utilized and unnecessary actions are not taken. Process redefinition or process redesign are also an integral part of the quality loop concept; if the metric is still out of the acceptable range after the remedial system steps have been executed, something may have changed in the business's overall environment necessitating a change to the actual process. This examination of possible changes to the process results in a systematic approach to a process redefinition or process redesign function.

When you combine these steps, you have created the foundation for your business's entire process quality initiative.

Example

Kenny, Larry and Robbie, all in their mid-60's, owned this large, industrial fastener supply company that had been in business for almost 30 years. Their main employees had worked for them for many years, so much of the company just worked on "auto-pilot," and each owner executed their responsibilities completely separate from the other owners.

Since everyone had worked for the business for many years, very few processes were documented, and most people carried everything around in their heads. This did not cause any apparent problem until something unusual happened.

When suddenly Larry was out for several months for a surgery, a key financial management process was overlooked and never occurred. As a result, the funds in their checking account plummeted, and the business was put at risk from a cash management position.

When Larry finally returned, he remembered the thing that he had forgotten to tell anyone about, and over time the organization returned to normal. However, this drove the company to implement the Structure of Success™ methodology, especially the use of Quality Loops so that if others had to cover for someone when they were out or the position was open, they knew exactly what to do and how to handle things if there were any problems. Thereafter, the documentation of Systems, Personnel, Metrics, and Quality Loops was instrumental in ensuring the company operated smoothly.

Complete exercise 11-5 in workbook

INCENTIVES

The final component of your execution is incentives, which reinforce the carrying out of the first four segments of your structured execution plan. Incentives and rewards induce a person, team, group, division, or the entire business to do things a certain way. If there were no incentives, anyone and everyone in your company could do everything as they see fit!

The objective of the use of incentives is that your business executes your strategy in a way that will result in your enterprise achieving its Vision.

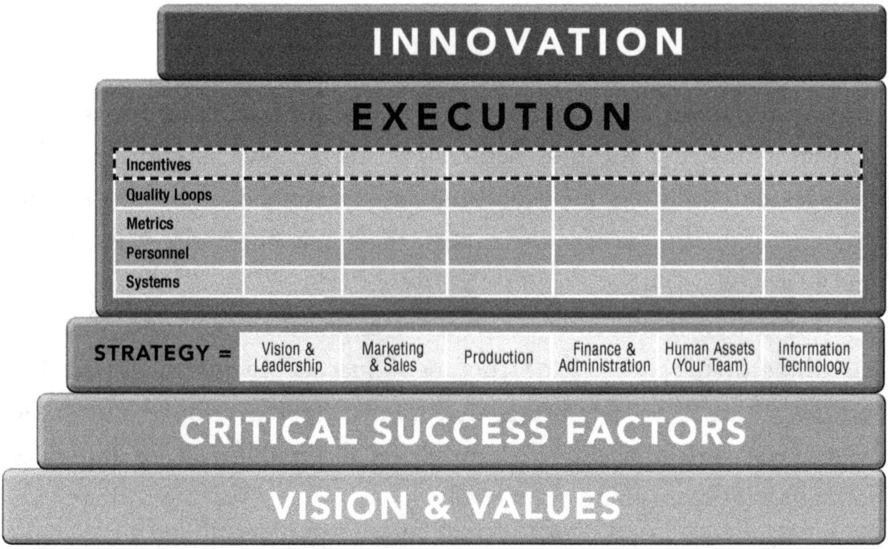

INNOVATION					
EXECUTION					
Incentives					
Quality Loops					
Metrics					
Personnel					
Systems					
STRATEGY = Vision & Leadership	Marketing & Sales	Production	Finance & Administration	Human Assets (Your Team)	Information Technology
CRITICAL SUCCESS FACTORS					
VISION & VALUES					

Fig. 11-6 Execution Area—Incentives

There are three different categories of incentives:

1. Financial incentives to the business or business owner. These types of incentives tend to be very global in nature. Some examples are increased business profit, increased compensation, more fringe benefits or additional funding of existing ones.
2. Financial incentives to non-owner employees or suppliers. These may be continued employment, a bonus, incentive compensation, or pay increase.
3. Non-financial rewards to employees or suppliers. For example, employee of the month, Friday off, dinner with the boss, or a recognition award.

There are two important things to keep in mind when you are creating your rewards. One, they need to tie directly to reinforcing the desirable behavior of the person, team, group, division, or the entire business. Two, they need to be aware of the reward so that it serves to reinforce adherence to the process.

Example

This plumbing manufacturer was started by four close friends who had never owned a business before. Two of the owners had worked in management positions for plumbing supply companies before, so they knew the industry, but for the others, their new enterprise was a whole new adventure for them.

This lack of management experience required the creation of almost everything that is part of the Structure of Success™ methodology for their company. One of the key things that needed to be developed and implemented was the proper use of Incentives for the manufacturing shop floor, both at an individual and team level.

As they started to develop individual and team Incentives to get everyone fully working together, they realized they also needed Incentives at the group and entire business level. Thereafter, they were able to implement both financial and non-financial Incentives to induce their personnel to perform in certain ways and effectively reward them for their behavior.

Complete exercise 11-6 in workbook

IMPACT OF COMPANY SIZE ON STRUCTURED EXECUTION IMPLEMENTATION

I am sure by now you are wondering if the size or complexity of your business affects the implementation of the five components of structured execution? The answer is yes because I have found that organizations fall into certain categories.

Before I continue, let me clarify three things regarding the categories below. First, these dollar amounts are not hard and fast as delineations because you could have a business that still is in start-up mode with

$500,000 in revenue, or a business with $250,000 in revenue that, because of the nature of the organization, it is operating as a small business.

Second, these are approximate amounts. For instance, once a business hits $300,000 in revenue, it does not magically become a small business; instead somewhere around the $300,000 mark in revenue, the nature of the organization, its growing complexity, and its increasing sophistication is going to move it into the next echelon of companies. This same concept of *approximate* amounts is true for each of the other categories also.

Third, I use these amounts because I have observed that businesses tend to hit a ceiling at the upper limit of each range, which may cause them to plateau and start to struggle with a common set of issues.

While I recommend that businesses of all sizes fully develop and implement all components of their structured execution, if you want to look at structured execution from a what is the "minimum I can get by with" standpoint, I suggest the following.

Businesses that fall into any of the five categories below (start-up, small, mid-size, large or enterprise) need to at least implement the five components of structured execution for each of their Critical Success Factors. Small businesses should also implement them for each of their essential functions; mid-size businesses should also implement them for all their major functions. Large and enterprise businesses should implement the five components of structured execution for every one of their functions because once you *have* risen above $10,000,000 in revenue, the risk to your business of not being fully systematized is enormous, and you can lose control of these sized businesses very quickly.

Category	Revenue Size
Start-up	$0 to $300,000
Small	$300,001 to $1,000,000
Mid-size	$1,000,001 to $10,000,000
Large	$10,000,001 to $100,000,000
Enterprise	$100,000,001 and over

Table 11-1

DEVELOPMENT OF YOUR FIVE COMPONENTS OF STRUCTURED EXECUTION

Now that we have discussed each of the five components of structured execution and the five categories of organizations, we need to further explore how you fully utilize them in your company?

Expanding on what was discussed in the prior section, it is imperative that all five components are completed for each of your Critical Success Factors. This is because, as you will recall, your Critical Success Factors are the make-or-break things that your organization must categorically accomplish to be successful, and proper and effective execution is key to accomplishing them.

Next you need to determine what other functions are *essential* to your business's success and then develop all the five segments of structured execution for them. Then, identify your *major* functions and develop all the five segments for them.

For all your remaining functions you need to at least create the systems and personnel segments. Once this is done, you want to analyze these remaining functions to determine whether or not they also require a metric, quality loop or incentives developed for them.

As you work on your remaining functions, keep in mind that some may be dependent, sub-functions of ones you have already defined. Therefore, from a hierarchical standpoint they may fall underneath one of your other functions. If this is so, you may be able to reuse some or all of previously defined personnel, metrics, quality loops, and incentives from the other functions.

Looking at this development endeavor from an overall standpoint, incentives are the most likely segment you might omit for a function, next comes quality loops, and finally metrics because these segments could have already been addressed in a higher-level function.

In summary, determining what steps are required for each of your functions is a hierarchical progression in which you start from the most comprehensive functions to the least comprehensive one.

Implementation Timeframe

Depending on the size and complexity of your business and how much time you can devote to developing your structured execution plan, it may take six months to two years to complete the work described above.

You most likely will find that you have some of these pieces already in place and all you need to do is review them for completeness and accuracy. Please do keep in mind that when you are working on the five components of your structured execution, you normally want to work on them in the order they presented in this chapter (systems, personnel, metrics, quality loops, and incentives) because each of them builds on the previous component.

Complete exercise 11-7 in workbook

CHAPTER SUMMARY

Leadership burn-out, which is caused by continual activity from company management that is not effective in moving the company towards its long-term goals, is a real and debilitating phenomenon. The antidote to this malaise is the use of a structured approach to the execution of the enterprise's game plan.

This structured approach to execution consists of five components.

1. Development of the systems that will enable the company to meet its operational targets on a consistent basis.
2. Determination of and hiring the personnel required for the systems to operate correctly.
3. Putting in place the metrics necessary to ensure that both the company's systems and related personnel are functioning properly.
4. Establishing and utilizing quality feedback loops that will assure personnel and management know what actions to take if the business's operations go awry.

5. Identification and implementation of incentives and rewards for employees adhering to the above items.

Together, the development and enactment of an entity's five components of structured execution will lead to leadership, management, staff, and customers obtaining what they desire from the company.

Chapter 12

Building a Better Mousetrap (Step #11)

• • • • •

The final building block of the Structure of Success™ is innovation, which has been getting a lot of attention in the business community and the press, and rightfully so. Various thought leaders say that the world has moved from the Information Age to the Innovation Age, and the businesses that innovate faster and better than their competition will be the ones that will prosper in the twenty-first century. Since you too want your company to prosper, we need to address the topic of innovation.

Fig. 12-1 Structure of Success—Innovation

What does innovation look like? The dictionary defines innovation as "the *use* of a new tangible or intangible thing, process or idea." In the context of this book, innovation includes inventions. Inventions are tangible things. Innovations can either be tangible or intangible. Listed below are some innovations that changed mankind:

- Airplanes
- Antibiotics
- Automobiles
- Compasses
- Domestication of the horse
- Harnessing electricity
- Light bulbs
- Living in cities
- Magnifying lenses
- Personal computers
- Printing presses
- Running water
- Steam power
- Steel
- Telephones
- The Internet
- The wheel

The definition that I will use for innovation in this book is "Doing something in a better way." This properly broadens the definition of innovation because many people only think of a new technology or invention when they hear the word innovation. That is way too narrow of a definition for harnessing the power of innovation.

While generally defined as something new, I include in the definition of innovation something old that has been rediscovered or reintroduced and used in a new way based on current needs. Take for instance community gardens or organic produce. These have been around since the beginning of time but have been recently rediscovered, so I include them as an innovation.

Innovation could be going back to the way you did something in the past that was in fact a better way than it is being done now. One such innovation is truly taking the time to understand and connect with your customer. Or, as many fast food restaurants learned from Starbucks, Apple Stores, and Panera Bread, trying to create a comfortable atmosphere where people will want to linger—and make additional purchases, as compared to making things more efficient.

What are the benefits of innovation? There are many, many benefits but the three major ones are:

- Revenue growth
- Cost reduction
- Improvement of customer experience

Revenue growth comes from differentiating your company from your competition. This enables you to beat your competition and separate your business from the rest of the pack. This could take the form of new products or existing products being delivered in a better way.

Cost reductions are garnered because with innovation you are doing more with less. You are operating in a more efficient, more productive way, thus saving money.

Improving your customers' experience in doing business with your company may not result in immediate revenue growth for your company, but it will in the long run. This is the kind of thing that makes them repeat customers who will refer your company to others. They become your unpaid sales force!

Ultimately the outcome from each of the above will be to increase your company's profits.

What is the alternative to innovation? We must all realize that change is inevitable. The world changes, your customers' desires change, your competition changes, technology changes—everything changes! You have a unique opportunity to harness change, even create it—it is called innovation.

Even unwanted change brings opportunities. You have the ability to decide; change can either be your friend or your foe. But be aware, if you do not properly deal with the innovation that is taking place around your company, sooner or later your business will become irrelevant. The worst thing to do is to ignore and try to hide from change—this is a recipe for disaster. Consider how change has crushed the pay phone industry, video rental business, or camera film market. If you embrace change as an opportunity to beat your competition and differentiate your company, change and innovation become your friend, closest ally, and a rally call for improving your enterprise.

The bottom line of embracing change and innovation is that you can use them to future-proof your business. To do this you have to decide to systematically incorporate innovation—doing something in a better way—into everything you and your business does. This way you do not fear the future but welcome the change it will bring with open arms.

INNOVATION SEES EVERY PROBLEM AS AN OPPORTUNITY

Where does innovation begin? What is its foundation? What fertile soil fosters innovation?

Have you ever thought of an invention or innovation and then saw it on TV and said to yourself or someone else, "I thought of that, they stole my idea!" In 1899, Charles H. Duell, the acting Commissioner of the U.S. patent office said, "Everything that can be invented has been invented." With 20/20 hindsight and over 100 years and many thousands of inventions later, we see how ridiculous this statement was.

In working with thousands of companies, practicing this in the nine companies I have started, and living this out in my daily life, I have found that the secret to innovation is to see every problem you encounter as an opportunity for an invention or innovation—which means we will only run out of inventions and innovation when we run out of problems!

As a professional speaker who regularly speaks on innovation and business planning, I sometimes ask audiences, "Who views themselves as creative?" Most times I get relatively few responses. That is so sad and totally wrong. Everyone is a very creative person!

All people are born creative. Just look at any young children; they are a curiosity dynamo. Furthermore, curiosity is the foundation of creativity and intelligence. Most people like to do new things—we don't want to do the same thing every day. Many people envision themselves as trail blazers, going where no one has gone before. If you tap into that curiosity, that desire to discover new things and longing to be a trail blazer, then you can be incredibly creative.

How do you do this? You begin this by seeing every problem that you encounter from the moment you awake in the morning to the time you go to bed as an opportunity for an innovation. For instance, your bathroom mirror fogs up from your shower, so you cannot use it after your shower. Next, in driving to work your coffee cup tips over and spills. When you get to work, you have to drive around to find a parking space.

All three of these are problems crying for a solution. How many other people do you think face these problems all the time? Billions. Your innovation could be mirrors that do not fog up. Coffee cups that have a magnet build into in the bottom, so they do not tip over. A GPS app could guide you to an open parking space. You see, it all depends upon the perspective you take with the problems you incur.

Unfortunately, most people see the problems that confront them in a completely negative light—an as obstacle, an impediment to their happiness or something that must be endured. As of 2018 there are about seven and a half billion humans in the world. Do the math—if you encountered a problem, how many other people do you think faced the exact same problem? Ten million, 50 million, 250 million, 500 million, one billion, or more! There is a ready market for the solution to the problems you face—in other words, the world is waiting for your company's innovation!

How do you implement this concept innovation in your life and business? You begin by taking everything in your day that does not go perfectly smoothly and ask, "How can I solve this problem?" By contemplating the problem, considering various solutions, and pondering on the efficacy of the solutions, you have the foundation of innovation. In this process, it may be useful to ask questions like the following as it pertains to the problem and alternative solutions:

- What if . . . ?
- I wonder if . . . ?
- Would this work better if . . . ?
- I can solve this if . . . ?
- What would it look like if . . . ?
- How would this work if I . . . ?
- If I did . . .

There are only three hurdles to the adoption of your innovation in the world:

1. How effective is your innovation (solution) in solving the problem?
2. What is the size of the market that needs your innovation?
3. How difficult is it to deliver the innovation to your market in a cost-effective manner?

Example

This aerospace component manufacturing company, that was owned by a venture capital fund, was founded on the concept of seeing every problem as an opportunity for an innovation. Furthermore, this philosophy continued to be a key to their ensuring growth.

The founder was an expert in finding ways to increase the efficiency of jet engines, and he and his team of engineers used the approach of seeing problems not as obstacles, but as opportunities for developing new and innovative ways to solve challenges.

This approach led the company to technological breakthroughs, then industrial process innovations, which in turn yielded manufacturing-cost efficiencies—the sum of which created a series of products that had both a better operational result, but also a lower acquisition price for the customer.

> **Complete exercise 12-1 in workbook**

HOW OUGHT THE WORLD TO WORK?

Let us take the concept of seeing every problem as a potential innovation to the next level. In Chapter 2 we discussed that the first step in developing your Vision was conceptualizing what your business is all about. Then in Chapter 9 we took this one step further by reconceptualizing your company so you can take your business where you want it to go. A key to reconceptualizing your company is innovation. An incredibly effective tool in combining reconceptualizing and innovation is to ask the question, "How ought the world to work?" with regard to your customers and their needs.

Determining the Ideal Solution for Your Customer

This method of jump-starting innovation within your organization begins with reflecting on "how the world ought to be" or "how the world ought to work" in the context of the environment in which your business operates. In this exercise, you want to focus on your customers and envision what the best way would be for them to have their needs met by your product?

At this point in this process, do not limit or even consider the meeting of your customers' needs in the context of your existing business. In fact, it may be helpful to pretend that your business does not even exist and think about your customers' needs from a theoretical standpoint!

This will require you to expand your thinking, reflect on and develop your thoughts regarding how an ideal world would operate as it would pertain to your market. What you want to do is to imagine in a perfect or ideal world, what would be the best possible way your customers' needs could be met?

It also may help you to reflect on the concept of excellence and how excellence would be manifested and delivered in your market. What you want is what great visionaries and leaders do—identify the true need of your target buyer and then capitalize on this need by providing the best possible solution for your customer!

To fully understand your customers' needs and how they perceive their needs, you need to get inside of their hearts and minds, which is part of the process of developing your Unique Selling Proposition that we discussed in Chapter 4. You may want to reread that section. Keep in mind that you may end up developing ideas or variations of the same idea as your idea solution.

Complete exercise 12-2 in workbook

Narrowing the Ideal Solution to a Certain Price Level or Target Market

The next step is to narrow your ideal solution to the best solution that can be provided at a certain price level, or to a target market that has product-pricing constraints. We began this process by considering the ideal solution from an unconstrained point of view because we wanted to think outside the box and not limit our possibility thinking.

While we started this process with an unlimited horizon, in reality unless your customer has an unlimited budget, we need to figure out a way to provide the absolute best solution to your customers' needs within their price constraint. In this second step, we are combining the economic realities of the market with our possibility thinking.

As an illustration, let's say that you are a dollar store. Unless you want to change your Vision for your organization, providing an ideal solution to your customers would be limited to one dollar. You would only be considering solutions that fall within your price level or target market, so you could not, for instance, sell furniture at your store.

Let us look at another example. If you were a mid-priced cruise ship line and were completing this second step, you would evaluate your innovation ideas you came up with within the target of providing the absolute best solution at a mid-market price level, not a luxury cruise ship price level. While completing the first step in the process, you did not want to limit yourself with pricing constraints, so unless you want to change to a higher-priced market, you need to filter your innovation ideas in this second step.

However, if you have come up with an incredible idea, you could decide to change your target market to the luxury cruise ship arena and pursue a business model for that market. This change would necessitate modifying the Vision for your business.

Keep in mind your ideal solution may change over time with advances in technology or changes in the environmental, energy, social, or political situations affecting your market. Consequently, one of your roles as the leader of your business is to keep an eye on these and other frontiers to evaluate how these changes may affect your ideal solution.

Complete exercise 12-3 in workbook

Deciding What You Are Willing to Change in Your Business to Provide an Improved Solution to Your Customer

The third step in this process is to come back to the real world and consider what this ideal solution would look like in the context of your company providing it. This requires you to look at all aspects of your organization and assess how willing you are to possibly change your entire business. These changes may include your business philosophy, model, and operations.

This consideration, analysis, and, envisioning should lead you to make decisions regarding how far you are willing to go in the process of creating an ideal solution for your customers' needs. Keep in mind that this third step automatically yields a continuum of options. You could choose to make the commitment to totally transform your business, do nothing, or do something in between.

The continuum of options may also include completely changing your business to focus on a new or different market for your product. There have been countless examples of businesses totally reinventing themselves (including many of the Fortune 1000 companies such as Kimberly Clark) to emerge from this process as a completely different business!

If you choose to do nothing or something in between, bear in mind two things. First, if you provide anything less than the ideal solution or at least a better solution than is present currently in the marketplace, the option remains open (and is a threat to your business) that one of your competitors could provide the ideal or a better solution than you are currently providing.

Second, if you do not sufficiently improve your product, you run the risk that your new, reconceptualized solution is perceived by your customers as not a significant improvement in meeting their needs. If this occurs, then the work, effort, and cost you incur to change your business to provide a better solution will not have your desired outcome and could result in a waste of your organization's resources.

As has been discussed several times with regard to innovation, it is critical to truly get inside of your customers' hearts and minds and thereby try to understand what is their perceived need? Therefore, an insightful thing to do is to pretend that you are your customer and ask yourself, "Would I buy my own product?" You can do this exercise with your current product and your contemplated improved solution.

To obtain value from this exercise, you must be brutally frank with yourself because it will provide you with tremendous insights into your business by showing you the gap between your customers' perceived needs and the solution you are providing. If you would not buy your own product, then you need to think about what you need to change within your business to induce you to buy your own product? In this case, considering "how ought the world to work" is ideal for solving this problem.

You should also be aware that net Financial Benefit (FB) from this process is your business's Desire for Change (DC) times the Attractiveness of the new solution (AT) minus the Costs (C) to develop a better solution. In other words, FB = (DC X AT)—C.

If you are not convinced of the need for change, or your new solution is not attractive enough to your target market, or the costs to change your business are greater than the benefit, then the net financial result of changing your business could be negative. Therefore, you need to prudently and carefully go through this process.

It is advisable to cycle through this process several times until you decide where on the continuum creating the ideal solution for your customers fall versus doing nothing or something in between before deciding what your go-forward plan will be. Keep in mind during this reiterative process, the bottom line you are focusing on is creating the ideal solution for your target customers *at a certain price/market level,* not with an unlimited budget.

Complete exercise 12-4 in workbook

Develop the Systems to Deliver the Improved Solution

Throughout this book, we have discussed the concept of systematizing your business, particularly your production area. With regard to innovation, you are looking to optimize your product delivery system so it can provide the most desirable solution at a certain price/market, and innovation can be a vital tool in the pursuit of this objective.

To achieve the improved result that you desire from this innovation exercise, you must engineer the quality—and other attributes your new solution needs—into the updated system that will produce the new product. This also requires innovation. The significance of this re-systematization step is that the outcome will take your business to a higher level because you are making the conveyance of your improved product consistent and at the exact level of quality that you have envisioned.

Complete exercise 12-5 in workbook

Identifying Other Changes You Need to Make

Lastly, you need to consider what other changes you may need to make (from your overall business philosophy, organizational structure, model, personnel, location, technologies employed, and operations) to provide the solution upon which you have decided. These additional changes may be related to improving your infrastructure or to optimizing your actual production process.

This Process Is Never Truly Finished

The reality is that this process of innovation is never finished. Meeting your customers' needs is a relative concept based on the technology, environment, economic circumstances, and customer situation present at that moment. These factors change over time.

Example

Henry was a very bright man in his mid-30's. Along with a group of investors, they owned an e-commerce platform company. Henry had a very strong Information Technology background and had worked in the e-commerce industry all his adult years.

Several years before, he had a brilliant idea about how to improve the targeting of e-commerce searches and marketing. Armed with this idea, he raised sufficient capital to start the company and acquire the skilled staff it would require.

In the process of developing their initial product, they worked through the process of identifying several ideal solutions for their target customer, which were e-commerce retailers. Next, they narrowed their solution down to a particular market that was determined by the price the e-commerce retailers were willing to pay.

Once they had introduced their initial product to the market and it had garnered enough market share, they started developing several more advanced products. This required Henry and his organization to determine what they needed to change in their existing product and within their organization to provide this improved solution. This required the development of new systems to deliver the improved software and the formation of several new companies to provide a greater bandwidth of products.

INNOVATION TEAMS

Now, let me introduce an incredible tool called *Innovation Teams* that can be instrumental in driving innovation throughout your organization. Innovation teams are internal teams of employees assigned the task of examining your company at various levels to find ways to increase revenue, reduce expenses, and improve your customer's experience. The goal is to make your company a shining example of innovation by tasking an innovation team with a specific problem or area of opportunity.

The result of using innovation teams throughout your company is developing new products, reducing costs, and creating experiences worth repeating for your customer. The innovation-team process is instrumental in accomplishing all three of these goals.

The Innovation Team Process

From the outside, innovation teams look a lot like typical brainstorming groups but in reality, they are very different. Traditional brainstorming groups are tasked with developing answers to various problems by immediately suggesting solutions. This approach has two main flaws. The first is that they are expected to get it done as quickly as possible, and the second is that this approach tends to be competitive so the participants in the teams may be unwilling to share their ideas for fear that their ideas would be shot down. Additionally, a problem with typical brainstorming is that the participants generally lack a true understanding of the problem.

Innovation teams are different because the initial session only addresses trying to fully understand the problem, not coming up with solutions. The objective is to ask deeper questions that force the team to get to the heart of the matter and be more creative, not just deal with surface symptoms. At the end of the first meeting, questions or areas are assigned to team members for them to research.

After the first meeting, the team then goes away to research the answers. The various research tasks could be done by one or more of the team members or some subset of the entire team. To complete the investigation, they talk with people in the company who have specialized knowledge of the area pertaining to the question. If appropriate, the analysis can include research outside the organization.

In the next meeting, each person reports the answer they found to their question. The team members ask each other more questions about what they discovered, and the team members go away to research this second set of questions.

The answers to the second set of question are then shared in the next meeting. This process of trying to fully understand the problem continues as long as is necessary through the question and research cycle.

During the questions, research, and answer cycle, solutions will surface that will need to be researched. The process continues and as solutions are proposed, questions are asked, research is done and reported. To avoid creating shallow answers and solutions, only when the true answers to the diagnostic questions are found should solutions begin to be proposed.

Whenever the team feels they have a sufficient understanding of the problem, they should start to create as many possible solutions as the they can develop. The goal is to come up with as many solutions as possible, so no narrowing process takes place at this time.

Once the group feels they have a sufficient number of solutions, the question, research, and answer cycle is used again to validate, modify, or dismiss an idea. This process can be used to develop new products or save money in producing a certain product—so the objective is to create as many ideas as possible. However, if the situation calls for only one solution, such as deciding into which country to expand or where to move your office location, then the question, research, and answer cycle is used to narrow the solution down to the best alternative.

There are three foundations for innovation teams to work correctly. First, you need a supportive, noncompetitive environment. Second, proposed solutions are not criticized, only researched and then the results are reported. Third, only when the team feels it has gained sufficient understanding of the problem and the issues surrounding it does the team begin to focus on solutions.

Listed below are two examples of this brainstorming process.

A Plant Nursery

A plant nursery company has experienced decreasing sales for the past five years. A typical solution that companies would use in a situation like this would just be to advertise more. However, instead of simply "throwing" money at the problem, they form an Innovation Team with members from Marketing, Sales, Operations, the Plant Nursery, Research & Development, Logistics, and Finance.

The team utilizes the question, research, and report process to identify and try to understand the issues. Their research unearths that people nowadays are less active than prior generations and spend more of their time interacting with electronic devices, rather than being outdoors. They also find that gardening has just fallen out of vogue and more and more people are moving into high density housing settings and unlike prior generations, they don't have room for large gardens.

Use of this unique process could generate innovative solutions to the above problems. For instance, creating gardening video games to get people attracted to the concept of growing plants. Also, in an effort to make gardening a "cool" thing to do, establishing teams of gardening "Ambassadors" that travel around the country to educate people about the benefits and fun of gardening.

Next, the company could decide to develop plants that take up less space and can be grown indoors, with lower light. Lastly, as part of the above gardening education program they could introduce people to "square foot" gardening that enables them to grow plants in more compact areas.

A Jet Engine Manufacturer

Another example would be a company that wants to develop a lighter weight jet engine which has more thrust per pound than prior engines. Instead of rushing to come up with a "solution" to the problem they establish an Innovation Team with members from Engineering, Aerodynamics, Avionics, Metallurgy, Composites, Research & Development, Finance, and Marketing.

The team then uses question, research, and report process to develop the best solution which could include developing a new jet fuel that eliminates the need for several components of the engine, thereby reducing the weight of the engine, while producing greater thrust.

As the innovation team works on a task, keep in mind the six basic ways to increase revenue:

1. Create new products
2. Develop new markets for existing products
3. Generate additional revenue from current customers
4. Develop additional sales and distribution channels
5. Improve your sales process and increase the productivity of your salespersons
6. Optimize your pricing and financing polices

Also, there are eight basic ways to reduce expenses:

1. Reduce production costs
2. Decrease salary and wage expenses
3. Reduce fringe benefit costs and employee administration costs

4. Cut worker's compensation expenses and health care costs
5. Reduce marketing, public relations, communications, and professional fees expenses
6. Decrease utilities, facilities, insurance, and equipment lease, rental, and maintenance costs
7. Trim auto and truck, travel and entertainment, supplies and services expenses
8. Reduce other costs

Choosing Innovation Team Members

A secret to how the innovation-team process produces extraordinary results lies in the configuration of its team members. The team needs to be cross-functional. The members must come from the various areas that are affected by the problem or that could benefit from a solution. By using a multi-dimensional team configuration, you get beyond the typical brainstorming approach and you can fast track your innovation by bringing in more perspectives.

Experts say that Thomas Edison could have eliminated his 10,000 failures in creating the incandescent light bulb if he had a chemist on his staff who could have guided him to use a carbon filament in an oxygen-free environment. This is great example of the power of a cross-functional team.

The optimal size of an innovation team is between five and eight people. Teams with fewer than five people don't have enough perspectives to provide a broad spectrum of viewpoints. You also want to keep the teams to eight or fewer participants so that the team can avoid bureaucracies, move quickly through the process, and have sufficient time for each person to voice her/his thoughts.

Avoid choosing people for the team who are comfortable with the status quo, have hidden agendas, or are political players within the company. The members should be out-of-the-box thinkers and chosen from the lowest level in your organization as possible because they will understand the problem the best because of dealing with it daily. Avoid using department heads because the entire process may become a turf war. Keep in mind the team members are likely your organization's next superstars.

The team should meet preferably weekly and at the same time, so this standing meeting becomes a part of everyone's work-week calendar. Research assignments are due at each meeting unless an exception has been made by the team beforehand. The team should continue to meet until the issue is resolved, and they should focus on only one problem at a time.

After solving the problem, they are tasked with, if the company needs to tackle another situation that requires the same team member skill set, the team can continue with their current configuration or it can be recomposed.

> One huge benefit of this cross-functional approach is that appreciation, trust, and cooperation is built across departments or areas in the company, thus understanding how the parts of the business fit together. From one perspective, even if no innovation was developed, the outcome of building understanding and cooperation itself makes the entire process worthwhile. So, the innovation itself almost becomes icing on the cake.

Management of the Innovation Team

While innovation teams function best at the lowest level within a business, they must be implemented with the support of the organization's leadership. The business owner or, in a larger company, its leadership and management *must* authorize, sanction, and recognize the team regularly by periodically publicizing its milestones and innovations through emails, speeches, and newsletters.

The management of the business must believe in the process and personally support it. Additionally, innovation teams will not work where company management in essence says, "This will fix my people because they are the 'problem.'" Nor will it work where management stands off to the side and hopes that the initiative will take care of all their problems. Innovation teams are not a "throw the dog a bone" exercises.

During the first meeting, the person who is leading the innovation team should lay out the objective and the ground rules for operating. If there is any history of the problem that would be beneficial for the team to know, the team leader should relay that to them. The management representative can also jump-start the first meeting with prepared questions to get the team off and running properly.

The business owner or company management representative should be at the initial kick-off meeting. Thereafter, it is a good to periodically attend a meeting if the members will feel free and open with you being there. By occasionally attending a meeting, you are demonstrating support of the innovation team while increasing your comfort level because of seeing their progress. Also, it will give you great insights into who may be your current or future star players.

Be sure to reward team members with a financial incentive to do the best possible job—a percentage of the cost savings or additional revenue or profit.

Generally, someone on the innovation team should oversee the implementation of the innovation for three reasons. First, the team member understands the innovation better than anyone else, so he/she can resolve any issues that arise during the implementation. Second, since the innovation team member has a vested interest in the innovation, she/he will be driven to make it a reality. Third, during the implementation, he/she would be the most knowledgeable person to identify any other related opportunities for innovations.

The Innovation Team Methodology Should Become a Systematic Part of Your Company

Once you are comfortable with and appreciate the results of using the innovation-team process, this methodology should become a systematic part of your company. You can have standing innovation teams working at the broadest level or they can be commissioned and recommissioned as is needed for focused objectives. The important thing is to use the innovation-team approach to effectively solve problems in a cross-functional manner, avail yourself of potential opportunities, or address threats to your company.

Example

The concept of using Innovation Teams was crucial in the growth of this movie and TV-show set-design and construction company. It was owned by several people in their mid-30's. Each of the owners and many of the employees had worked in the film industry for numerous years, and because of its growth in the state of Georgia, they decided to launch out on their own about five years previously.

Since owning a business was new to them, and they each had done movie and TV show set design and construction in their own unique way, the use of Innovation Teams was instrumental in determining the best approach to each of the types of projects they were landing. When the company started, it consisted of less than eight people, so everyone became an Innovation Team member, and they followed the proper rules for its use.

Once the company got up and running, the use Innovation Teams changed to be focused on a particular problem or new project type. At that time team members were chosen from each of the departments that could be impacted by the issue or project. Because the company had such a positive and beneficial experience from the use of Innovation Teams, they made its use a standard operating procedure for their firm.

Complete exercise 12-6 in workbook

AN INNOVATION BOX

One of the simplest ways to encourage, foster, and implement innovation is by using an innovation box. The most important factor in making an innovation box a useful, functional tool is to *act* on the suggestions. Company management should meet with the people submitting the innovation. They should discuss the idea and if appropriate form a committee or innovation team to examine the idea further. You can place innovation boxes throughout your company or have a virtual one by using your website or an innovation box email account—Innovation@. However you set it up, be sure to monitor it regularly.

Acting on the innovations that are submitted communicates to your staff that their opinions are appreciated, valued, and used in the business.

The problem with a non-systematic approach like the above is that if there is hardly any innovation volume, it is very easy to lose control of tracking your innovations.

Additionally, as you will see below, this approach lacks a number of innovation pipeline management features you may find very desirable. Therefore, for larger organizations, the use of innovation pipeline management software to track ideas and innovations is very advantageous.

A systematic example of innovation pipeline management software that addresses these issues is www.BriteIdeaLab.com, which includes two software applications. One system, Brite Idea Lab, collects ideas from an organization's customers and the public and then routes the ideas to the company's internal idea collectors.

This system also includes the utilization of service providers who can deliver resources to idea submitters to further develop their ideas. Ideas that can be submitted may either be: just an idea, one for which a prototype has been developed, an invention that is somewhere in the patent process, a start-up business with innovative ideas or an existing company that has innovations they want to provide to another organization.

The second system, i-Lab, collects ideas from the enterprise's employees, suppliers, and their sales channel, and then passes the ideas on to the appropriate personnel within the organization for evaluation. Both systems use keywords and other data in the submitted ideas to match and direct ideas to the person within a company in charge of the pertinent innovation area who is looking for that specific type of idea.

To manage the interface between idea submitters and collectors, both software applications use profiles built by the idea collectors regarding what they are looking for. These software packages and the matching algorithms inside of them are basically "match.com" between anyone with an idea and those organizations and companies looking for ideas.

> An atmosphere of innovation must originate from the business owner, leaders, and management of a company. While innovation should occur at all levels within an organization, it must be sanctioned, supported, and celebrated from the top of an organization down.

Complete exercise 12-7 in workbook

SYSTEMATIZING INNOVATION

A 2019 survey by Implement Consulting Group, asked a large number of companies this question, "My organization prioritizes innovation as a key strategic factor for success." and received this response:

- Strongly agree: 23%
- Somewhat agree: 43%
- Neither agree nor disagree: 11%
- Somewhat disagree: 17%
- Strongly disagree: 6%

So, a full 66% of respondents view innovation as a high priority.

However, a previous 2014 survey by thoughtLEADERS, LLC, asked their readers, "How much time per month do you dedicate to innovation and generating new ideas?" and got these answers:

- A significant amount (3-5 days/month): 20%

- A moderate amount (1-2 days/month): 20%
- A small amount (2-4 hours/month): 36%
- Almost none: 24%

In reality, while companies state that innovation is highly important, the results show that 60% of people spend virtually no time on innovation within their companies. How can a business develop new products and improve its processes and thereby beat its competition if it does not spend sufficient time on innovation? The following two foundations ensure that time is regularly spent on innovating in a business.

Innovation Is Important

A business's leadership and management must stress to everyone in the organization how crucial innovation is to its future. Communicating the importance of innovation is a top-down effort that must emanate from the company's leadership. Innovation should occur at all levels within an organization, and the expectation should be set that each person within the company should be regularly developing new products, improving its processes, and identifying ways to create better customer experiences.

Innovation Is a Continuous Process

Innovation must be built into your company's processes. It cannot be optional.

One way to do this is to periodically bring all the people who are involved in a system together and ask them for suggestions about how to improve the process. This initiative can be tied to the use of innovation boxes where innovations that are submitted are given to the group of people who are executing the process or overseeing its execution for evaluation.

> Entrenched systems and the status quo are
> the enemies of innovation.

Example

This bio-engineering company had been started by a group of bio-engineering engineers and scientists about eight years before, and now it was primarily owned by a group of outside investors. The company had faced many roadblocks in trying to fully develop their first product, and just now it was coming to market.

The use of Innovation Teams had been a fundamental function in their company, and now that their first product was ready to hit the market, leadership took the specific step of communicating and committing to the belief that innovation was important and foundational to the company.

Furthermore, their leaders and managers issued a statement that devoted the company to innovation as a continuous and fully integrated process that would be one of their guiding principles and key values.

REWARDING INNOVATION

The final ingredient of innovation is properly rewarding people's creative behavior.

People do what they are incented to do. That is the whole idea behind commissioned salespeople, piecework, or pay for performance. Studies show that highly achieving innovative companies recognize and/or reward their people who contribute to the organization's innovation efforts.

Recognizing and rewarding innovation should begin with an employee's job description by including it as an expected activity. Performance objectives should stress the creative aspects of their position. Similarly, performance reviews need to include an evaluation of what innovation efforts the person has demonstrated and the results.

Listed below are some ways to reward your personnel for coming up with innovations, reinforce their creative behavior and say "innovation is important" in your company.

Financial

Recognition and rewarding the innovator are an integral component of a successful innovation program.

Rewarding employees for focusing on innovation can involve many actions, some of which are listed below. Bonuses can be paid either in hard cash by giving out $50- or $100-dollar bills, or via check. Or, you can pay them a percentage of the revenue or cost savings related to the innovation. They can be provided with gifts, prizes, trips, and other options as financial rewards for innovation. You can also give them a raise or promote innovators with the resultant increased compensation.

Nonfinancial

Many innovation experts consider nonfinancial recognition as more effective than monetary rewards or prizes because it is easier to administer than a financial-based reward system. Therefore, nonfinancial recognition may be the most important element in fostering innovation.

Ways that don't include outright expenditures are recognition: Innovation of the Month, Innovation Team of the Quarter, Employee of the Year. Awards, plaques, honors, and mention in company publications are great incentives, as well as additional vacation or time off. Leading-edge companies like Google give their personnel regular time off to develop ingenious solutions to problems.

At Kraft Foods, Division General Managers award employees token light bulbs for creating ideas; there are also awards for Innovator of the Month and Innovator of the Year.

An underlying tenant in the rewarding process is to celebrate your innovation successes. This is part of making innovation fun. Being innovative takes both time and energy and striving for improvement must be made fun so that it does not become a drudgery and fizzle out.

Example

Louise and her husband Curt, both in their mid-40's, owned a recruiting and contract placement company they had started 10 years before. Both Louise and Curt had already been in the recruiting industry for many years, therefore they had a great number of contacts. Because of this, when they began their enterprise, which focused on Accounting and Finance personnel, it grew very rapidly.

Because recruiting and contract placement companies tend to be very generic, it is quite difficult for companies to differentiate themselves from each other. Therefore, Louise and Curt went to great lengths to establish an innovative environment that would be an excellent breeding ground for creative ideas that would enable them to distinguish themselves from their competition.

This effort began with Louise and Curt making sure to include the expectation of innovation within each employee's job description. Their staff responded to this by coming up with various innovative ideas. Then they included financial rewards in the form of both flat-amount bonuses as well as sharing a percentage of the revenue or cost savings related to the innovation.

They tied financial rewards and nonfinancial recognition together by entering the winner of the "Innovation of the Month" in a yearly innovation contest, which involved various prizes and a grand prize of an all-expense-paid vacation.

Complete exercise 12-8 in workbook

CHAPTER SUMMARY

Innovation, which is necessary for a business to separate itself from its competition, starts with seeing every problem or situation within the company that does not go optimally as an opportunity for innovation. Taking this concept one step further, to transform an enterprise via innovation, one wants to ask (with regard to how your customers should get their needs met), "How ought the world to work?"

The ensuing determination of the ideal solution for your customer, narrowing the ideal solution to a certain price level or target market, deciding what you are willing to change in your business to provide an improved solution to your customer, and developing the systems to deliver the improved solution can revolutionize a business.

Implementation of innovation teams can be instrumental to improving a company, but to get effective results, the business has to properly chose innovation team members and effectively manage the innovation team process. Optimum results can be obtained from innovation teams by utilizing them as systematic part of your company.

While an easy place to start with innovation is the creation of an electronic "innovation box" to obtain the desirable results from innovation, it requires a systematic and ongoing commitment to innovation. This is because results of innovation should not be "a one hit wonder" but should instead produce an ongoing stream of innovation. This systematic approach to innovation includes properly rewarding personnel for their innovations, with both financial and nonfinancial incentives.

Chapter 13
Putting It All Together (Step #12)

• • • • •

I n this final chapter, we will pull everything together that we have considered in this book and provide you with the final tools to catapult your business to a whole new level, make you a world-class leader, and take you down the path to creating the business of your dreams! We are going to examine how to create the organization to accomplish your Vision by preparing your business for the future.

Just like Henry Ford did with the mass-production of the automobile, Sam Walton did by re-inventing the retail landscape in America, and Michael Dell did with creating an organization to deliver reasonably priced, custom computers to the masses—by pulling together all the facets necessary to create a *system* to accomplish their overall objective—so you want to take a systematic approach to moving your company from where it is today to where you want it to go.

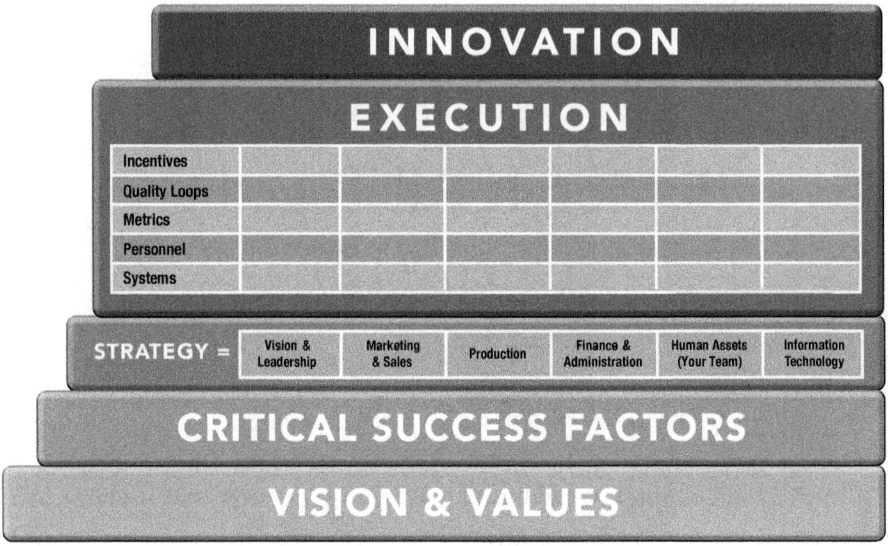

INNOVATION						
EXECUTION						
Incentives						
Quality Loops						
Metrics						
Personnel						
Systems						
STRATEGY =	Vision & Leadership	Marketing & Sales	Production	Finance & Administration	Human Assets (Your Team)	Information Technology
CRITICAL SUCCESS FACTORS						
VISION & VALUES						

Fig. 13-1 Detailed Structure of Success

By using all aspects of the Structure of Success™ you want your company to operate just like a well-tuned race car engine with all its cylinders firing properly and in the correct sequence. To do that you need to systematically execute the daily tasks necessary to accomplish the Vision for your organization.

As we considered in Chapter 1, a business is like an intricate jig-saw puzzle where one piece of the organization fits with another piece, and when all the pieces are put together properly, they are able to operate correctly and achieve the company's goals. The totality of the prior 11 steps we have examined yields a 12th step where the end result you obtain from your company operating via Structure of Success™ is greater than the sum of your organization's parts.

Let me share two examples of a company using a comprehensive systematic approach to operate—one a relatively small company and one a very large one.

One of our clients, an HVAC company, created a compelling Vision, comprehensive strategy, Time-Sequenced Vison and structured execution to perfect their operations in the HVAC world and then expand into electrical, plumbing and home performance. They became the largest and highest-rated company of its kind in state of Georgia.

Second, as I mentioned in Chapter 1, if you look at any company that has been truly successful, you will find that they have in some way done what is included in this book. Amazon is a great example. From top to bottom, starting with having a compelling Vision, a comprehensive strategy, an engaged workforce, utilizing structured execution and applying innovation to its operations, it has changed the face of America and is now beginning to change the world. They have done this as a result of implementing the principles contained in this book and creating an entire economic system to accomplish their goals.

An interesting by-product of creating an entire economic system with your company is your brand ends up becoming very well-known because of creating an experience your customers can expect and rely on. The two companies described above are great examples of this.

By this point in this book, you should have recalibrated the Vision for your company. We will now take the organization you have in place and mold it into what you will need to achieve your five-year Time-Sequenced Vision. This task includes fully systematizing your business and managing the execution of your strategy using metrics.

UPDATE THE STRATEGY FOR ACHIEVING YOUR RENEWED VISION

With your renewed Vision in mind, now it's time to re-examine your strategy by completing the following five steps:

1. Review, and revise if necessary, your existing Critical Success Factors

2. Update your Time-Sequenced Vision

3. Apply your renewed Vision, revised Critical Success Factors and updated Time-Sequenced Vision to your analysis of the six areas of your company

4. As necessary, update the five components of your execution plan

5. Utilize innovation within your company to beat your competition and differentiate yourself from your rivals

While we discussed having business planning retreats and reviewing and recalibrating your Vision every six months, most businesses only complete a comprehensive review of their strategy and organization on a yearly basis. This is unless they are a large company that requires a complete semi-annual review, or they have a very complex or very dynamic situation that requires semi-annual reviews.

The First Three Steps to Figuring Out How Your Business Must Work

To answer the somewhat daunting question, "How do I structure my business for it to operate correctly in the future?" you start with the following.

1. **Recalibrate your Critical Success Factors**—The first task is to review and possibly update your Critical Success Factors based upon your recalibrated Vision and the delivery of your desired solution to your customers. If your Vision has changed because of the analysis you performed in Chapters 9 and 12, it is very likely that your Critical Success Factors will also change. But even if your Vision has not changed, you should perform a summary review of your Critical Success Factors to ensure that they are all still valid and they do not need to be updated.

2. **Revise your Time-Sequenced Vision**—The next task is to review and revise your Time-Sequenced Vision because if either your Vision or Critical Success Factors have changed, you need to update your current Time-Sequenced Vision. Since your current Time-Sequenced Vision reflects your goals and objectives from a year ago, and that means that your one-year Time-Sequenced Vision should now be accomplished. This means that you must roll all your other Time-Sequenced Vision objectives forward a

year. As you roll them forward, there may be mile markers for goals and objectives that have not been accomplished that will need to be reviewed and either left in the updated plan as is or possibly revised or deleted.

3. **Update your analysis of the six areas of your business**—In light of your renewed Vision and Critical Success Factors, the final task is to review and update your analysis of the strengths, weaknesses, opportunities, and threats in each of the six areas of your business:
   • Vision and Leadership
   • Marketing & Sales
   • Production
   • Finance & Administration
   • Human Assets
   • Information Technology

Example

Oscar and his wife Kate owned and operated this large moving company, and they were in the process of passing the business to their son and daughter. They had started the company over 30 years before, and it had grown to be one of the largest moving companies in their metropolitan area.

Their son and daughter had worked in the company in various roles, although not in decision-making roles. However, they were quite familiar with its operations. Oscar, Kate and their son and daughter wanted to take this opportunity to completely reassess its operations and direction. In recent years the parents had been less active in its daily operations, so a number of things had slipped in the business.

Therefore, they examined the company from the top down by considering their Vision for its future, Critical Success Factors, and Time-Sequenced Vision. While they did not change its overall Vision, they did revise its Critical Success Factors and Time-Sequenced Vision to bring it into the digital age and update the strategy for a number of aspects of the six operational areas of their company. This included trying to elevate the company's image and the professionalism of its moving crews, that had suffered in the past few years.

As of result of these actions, the son and daughter were more comfortable with taking over the company and were gratified that they were not saddled with a reclamation project of the company from day one of their ownership.

Complete exercise 13-1 in workbook

UPDATING YOUR ORGANIZATION TO ACCOMPLISH YOUR VISION

What does it mean to "Create the organization to accomplish your Vision"? It means just that, to create your entire operating business in the real world for everyone to see and interact with!

The Visible and Invisible Parts of Your Business

There are two parts to your business: the visible and invisible portions. Drawing from the overall structure of your company, six areas of your strategy, and the five areas of your structured execution, there are six elements that comprise the invisible portion of your business, which are your:

- Vision
- Critical Success Factors
- Strategy
- Metrics
- Quality Loops
- Incentives

Drawing again from the above areas, there are eight elements of your company that comprise the portion of your organization that is visible to your customers or the outside world, namely:

- Leadership
- Marketing & Sales
- Production
- Finance & Administration
- Human Assets
- Information Technology
- Systems
- Personnel

The above eight elements are the ones your customers see and know about; to them these areas are your "business." Of these eight functions, your systems and personnel are the ones that must correctly interact with your customers for you to have a thriving business. This is because your systems accomplish everything your business does, and your personnel execute these systems. This is true for your company now as well as how you want it to operate in the future.

Creating Your Future Organization

The re-creation of your organization to achieve your renewed Vision involves determining what your future organization needs to look like.

Of the five components of your organization, your systems and personnel are the most important areas because they are the most visible ones to your customers; therefore, you need to determine the systems and personnel resources that will be required by your company in the future. This is not a daunting task because you know your current systems and personnel resources; therefore, the task at hand is to create the roadmap to move your operations from where they are at today to what you want them to look like in the future. There is a very straightforward, two-step method to creating the organization that will achieve and accomplish your renewed Vision and five-year Time-Sequenced Vision.

First, review in detail your renewed Vision Statement, definition of your Critical Success Factors, and the goals and objectives included in your five-year Time-Sequenced Vision and then create a well-defined personnel organization chart that would reflect what your business would need to look like from an organization standpoint in five years to achieve your five-year Time-Sequenced Vision. For this exercise to be effective, for each position that needs to appear in your projected personnel organization chart, you need to include the position title and a general list of the responsibilities.

Once this is done, it is a fairly easy task to also create projected personnel organization charts for one, two, three, and four years from now. These additional charts can be used for planning purposes as you move forward. I suggest you print out these projected charts and keep them in a place where you can periodically review them for guidance and inspiration. By doing the tasks above, you will be alerted to issues, challenges, and decisions you are going to be faced with in the future.

Second, using the detailed five-year personnel organization chart above, at a general level, create the systems/plans that you would need to have in place to achieve your five-year Vision. This requires that you examine the current operational setup of your company and see what you need to change to get your business from where it is at today to where it needs to be to support your future General Vision and Time-Sequenced Vision.

When this is completed, you have a picture of what your business will look like in the future, and then you can work backwards to the present with the intention of changing your current organizational structure to move it toward your Time-Sequenced Vision.

After this step is finished, when you are ready to actually hire the people who will be needed in the future, all you need to do is to expand the general systems/plans to develop the needed detailed processes.

> The key concept that we are talking about here is "change" and your ability as a leader to change your business to what it will need to look like five years from now to achieve your Vision.

Complete exercise 13-2 in workbook

Abdication versus Delegation

Closely related to the subject of creating and managing your current and future organization is the issue of abdication versus delegation. What is the difference?

When you place an individual or a team in charge of an area, system, or process and say to them, "Here it is, take it, it is all yours and only call me if there is some major problem," you have abdicated your authority over the function. Whereas, if you say to them, "You are in charge of this area (or operation), and I would like to sit down with you periodically to review how things are going" (you decide how often), you have now delegated your authority.

There is a huge difference between abdication and delegation.

Many times, business owners, leaders, and management personnel end up abdicating various areas of their company because they either don't want to deal with a particular area or they feel they are too busy to be involved in the area.

The issue is that when you abdicate control to employees and then have to speak to them because a difficulty is occurring, they may feel you are intruding on their space and may say to you, "I have it under control, don't you trust me?" The problem with this situation is that no forum has been set up to review their performance.

How do you avoid this happening? When you put someone in charge of an area, simply say "I would like to meet every _____ to review how things are going." You fill in the blank in determining if you want to meet weekly, bi-weekly, monthly or quarterly. Also, you should define what will be covered during the meetings and if any metrics for the area will also be discussed.

Establishing these meetings should not be a problem for the person being promoted or put in charge of an area, because when he/she receives the promotion or increased responsibility, a large amount of goodwill is produced, and, therefore, setting up the periodic meetings will be considered simply part of the package that comes with the new responsibilities.

Thereafter, when you meet, you are keeping your word, and virtually anything is fair game to be discussed during the meeting. This is effective delegation.

Abdicating something often comes back to haunt you. Therefore, don't cut yourself out of the control and communications loop—delegate responsibility for something but make sure you set up regularly scheduled meetings to review the status of the area.

Example

This mid-sized trucking company, and its father-and-son owners, were just completing a Structure of Success™ assessment of the business, and as a result they wanted to expand the company significantly. During this process they had made the decision to expand from the 30-tractor trailer operation they had, into also offering logistics and warehousing services.

These changes required additional capital, infrastructure, management expertise, and personnel. While the logistics and warehousing operations would start small, hopefully they would grow considerably. Therefore, projecting the staff and management structure the new entities would require was a necessity.

To address this, they used the tool of creating their future organization on paper by developing a personnel Organization Chart for the two new enterprises as well as their current company. They used a five-year planning horizon for this effort and then used this to work backwards to develop Organization Charts for three-year and one-year time periods. They also established general Job Descriptions for the positions in the five-year organization chart. They were very pleased with the planning results, and these efforts enabled them to get a good feel for what it was going to take to make these new ventures successful.

Complete exercise 13-3 in workbook

WORKING ON THE FUTURE OF YOUR BUSINESS

What does the concept of working *on* versus *in* your business involve regarding the future of your business?

Here are a few earth-shattering concepts that will transform how you approach your business!

How You Produce Your Product Is More Important Than Your Product

The "methodology" (strategies, systems, processes, metrics) used for delivering your product can actually be more important than the product itself. This means your primary focus should be on the systems that produce and deliver your product, which, if perfected, will produce your desired solution every time.

McDonald's* is a good example of utilizing a systematic approach to operating a company.

What is McDonald's product? Hamburgers and French fries? Not really. When a person buys a McDonald's franchise, they are purchasing a system that has been proven to provide a consistent experience to customers. For example, no matter where you are in the world, their hamburgers and French fries taste the same.

The operation of this systematic methodology of providing food and drinks is being played out before our very eyes, as they have added salads, various coffee beverages, pastries, and most likely many more items to come.

Let's say that you are an engineering firm with a large engagement to complete. You find not only that the engagement is running behind but that there are many design flaws in the work that has been performed.

To resolve this problem, you have all your employees work overtime to catch up, you pull one of your managers off another project, and you personally get involved to salvage the engagement. You complete the project and deliver it to your customer, and they are very pleased with the results. You may view the engagement as a success; in reality it was a dismal failure. Why was it a failure? Because your systems failed your company miserably.

Here is another example. Suppose your business is a bakery that specializes in large wedding cakes. For Saturday June 15, you are scheduled to deliver three large wedding cakes. On the Thursday before the 15th, your staff bakes the cakes. Friday morning, they ice and decorate the cakes. Friday afternoon you review the order and discover that the chocolate cake is in fact supposed to be a marble cake—the bride's family referred to the cake as "chocolate and vanilla" but it was written down as chocolate.

Although you have a procedure that calls for verifying all wedding cake orders in writing with the person placing the original order, this process was not followed. So, at the last minute, the cake had to be thrown out and entirely redone. The customer ends up being very pleased with the cake. However, just as in the previous situation, your company failed to execute properly, since the cake-verification process you have in place was not followed.

Systems Are the Solution

When someone interacts with your organization, for the most part, they are interacting with the systems of your business. Therefore, if you perfect the systems used to produce your solution (your product), then as a consequence, you will produce the desired solution for your customer.

> Your business will not automatically produce a *perfect* product unless you optimize and perfect the systems for delivering the product to your customer.

Here are three basic reasons for systematizing your company:

1. Systems are required to grow your business and are absolutely required to scale (substantial growth) your company.
2. Even if you are trying to achieve only slow growth for your business, to have the time to concentrate on managing your company, you need to put the proper systems in place, or things you delegate to someone else may not be done properly.

3. Whether you intend to grow or not, systematizing allows you to spend more time on the things in your company you enjoy. It's clear that unless you want your business to stay very, very small, you cannot do everything yourself. If you operate a big fruit-stand type venture, it is likely you will burn out. Creating a systematized "economic factory" provides you with the enduring freedom and flexibility in your company you desire.

Re-systematization is pivotal in taking your business to the next level. As we discussed in Chapter 11, all organizations have natural limits or ceilings involuntarily built into their companies. For instance, in having worked with various businesses in the HVAC industry, we have found when a company goes from one to two or three crews, a fundamental change takes place in the operations of the organization, and it must change its processes to handle the expansion.

Once it goes to five crews, the systems that served it at the three-crew level need to be updated. When it grows to ten crews, the company needs to reorganize its systems because the ones that worked well at the lower level will not support all the complexity of having ten crews.

The reason for this *ceiling* experience is that while systems are your friends, they can also be your foes. By this I mean your systems will take your company to a certain level of size, but then they become an impediment to future growth. I have seen companies that have been stuck at the same level for five or more years because no matter what actions they have taken, they cannot punch through the revenue plateau they are facing as a result of not having redeveloped their systems.

By properly re-systematizing your business for future growth, you ensure that as your volume grows, the quality of your product does not decrease, and you are able to break through the ceilings you are facing.

Systems, Metrics, and Quality Loops

Quality loops, which we discussed in Chapter 11, play a key role in re-systematizing your business in that they use your metrics to correct the execution of your systems/processes when they are not functioning properly. Quality loops also provide you feedback to determine if your systems may need to be re-engineered or redesigned.

This entire area of resystematizing your company is one of the components of instilling innovation in your organization. While the expansive topic of innovation is outside of the purview of this book (my next book will cover how you weave innovation into the very "DNA" of an organization), I would like to discuss the concept of "being the best in the world" that Jim Collins covers in his book *Good to Great,* as it relates to systems.

While being the best in the world is a lofty goal, it is not realistic for all but the largest companies. However, by properly systematizing your business, you can become the best in your city [fill in the blank], then the best in your county, then your geographic area, then your state, etc. The concept of being the best (or the foremost expert) is still applicable to smaller businesses; you just enlarge your target area by being the best in it as your enterprise grows.

> The important thing is that you should not accept mediocrity in your company, but instead to use the concepts in this book and the companion workbook to "be the best" and thereby create the business of your dreams.

Proper Systems Produce a Sustainable Competitive Advantage

This entire subject of systematizing your business takes us to the next logical step on our journey of working *on* your business. This involves combining the third role of a leader, creating the organization to accomplish your Vision, with the concept of systematizing and resystematizing your business to develop a sustainable competitive advantage as we discussed in Chapter 5.

The key to having a *sustainable* competitive advantage is the use of systems throughout your company so you can duplicate the desired results time after time.

Example

The concept of how you produce your product being more important than your company's actual product was very insightful to the husband and wife owners of this tool rental company. The company was beginning to explore creating a franchised structure, therefore they needed to create an operation that was so attractive other people would be interested in becoming a part of it.

After completing Structure of Success™ process, they realized that developing robust systems was a necessity, because how they actually provided their service was just as important as the service itself. Therefore, once they had the proper Systems in place, they added the Metrics, Quality Loops, and Incentives that would be required for proper ongoing execution of their processes.

These actions provided them with a sustainable competitive advantage in the marketplace, which in turn enabled them to pursue franchising their company. Not only that, but having effective Systems in place enabled the owners to spend more time away from the business at their vacation home.

> **Complete exercise 13-4 in workbook**

YOUR BUSINESS IS YOUR PRODUCT

Let us take the concept above, "How you produce your product is more important than your product" to the next level.

I will begin by asking the question, "What is your product?" You may answer that it is lawn mowers, engineering services, or commercial construction. However, in reality your product is a system that produces lawn mowers, engineering services, or commercial construction.

Earlier in this chapter, we looked at that the concept that your product is a system that provides your product, not just your actual product. Let us take this concept one step further—you should view your business as product sitting on a shelf that is available for someone to purchase.

When you go to a store to purchase something, you shop by comparing the features of each product, its claims, its price, its packaging, etc. to determine which product is most attractive to you.

You should evaluate your company in the same way. Your overall goal should be to create an organization that is very attractive to a potential purchaser and is more attractive than other businesses that are also "sitting on the shelf" for an investor to buy. What you should be trying to do is to create a business for a potential "customer" to buy, whether you are planning to sell your company or not (sooner or later most likely you may want to sell it).

If you apply this concept of trying to make your company more attractive than other businesses that are also "sitting on the shelf", you will end up being driven to make it the best it can be.

By doing this you will avoid falling into the status quo by being complacent with your company the way it is now. This will lead you on a quest to be continually looking for ways to improve your business and make it the best it can be.

What are some of the ingredients of an attractive business? First are significant current profits. Second is a high potential for increasing future profits. Third is the existence of properly functioning systems. Fourth is a fully engaged, stable, and contented work force, which is something that is often overlooked by many business owners. There are other ingredients, but that is another subject. By employing this concept of trying to make your company more attractive than other businesses, you will accomplish the four items above.

SUCCESSION/EXIT PLANNING

With regards to your business sitting on a shelf as a product for someone to acquire, there are five basic succession "strategies" you can employ, namely:

- Sell it to an outsider or another owner
- Sell it or gift it to a family member

- Sell it to your employees or to an ESOP
- Run it for the rest of your life
- Shut it down

While the area of succession planning is outside the scope of this book, the concept of "your business is your product" that was discussed earlier in this chapter, which is built on the implementation of what has been presented in this book, will create an enterprise that will create a high likelihood of first option occurring.

If you decide to pursue the second option, you want to provide your family member with a company in a desirable condition, and likewise, implementing what has been covered in this book will provide for that outcome.

If you decide to sell your company directly to your employees, or to them via an ESOP, you want to provide them with an operation that will present them with the greatest opportunity for continued success. Once again, the use of the Structure of Success™ methodology will accomplish this.

Obviously, the fifth option is to be avoided and if none of the first three options become a reality for you, application of what has been discussed in this book is crucial because you want to have an enjoyable and profitable business to run the rest of your life, as compared to a stressful or unprofitable one. Please note, there are businesses that can put you in an early grave because of the burden of operating them.

Don't forget, your Human Assets are part of your product.
A person who would be interested in buying your business is going to focus on the quantity of and correctness of your work force, the skill sets present in your human assets, and the morale and satisfaction of your personnel. If any of these are found lacking, that will diminish the value of your business or even make it unsaleable.

Example

Bruno, a soft spoken, yet determined man in his early 60's, owned a manufacturing company that was a shining example of the concept that how you produce your product was more important than the product itself. Bruno was nearing retirement, and he was looking to sell his company, retire, and spend more time sailing his ocean-going yacht.

Over a number of years, he had created a systematized company that produced its product in a near flawless manner, which required very little staff. So, when he met with several business brokers, they were very impressed with his business that was just sitting on a "shelf" as a product, available to a purchaser.

He had put all the items together necessary to make the company appealing to a purchaser. Its desirable product, market share, profits, low overhead, in-place workforce, and overall systematized operations made it very attractive.

During its lifetime, he had not been complacent about the business's operations. He had been persistent in trying to improve his company's functions, which resulted in it being more attractive than other businesses that were also listed with various business brokers. Therefore, as his company was "sitting on the shelf," it had a distinct advantage in competing with other businesses for a buyer.

Complete exercise 13-5 in workbook

OVERSEE YOUR BUSINESS'S OPERATIONS AND MANAGE IT VIA METRICS

Once you have systematized your business, having the appropriate metrics in place and responding to the metrics that are off target is key to operating a company that it is not a burden to its leadership. This results in upper management managing the operations of the business by monitoring its metrics without having to be immersed in all the nitty-gritty details of the organization.

Monitoring Your Metrics

In Chapter 11 we discussed metrics in detail, including how many metrics your company should have. The question I would like to focus on now is how many metrics should you as a business leader track to manage your company? Studies have shown that the maximum items a person can track and be responsive to is 10-12.

Therefore, I recommend you identify 10-12 core metrics that will give you the most comprehensive view of how your company is operating and review them daily, every other day, or at least weekly. I cannot imagine not monitoring a key metric at least once a week. As we discussed previously, a digital dashboard is a great software tool for monitoring your metrics. A digital dashboard displays data from your accounting system, processes used to operate your company, and other sources by using graphics, charts, gauges and other visual indicators. It enables you to monitor your organization's performance by displaying your key metric values, projected amounts, and historical trends—all in real-time. In this way you can easily keep track of and if necessary, take action on the operations of your company.

Example

This gutter cleaning and installation company was owned by Sally. Sally was in her mid-40's, had completed fully systematizing her company, and now was ready to move on to maintaining what she and her management team had put in place.

To do this they knew they needed to identify the Metrics to put in place, and the related Quality Loops to respond to any Metrics that could go off course. In this way, the managers could oversee operations without having to be submerged in the company's details.

To achieve this, Sally identified the 12 core Metrics that would provide her with the most comprehensive view of how the business was operating. For instance, three of them were: daily number of sales inquiries, number of completed gutter cleanings per day, and gross amount invoiced per day. She accumulated and reviewed the data from these 12 Metrics on a weekly and monthly basis. Lastly, Sally had a digital dashboard created for easily monitoring of these metrics.

In a similar way, each of her managers identified their key Metrics and started monitoring them on a daily, weekly and monthly basis. As a result of these actions, Sally and her management team were able to effortlessly track and then take appropriate action regarding their ongoing operations.

> **Complete exercise 13-6 in workbook**

CHAPTER SUMMARY

The overall goal for your company is to take a systematic approach to moving your business from where it is today to where you want it to go. There are five steps to implementing this concept, which involves properly and fully systematizing the parts of your company that interact with your customers.

Perfecting the systems, you have created to produce your product becomes a hugely attractive feature of your business, increasing its value in the marketplace and making it more alluring to a potential purchaser.

To enable your company to achieve its five-year Time-Sequenced Vision, you want to determine what your future organization needs to look like in terms of systems and personnel. You want to realize that how you produce your product is more important than your product, which will change how you view your company. Relatedly, you want to view your business as a product "sitting on the shelf" for someone to buy, which will lead you to focus on ways to make it more attractive to a potential buyer than other businesses. Lastly, you want to oversee your business's operations and manage it via metrics.

If you do these things, you will become a world-class leader with a fully and properly organized company that has maximized its value by creating an economic system to produce its product.

Conclusion

• • • • •

We have covered a lot of territory in this book by examining every aspect, wall to wall, stem to stern, top to bottom, how a business should operate. We have also looked at how various people interact with and are impacted by a company.

The objective of this has been that your business becomes a blessing to you and not a burden because if a company is not operated correctly, it can be very frustrating, economically draining, and can lead to various physical and emotional health difficulties.

But, if an enterprise is managed properly, it will yield fulfillment, wealth, and financial and lifestyle freedom for those associated with it.

Let me share a good example of what outcome this book can produce. A long-time friend of mine, Will, started his own construction company several years ago. During the prior 30 years he worked in a very stressful job in a large organization, and now, with his own business, his wife recently told me that this was first time he has been happy at work in his entire adult life. Will's use of the Structure of Success™ led to this result. Yeah for Will!

Most importantly, the concepts we have considered are applicable to businesses of any size. For example, a friend of mine, Ed, is in upper management with a Global 100 company, and he has told me many times the principles contained in the Structure of Success™ are directly applicable to any sized company, including his Global 100 company.

From a personnel standpoint these concepts are even more important to large companies and major corporations, because many people who work for these companies, like Will had been, are very unhappy and unfulfilled with their employment situation. Use of the comprehensive approach detailed in this book can and will change these work environments into desirable places to work.

As we have seen on this journey, to create a business that operates optimally, there are 12 aspects of a company that need to be examined.

The first of these 12 steps began with identifying your values—what is important to you in life—because a business should reflect who you are. These values are then used to identify the Vision you have for your company. Your Vision is the direction you want to take your enterprise, in other words, what does a successful and thriving business look like to you?

Step 2 was to identify your company's make-or-break factors, its Critical Success Factors and then to use these to develop a Strategy for achieving your Vision. Steps 3 to 9 involved fleshing out your Strategy for the various operational areas of your company.

Step 10 focused on executing your Strategy in a structured, systematic way so you have assurance you will achieve your Vision. Step 11 involved utilizing innovation advantageously to beat your competition and separate your business from the rest of the pack.

Lastly, Step 12 showed how to put Steps 1 to 11 together to create an economic system that will allow your company to operate in a predictable manner so that it generates the financial and lifestyle freedom you desire.

Some people ask, "How does this book and its predecessor, *Creating a Thriving Business*, relate to each other?" To answer that question, let me use an American Baseball analogy.

Creating a Thriving Business showed how to get to first base, how to start a business from scratch, using our unique Structure of Success™ methodology. Then it looked at how to get to second base: making sure the business has traction, is viable, successful, and thriving. Hence the title of the book, *Creating a Thriving Business*.

If you are starting a new business, I highly recommend you acquire *Creating a Thriving Business* because it covers material that is not covered in this book, and it will provide you with great insights if you are not already "standing on second base" with your business.

This book shows you how to scale your business and take it to the next level. When you combine the material presented in this book with the content from *Creating a Thriving Business*, you will possess both a firm foundation for your company and the means to take it wherever you want it to go.

Scaling your company could take the form of organic business growth, additional products, multiple locations, franchising it, overseas expansion, vertical or horizontal integration, etc. By using the concepts we have covered, the outcome from this effort is that figuratively you reach third base with a successful, scaled business.

As we have seen, Steps 1 to 11 enable you to establish a compelling Vision for your business, identify its Critical Success Factors, develop a Strategy for achieving these, execute that Strategy in a systematic way, and apply innovation to your company - thereby providing you the ability to scale your operation to level you desire.

Lastly, as was discussed in Step 12, how do you get your business working exactly as you want it to?

That is, you are working X number of hours and making Y amount of income? Your employees are fully engaged in your business. You have an exit strategy in place. You are impacting society in a desirable way. In essence, you have the business of your dreams, which using our baseball analogy, takes you to home plate. The Structure of Success™ concepts presented throughout this book will enable you to successfully reach "home plate" with your business so your company is operating just like you want it to.

Creating the business of your dreams results from employing the Structure of Success™ methodology within your company. With regard to impacting society, as was detailed in various sections, it is important that an enterprise should in some way shape, form, or make the world a better place because that is part of having a meaningful life. The approach we have examined in this book is constructed in such a way as to establish socially responsible businesses that will make the world a better place.

So, now armed with Structure of Success™ methodology, go forth and create the business you have always hoped for, the business of your dreams!

About the Author

· · · · ·

George Horrigan is Founder and CEO of Fountainhead Consulting Group, Inc. and has over 25 years of experience as a business planner, innovation expert, and CPA. During his career, he's had a consistent track record of showing people how to start, grow, manage, and take their company where they want it to go. Over the past 21 years, George has shown over 1,200 business owners or leaders either how to grow an existing company or start a new one.

Besides being a noted business growth, scaling, and planning expert and recognized thought leader, he personally has started and operated nine companies which has allowed him to understand the mindset and mentality of an entrepreneur. He brings both professional and personal perspectives on how to create the business a person is longing for.

George is also an inventor and noted innovation expert, which he brings to bear in showing people how to grow and scale their enterprises. *Work Less, Make More, and Have Fun in Your Business* is his fourth book and his third one, *Creating a Thriving Business,* received wide acclaim. He holds a BA in Accounting, Master's Degree in Financial Information Systems, and multiple professional certifications. He is an author, speaker, frequent broadcast media guest, and has been recognized in a number of Who's Who National Registries. George lives in Atlanta, Georgia.

FREE SPECIAL BONUSES

To assist you in creating the business of your dreams, Fountainhead Consulting Group, Inc. is providing you with the following free resources that will speed you on your way to be able to *Work Less, Make More, and Have Fun in Your Business.*

These special bonuses include:

- A downloadable, expandable Organization Chart, so you can start to create an Organization to accomplish your Vision
- A *Structure of Success* Implementation Guide
- A free 30-Day free subscription to *i-Lab Innovation Management Software* so you can collect and implement innovations that will enable you to beat your competition and separate your business from the rest of the pack

To claim your free bonuses just visit *www.FountainheadConsultingGroup.com* and select *Resources*, then *Book Bonuses*, then select *Work Less, Make More, and Have Fun in Your Business*, and enter "dream" to access your free bonuses.

ADDITIONAL RESOURCES

Please visit *www.FountainheadConsultingGroup.com* to find a number of resources that will assist you in being able to *Work Less, Make More, and Have Fun in Your Business.*

Also, we have established an international network of Management Consultants who have been trained on the *Structure of Success* methodology that can assist you in creating the business of your dreams, so that you will be able to *Work Less, Make More, and Have Fun in Your Business.* Please visit us at *www.FountainheadConsultingGroup.com* and select *Resources,* call us at (770) 642-4220, or use the *Contact Us* function on our website to learn more about these resources. George Horrigan can be reached via email at *george.horrigan@fountainheadConsultingGroup.com.*

A free ebook edition is available with the purchase of this book.

To claim your free ebook edition:

1. Visit MorganJamesBOGO.com
2. Sign your name CLEARLY in the space
3. Complete the form and submit a photo of the entire copyright page
4. You or your friend can download the ebook to your preferred device

Morgan James BOGO™

A **FREE** ebook edition is available for you or a friend with the purchase of this print book.

CLEARLY SIGN YOUR NAME ABOVE

Instructions to claim your free ebook edition:
1. Visit MorganJamesBOGO.com
2. Sign your name CLEARLY in the space above
3. Complete the form and submit a photo of this entire page
4. You or your friend can download the ebook to your preferred device

Print & Digital Together Forever.

Snap a photo

Free ebook

Read anywhere

Printed in the USA
CPSIA information can be obtained
at www.ICGtesting.com
JSHW050021041223
53142JS00013B/10